How to Organize

Group Travel for Fun and Profit

*The Complete Group
Tour Leader's Manual*

Carl Meadows

ETC Publishing, Inc.
2254 Emerald Drive
Castle Rock, CO 80104-2703

I

Is There A Group Travel Leader In You Waiting To Be Discovered?

Before you buy this book, take this simple test...

Would You Like To:

#1. <u>Travel for free?</u>

#2. <u>Make money</u> while you are traveling (for free)?

#3. Meet new and interesting people?

#4. Take three, four, or more, free vacations a year?

#5. Travel with small groups of people to exciting destinations in the USA or around the world?

#6. Develop life-long, sincere friendships?

#7. Be upgraded to First or Business Class when you fly?

#8. Stay in deluxe hotels and resorts wherever you go?

#9. Have a private guided tour of almost any city (the choice is yours) in the world?

#10. Have a circle of friends that want to travel with you (if you invite them) on your next trip?

#11. Be a social travel leader to grateful friends and followers?

#12. **<u>Most importantly</u>, have control of your own time and destiny?**

If you answered <u>YES</u> to eight or more of these questions...

CONGRATULATIONS...
YOU ARE A BORN GROUP TRAVEL LEADER!

How to Organize Group Travel for Fun and Profit...

JOE & JAN MCDANIEL, ELEPHANT TALES TOURS, LLC
"Jan and I have read your book and thoroughly enjoyed it. You have given us so many ideas that we can hardly stand it!!!"

TOMMY SMITH, GREENSBORO, NC
"I got your book on Saturday and I could hardly put it down...it was exactly what I have been looking for. I finished reading it (for the first time) Tuesday. Thanks for writing it!"

DICK KISKER, CONFERENCES INTERNATIONAL
"Read and study this book. All of the group travel organizations and contacts you need to succeed are listed, and they're just a telephone, fax or e-mail away!"

DONNA ROBBINS, DONNA'S PERSONALIZED TRAVEL
"Super book! I just wish I would have had this information when I first got started in the group travel business!"

TERRY WALLACE, TRAVEL ABOUT WITH MS. TERRY
"This book is a wealth of information! Easy to read, easy to use, and loaded with important 'do's and don'ts' for the group our leader."

MELODY FEE, OUTSIDE SALES SUPPORT NETWORK (OSSN)
"A vital book for outside travel & tour agents interested in developing group travel as a major part of their business."

MARGIE ROBINSON, UNITY BAPTIST CHURCH
"...a great book! All my questions on how to get started and grow are answered. Thank you!"

SUSAN LASH, PASSPORT TRAVEL
"The reference section by itself is worth the price of the book!"

DICK INGERSOLL, SUN & BREEZES TRAVEL
"I recently completed your book and got so inspired I headed out to setup a group. The book was enjoyable, informative and motivating. Truly a good value product."

How to Organize Group Travel for Fun and Profit...

MARK GAUGHAN, SHOPPING SAFARIS.COM, INC.
"Carl, your book was a godsend! I used it as my bible launching my new company. It was like a 'one stop shopping center' for a new group tour company."

TERRY BYRNES, SURADIX INCENTIVES
"Thank you for writing How to Organize Group Travel for Fun and Profit. Because of your book, I now run a group tour business out of my home and travel to places I never thought I would ever see. After 28 years as a corporate executive I am finally living the life of freedom that I have always dreamed of. Thank you again!"

CINDY BRODHECKER, TOUR PROMOTION MANAGER - MTS TRAVEL
"This book is a treasure chest of information, ideas and opportunities. As you open the lid and look inside you are dazzled by the sparkle of its many treasures. As you dig deeper you realize that your dream of the treasure of travel can be a reality. All of the answers are found in this book. One of the gemstones to be found is 'When you find a travel agency that understands the needs of a group travel leader, hold on to them!' Working with an agency that will custom plan your tours and make you the Star of the tour is truly a 'diamond' to behold."

CLIFF JOHNSON, MOTIVATION FOR MINISTRIES, INC.
"For people interested in learning the group travel business, this is the book! Whether you are just getting started or already an established group tour leader, How to Organize Group Travel for Fun and Profit will have something you can use; How to get started, what organizations to join, how to get established and recognized as a qualified group travel leader. The business is covered from A to Z with valuable information. Great job, I know your book will be a big success!"

JANE BERTSCHINGER, SMART TRAVEL
"I just finished your book and just wanted to let you know I found it an excellent resource for someone new to the travel industry. I am a school counselor and I plan to use the information in your book to help me market a trip for this summer."

ALSO,

Read this letter from someone who has taken the information from this book and made his travel dreams happen...THEN YOU CAN DO IT TOO!!

SeaVision, Inc.
CONFERENCES AT SEA

Dear Carl,

    This is just a note to say "thank you very much" for introducing me to the wonderful opportunities in the group travel business.

    When you first mentioned this to me a few years ago, I never imagined that today, I would have my own successful seminar company and be traveling all over the world on cruise ships giving lectures to my fellow optometrists. Your guidance and continuous encouragement was invaluable to me in the establishment of my SeaVision business. My last conference in Greece (cruising the Greek islands of the Mediterranean) was absolutely fantastic...the highlight of my conferences so far!

    Traveling, cruising, providing certified continuing education to optometrists from all over the USA and Canada *and* making money at the same time, is almost too good to be true!

    I also wanted to say that it was a pleasure proof reading your new book "How to Organize Group Travel for Fun and Profit." I hope that my input was helpful. Everything you did to help me get started has been compiled in your book. Congratulations! I know that it will be a great success and will inspire many people to take advantage of the group leader opportunity.

    Thank you once again for opening up a new world for me!

Sincerely,

John L. Schachet, OD
President, SeaVision, Inc.

FOREWORD

by Charlie Presley, President
Group Leaders of America (GLAMER)

Carl Meadows grew up dreaming of traveling the world. Medieval castles, exotic islands, sailing the seven seas...no destination or adventure was beyond his imagination. Today, Carl has sailed the seven seas (in style), visited exotic islands around the world from Maui to Mykonos, and roamed more castles than you could catapult a stone at.

As excited about being in the travel business today as he was thirty years ago, Carl wants to share his good fortune and travel knowledge with anyone who also has a true desire to travel. Carl's book, "How to Organize Group Travel for Fun and Profit," is filled with common sense advice on how to get started in the group travel business, how to stay on top, and how to expand and grow.

Carl and I have a lot in common as we both recognized some time ago the growing importance of the senior group travel leader. The senior population is growing at a phenomenal rate and many have a strong desire to travel. My mission, as President of GLAMER, is to help these people accomplish their travel goals by bringing them together at the GLAMER seminars and trade shows held annually through out the USA.

Carl's mission is also to help as many people as possible accomplish their travel goals. He is doing this through his book. Whether you are just getting started or already an established group travel leader, this book will be a valuable business tool to you for years to come. The extensive contact and resource section is worth the price of the book alone. You will want to keep this book handy to refer to over and over again.

Best wishes for a successful life filled with wonderful travel memories!

Sincerely,

Charlie Presley
President

VI

How to Organize
Group Travel for Fun and Profit

The Complete Group
Tour Leaders Manual

Published by:

ETC Publishing, Inc.
2254 Emerald Drive
Castle Rock, CO 80104-2703
Tel: (720) 733-2003
Fax: (720) 733-2046
E-mail: etcpublish@qwest.net
Web: http://www.etcpub.com

Cover design: Foster & Foster, Inc.

Printed and bound by: Graphic Image Group Inc. / Glen Ellyn, IL

Library of Congress Card Number: 00-190256

Library of Congress Cataloging-in-Publication Data

Meadows, Carl
How to Organize Group Travel for Fun and Profit: how to start and manage your own group travel club as a home based business. Includes travel industry references, glossary and index.

1. Travel
2. Group Travel
3. Home Based Travel Business

ISBN 0 - 9670380 - 0 - 6 / $29.95

By Carl Meadows

A Note About the 2nd Edition Revisions

As I mentioned in the first edition of *How to Organize Group Travel for Fun and Profit*, business trends today are constantly changing and the group travel business is no different. The additional 32 pages in the second edition are basically made up of new trends I see happening in the group travel industry...new trends that can lead to golden opportunities. Also, additional support and educational contact information, e.g., a couple of great group travel leader schools I did not know about when I wrote the first edition, a new section of destination management company (DMC) contacts, and more information on niche group travel opportunities, etc.

The first edition was positively received by the ever growing number of people who are determined to fulfill their travel dreams. They recognize that being a group travel leader and establishing their own personalized travel club is a fantastic opportunity to finally do something about it. My travel colleagues from the supply side of the travel industry (airline, cruise line, hotel-resort representatives and DMC's) also gave the first edition great reviews, accompanied by suggestions which will add greatly to the second edition.

So, much of the additional information in the second edition does not come directly from me, but from many of my professional travel friends who are as equally interested in helping individuals get started in group travel business. One of the few businesses today that can, if worked properly, provide a lifestyle that most people will only ever dream of.

I am pleased with the additional information in this second edition and know you will be too. The feedback from the people who have bought the first edition of *How to Organize Group Travel for Fun and Profit* was overwhelmingly positive. Because of the great, enthusiastic response I received, I am more optimistic than ever about the continually growing opportunity for individuals to become group travel leaders and fulfill their own life-long travel dreams.

CM

CONTENTS IN BRIEF

- To find out about the most satisfying, fun-filled, home-based business in existence today, and learn if you have group travel leader qualities:
  Read Chapters One & Two

- To find out why the group travel leader opportunity is so great, and why you should consider it:
  Read Chapter Three

- To find out how to set up a group travel club business, get established as a group travel leader, and develop a three year plan of action for your travel club:
  Read Section II (Chapters Four, Five & Six)

- To find out about tour and travel supply contacts, who they are and how to use them, how to cost and price your tours:
  Read Section III (Chapters Seven, Eight, Nine)

- To find out about one of the most exciting and profitable growth areas in the leisure travel market today:
  Read Chapter Ten

- To find out how to become knowledgeable about the tour and travel industry and educational opportunities:
  Read Chapter Eleven

- To find group travel leader organization membership information:
  Refer to Reference Section / Organization

- To find group travel publication and subscription application information:
  Refer to Reference Section / Publications

TABLE of CONTENTS

Pre-Chapter Section

FOREWORD VI

CONTENTS IN BREIF IX

TABLE OF CONTENTS X

HOW TO USE THIS BOOK TO YOUR BEST ADVANTAGE XV

ABOUT THE AUTHOR XVIII

SECTION I

THE OPPORTUNITY

CHAPTER 1   The "BOOMING" Group Travel Business 19

The ultimate travel business 20
The three main objectives of this book 22
Ten is the magic number 23
The small, personalized travel clubs 24
The world (literally) is at your doorstep 25
Go for the gold 26
How the business of travel is changing 27
Bad news, good news 27
Survival of the fittest 29
The trend 30
Catch the wave! 31

CHAPTER 2   Are you Qualified to be a Group Travel Leader? 33

The three essential qualities of a group travel leader ... 33
A classic example 35
Beneficial careers that compliment the group leader 37
Feel honored, they're asking you "the Question!" 41

CHAPTER 3   Group Travel Leaders Needed 43

What's age got to do with it? 44
Special organizations for group travel leaders 45
Special publications for group travel leaders 47
Benefits of group travel leader organizations 49
Independent agents and group travel leaders...rejoice! 51
Wait...here's another great connection! 52
Quality contacts important to your business 53
Age is not a factor for ultimate success 54

TABLE of CONTENTS

SECTION II

HOW TO GET STARTED

CHAPTER 4   **Opportunity's knocking!** *55*
Setting-up Your Group Travel Club Business *57*
Getting started *57*
Business is business.. .... *59*
Tax advantages of a home-based business *60*
Setting up your office *64*
Who's going to be your Gutenberg? *70*
Get ready to open the doors! *74*

CHAPTER 5   **Establishing Yourself as a Group Travel Leader** *75*
Start earning commissions now! *75*
3 simple steps *75*
Cruising...instant agent, instant commissions! *77*
You're off and running! *84*
Decisions, decisions, decisions *86*

CHAPTER 6   **Where in the World Do <u>You</u> Want to Go?** *87*
How hard do you <u>really</u> want to work? *87*
Consider these questions *88*
Pick a place...any place *90*
See the USA...or UK? *92*
Three year plan of action *93*
Three Year Travel Plan - DRAFT #1 – Explanation *94*
Three year Travel Plan - DRAFT #2 – Example *96*
It's good to be the group travel leader *99*

SECTION III

TOUR & TRAVEL PLAN OF ACTION

CHAPTER 7   **Developing and Qualifying your Contacts** *101*
How to chose and who to use! *101*
One out of four – pick your option *102*
When to use a travel agency *104*
When to use a tour operator *104*
When to use an international DMC *109*
When to book direct with travel suppliers *111*
And in the beginning *113*
More about USA tour operators *114*

TABLE OF CONTENTS

SECTION III - continued

CHAPTER 7   **Developing and Qualifying your Contacts** – cont.
More about international DMCs 117
"Who do you use?" 118
Who do I use? 119
Can you tell I love my DMC's? 129
"What you know and Who you know are
equally important 129

CHAPTER 8   **Getting Group Tour Quotes** 131
How much was that again? 131
Group Proposal Request form /Explanation 132
Group Proposal Request worksheet 140
Getting a quote 145
Who to use, or not to use...that is the question! 146
Why use a travel agency when I can book direct
with a tour operator or DMC? 148

CHAPTER 9   **Making Money and Selling Tours** 151
The name of the game! 151
How much can I put in the bank? 152
Making money 153
Spending money 154
What did I leave out? 159
Finally! 162

CHAPTER 10   **Sailing the Oceans Blue** 165
"The best of the best" 165
Become a cruise expert 168
Go to school by taking a cruise 174
How to "jump start" your cruise counselor career. 177
Come aboard! 178
Yo ho ho and let's have a martini 179
Cruising the Great Rivers of the World 180
By the way 186

SECTION IV

BE SMART, WORK SMART AND LIVE SMART

CHAPTER 11   **Learning the Globe, the Trade, and Escorting** 187
Say, exactly where is Khartoum anyway? 187
It's not only what you know...it's who you know! ... 188
What you know 188

TABLE OF CONTENTS

SECTION IV - continued

CHAPTER 11　**Learning the Trade** – continued
Who you know *194*
Escorting tours *195*
There's no magic to escorting *197*
Work with the people you like! *198*
Good complications? *199*
A word about attitude *203*

CHAPTER 12　**Thoughts, Observations, and Miscellaneous
Information** **205**

CHAPTER 13　**Committing Group Travel Leader Suicide** **235**
How to commit it and how to prevent it *235*
The Great BS Syndrome Plague of the 1970's *237*
How to commit group travel leader suicide *238*
*How to prevent committing group travel leader
suicide* *239*
Group travel leader suicide – The consequence *239*

CHAPTER 14　**Living the Good Life** **241**
"If things were any better, I'd need a twin! *241*
"Fam" tours, educational tours & site inspections ... *243*

SECTION V

REFERENCE SECTION INDEX 251
REFERENCE SECTION OVERVIEW 252
GROUP LEADER ORGANIZATIONS 253
GROUP LEADER PUBLICATIONS 259
AIRLINES 265
CAR RENTAL AGENCIES 276
CRUISE LINE COMPANIES 279
DESTINATION MANAGEMENT COMPANIES (DMC) 286
HOTEL CHAINS & REPRESENTATIVES 293
MOTORCOACH COMPANIES 302
RAILROAD COMPANIES 318
TOUR OPERATORS 321
TOURISM OFFICES - INTERNATIONAL 352
TOURISM OFFICES - UNITED STATES 366
TRAVEL ASSOCIATIONS & ORGANIZATIONS 376
TRAVEL GLOSSARY 382
TRAVEL & TOUR RELATED WEBSITES 391
INDEX 393

DEDICATION

This book is dedicated to all of the people who have asked me over the past 30 years…"By-the-way, how did you get started in the travel business?"

- When you see a shadowed box like the one below, please pay close attention to the information in bold print within the box.

> *NOTE! Messages or important points I want to emphasize may be repeated and highlighted in italic type style in this box. Please read and consider this information carefully!*

- As you read, make use of the margins for notes. Also, keep a highlighter and red pen handy so you can highlight, underline or circle any information or ideas that you may want to review again later. Make notes to yourself, mark and highlight any sentences, paragraphs, or sections that inspire you or set your imagination into high-gear. Sticky notes and colored stick-on tabs are useful in case you want to color-code certain areas of interest. Color-coding is a great system for *fast referencing* parts of the book that you will want to return to at a later time.

- Read this book more than once. You will find that each time you re-read this book, something you missed the first time will probably grab your attention.

- Keep this book nearby as a travel industry reference guide. Most of the travel supplier contacts that you need to get started are listed in the reference section. As your travel knowledge grows (along with your club membership), you will establish your own personal contacts and can add these to the books reference list.

- All of the group travel organizations, publications, books, tour and travel supplier contacts mentioned in this book are listed in the Reference Section at the end of the book.

- Most of all, have fun reading this book, and remember that imagination is a major ingredient in your success. So, let your imagination be vivid, let it take control, let it put your desire to travel into *overdrive*. It is important you that you *SEE* in your mind the end result you want to achieve. Remember; it is hard for the eyes to see when your imagination is out of focus!

ACKNOWLEDGMENTS

First of all, a big "THANK YOU" for the gracious hospitality and friendship of the multitude of people I have met in my travels around the globe. It is because of these fond memories and special experiences that I write this book.

The input from many of the group travel leaders, suppliers and destination management companies, that I know and have worked with over the years, was terrific. These successful group travel leaders and travel experts added much to the overall completeness of the book. Thank you!

A special thanks to Ellen Schulz, Michael Nossaman, Nevell Razak, Rich Owens, Wayne Sica, Mary Wiedenmann, and Dick and Carol Starnes for their technical guidance, support and editing. A very special "thank you" to Peter and Cindy Cranstone whose time and effort on this project was invaluable. All of these peoples' specialties were a great help since *my real specialties* are in the area of eating, drinking and traveling.

Finally, a great big "THANK YOU" to my wonderful wife, Anne, who not only inspired me to write this book, but has *totally* taken care of our group travel business while I did it. Maybe she can write the next book and I'll work for a while!

CM

WARNING - DISCLAIMER

This book is designed to provide information in regard to the subject matter covered. It is sold with the understanding that the publisher and the author are not engaged in rendering legal, accounting or other professional services. If legal or other expert assistance is required, the services of a competent professional should be sought.

It is not the purpose of this book to reprint all the information that is otherwise available to the author and/or publisher, but to complement, amplify and supplement other texts. You are urged to read all related material available to you and learn as much as possible about the group travel leader/group travel club business.

The group travel business is not a get-rich-quick scheme. Anyone who decides to start a travel club and become a group travel leader must expect to invest a lot of time and effort in order to have a solid travel club. Many of the group travel leaders who understood this, have built successful, solid, growing, and rewarding travel clubs.

Every effort has been made to make this book as complete and accurate as possible. However, there may be a mistake either typographical or in content. Therefore, this text should be used only as a general guide and not as the ultimate source of group travel information. Furthermore, in the computerized world of today, the business of travel changes constantly, so this book contains information on group travel only up to the printing date.

The purpose of this book is to inspire, inform and educate the reader to the great opportunities that owning and managing a travel club can offer. The author and ETC Publishing, Inc. shall have neither liability nor responsibility to any person or entity with respect to any loss or damage caused, or alleged to be caused, directly or in directly by the information contained in this book.

ABOUT THE AUTHOR

Author sailing past the famous Sydney Opera House on the luxury sailboat, *Solway Lass.*

Sydney Harbor / Sydney, Australia - 1998

Carl Meadows is an acknowledged expert in several areas of the travel industry. Starting in the travel business in 1970 as an outside sales representative for a local Kansas City travel agency, Carl went on to become Director of Group Sales for one of the largest franchise travel agencies in the U.S.A. During his career, Carl has owned and operated successful travel agencies, produced international conferences and tradeshows, and was the Executive Director of a major international association. Since 1984, Carl and his wife Anne, have owned and operated ETC Services, Inc., a group travel company specializing in international travel, conference and convention meeting planning, and corporate incentive travel. Carl is also a consultant to the group travel leader community. Currently, Carl and Anne are happy, healthy and living in Castle Rock, Colorado.

CHAPTER 1

The "BOOMING" Group Travel Business

The small, personal travel club..."Catch the Wave!"

Donna Robbins is semi-retired and travels around the world in fine style. She travels for *free,* and at the same time, *makes money.* Donna has goals, several goals, but the main one is to travel to places around the globe which *she has always wanted to visit and tour* but could not afford. Now, however, Donna is realizing her goals and travels where she wants, when she wants, several times a year. How has she managed to accomplish this? She does it through her travel club, Donna's Personalized Travel. She does it as a *Group Travel Leader.*

If the story about Donna Robbins and her travel club is appealing to you, keep reading and find out what being a *Group Travel Leader* is all about. Donna is a classic example of thousands of ordinary individuals and couples who have decided to finally fulfill their travel dreams and enter into the leisure travel business...specifically the *group* leisure travel business.

The ultimate travel business

After working in just about every facet of the travel industry for the past thirty years, I have discovered what I believe is not only the ultimate travel business, but also is one of the easiest areas of travel to get started in. It is also the one which has the most growth potential and the best opportunity to make money...*group leisure travel.*

Being the organizer and leader of your own tours, you get to go to the best destinations that the world has to offer, have the most fun while doing it, and make money on top of it. The reason the tours are to the best places in the world is because <u>you</u> get to pick where you are going!

Although I consider group travel "the best of the best" in the travel industry, there are many other areas of the travel business you could consider. Listed below are a few that may be of interest to you. The categories are diverse and opportunities abound for anyone wanting to get involved:

- Destination Management
- Cruise Specialist
- Corporate Meeting Planning
- Convention Management
- Seminar and Conference Management
- Incentive Travel

All offer great opportunities and rewards for anyone willing to <u>put in the time and effort to learn these specialized travel trades</u>. Depending on where you are in your stage of life and how strong your interest truly is in travel, the key to your success in getting started in the travel business will be to analyze and investigate these different travel categories to match them with your strengths and weaknesses. Some of the categories listed (and there are many more) will take a considerable amount of education and training over a long period of time. If you are in college at this time, this could be a smart career decision for you. However, if you are retired, or close to the end of your working career, you will probably want to find an area that offers a more leisurely entry...something that fits your lifestyle a little better and lets you use the social and business skills you have developed over the years to your best advantage. If you have been in a career where interacting with other people was required, such as sales and marketing, public service, the hospitality industry, teaching, etc., then you already possess many of the skills needed to be successful in the group travel business.

If you are a senior, a travel club can be a great hobby or a full-time business, depending on how active you want to be and what your goals are. Whatever level of commitment you choose can be attainable with the guidance of this "how to" manual.

NOTE! This book was written to help anyone, at any age, who is interested in exploring travel either as a career or for a fun, full-time or part-time business. However, the main objective of How to Organize Group Travel for Fun and Profit is focused on showing the semi-retired and senior citizen population (this includes baby boomers and older) the easiest way to "get their feet wet" without making a major investment of cash or having to commit to long-term schooling.

Throughout *How to Organize Group Travel for Fun and Profit,* I will recommend other reference and travel related books that you may want to consider purchasing for your personal library. These books will provide additional travel education for you as well as more extensive travel resource contacts. Why or when you obtain these additional books depends, of course, on your decision about how active you want to be in the group travel business.

Chapter 1   **21**

For individuals wanting to be a casual group travel leader, *How to Organize Group Travel for Fun and Profit* will provide more than enough guidance for you to be successful. For those who want to really catch the group travel leader *"wave"* of opportunity, continually gaining knowledge about the travel business will be a must, so reading and studying about the travel business will be very important. Initially, while deciding where you want to position yourself in the industry, the public library can be a great source of information for you. Another way to get informed about the group business is to subscribe to the various group travel leader publications and/or join one or more of the group travel leader organizations.

NOTE! All of the books, publications and organizations that are mentioned throughout the various chapters will be listed again in the Reference Section of this book. A complete A-Z listing is provided for your convenience.

Meanwhile, this is the first book you will need to help you get your new career (or hobby) started in the group leisure travel business.

How to Organize Group Travel for Fun and Profit **has three main objectives:**

1. To help you understand the way the business of travel is changing dramatically and why now is the time to start taking advantage of these great opportunities

2. To help you make a smooth transition from your present position to that of an acknowledged group tour leader

3. To help keep your new business (or hobby) on track

Giving you guidance from start to finish, this book will show you:

- How to structure and operate a group travel business as a home-based operation

- How to get started in group leisure travel

- How to get established and be recognized by travel and tour suppliers as a viable group tour operator

- How to help accomplish your travel and monetary goals

- How to fulfill *your* travel dreams

Ten is the magic number!

Getting a group of ten to forty people to agree to travel together on the same dates and to the same destination probably seems like a pretty hard task to you at this time. Admittedly, it does take some finesse, but it's easier than you think once you have a fundamental knowledge of how to package and market your tours. I will go into much more detail about this subject in later chapters, but for now, I want to pass along some information that should put your mind at ease and keep you reading.

The first thing you should know is that you only need ten, that's TEN, people to be eligible for discounts on travel. Sometimes it's even less than ten, but for now let's use ten as the magic number. This includes major national and international airlines, hotels, railroads and some cruise lines. Most cruise lines, as a norm, offer one free for every fifteen full paying passengers (this means the sixteenth passenger goes free). Some cruise lines offer special cruises occasionally at one free for every ten passengers (eleventh passenger goes free).

Now, think about this; You could be on your way, to almost any of your "dream destinations" *if you could just get ten individuals* from the list below:

- family members
- close personal friends
- neighbors
- high school & college friends
- business acquaintances

OR <u>five couples of</u> :

- golf partners
- bridge and dance partners
- bowling and bingo friends
- fraternal and social club member acquaintances

That's it! Ten people, and you could start traveling for free and making money while you are on the trip! Think of all the people you know, that you work with, that you associate with on a daily basis, and you will realize that this is *a very achievable goal.* As your groups grow in size, so do the discounts, perks and benefits as well as your potential to make more money.

Again, all of this will be covered in more detail in the chapters. I just wanted get you started thinking about how few people it will to take to get your travel club up-and-running and to start you on the road to new adventures.

Small, personalized travel clubs

To get the "Big Picture," it is important that you understand the nature of the inevitable group leisure travel explosion that will happen during the next decade. There is a new trend evolving in the travel industry today that is going to have a profound effect on thousands of ordinary people not currently involved in travel. The trend is that of *small* groups of people (10 to 40) traveling together. **This is not exactly a new concept, I admit.** But the real story is <u>the evolving</u>

major trend of emerging *small, personalized travel clubs* owned and managed by an independent *group travel leader or leaders.*

Group travel leaders are a growing number of people who are interested in traveling, enjoy being a leader, and who are now actively involved in organizing tour groups through their church, AARP chapters, senior and community centers, etc. *The new area of real growth, however, is coming from people who operate their OWN tours through their OWN personal travel clubs. The incentives for the group travel leader are many, including free travel, extra income, educational opportunities, religious studies, cultural enlightenment, adventure, making new friends, etc.*

The good news is that this phenomenal opportunity is not reserved only for affluent retirees anymore, but for anyone (from teenagers to senior citizens) interested in travel.

> *NOTE! The new area of real growth, however, is coming from people who operate their OWN tours through their OWN personal travel clubs. A personal travel club is one of the best home-based businesses you can be involved in today. This is an especially attractive option for retired and semi-retired people.*

Starting now, the world is at your doorstep!

Anyone who has a desire to travel can now be in the travel business. If you are younger and still working, this is a great way to have one or two annual vacations for free and make extra money at the same time. If you are retired or semi-retired, it is a wonderful way to experience the places you have always wanted to see, but never had the time or money to visit. A major plus is that it's *your decision* on how involved you want to get and how hard you want to work. In other words, the number of trips you want to take each year, length of the trips, how many tour participants you want to handle on each tour (group size), etc. is totally up to you.

For years, exotic travel has been reserved for the "rich and famous." Not anymore! Anyone with a desire to travel today can make it happen by becoming a group travel leader and starting a group leisure travel club. During the past ten years, travel has become more and more affordable to the masses. Intriguing areas of the world that people only dreamed of traveling to are now getting more accessible day-by-day and are ready to be explored by you...the group travel leader!

What is the reason for this great opportunity? The number of people able to travel today is absolutely exploding because of the "baby boomer" factor. In the year 2001, over one hundred million US citizens will be over the age of fifty. *One Hundred Million!* Today, adult Americans are healthier, wealthier and more active than ever. The "baby boomers" especially fall into this category as most want to live life to the fullest and traveling is very high on their agenda.

Thousands upon thousands of people are able to take several trips a year these days. A *majority* of these people will be looking for someone to provide a travel and tour service for them. As the trend evolves, most will prefer to travel with a small group of people, organized by someone who has a personal interest in them and the area they are considering. *That is where you enter the picture if you are a leader*...as most people prefer to follow, not lead. Providing a personalized travel service, in the form of a travel club (*your* travel club), has a value which more and more people will be searching for during the years to come.

Go for the gold...

By the time you finish this book, you will have all the information needed to make a logical decision on whether you wish to pursue a group travel leader career or whether you prefer to simply find a good travel agency or independent travel club that fills your travel requirements. Whether you think you are a born leader or not, *if you have a desire to travel, like people, and have an out going personality*, give this great opportunity a try...*go for the gold!*

> *NOTE! Over 100 million people will be age fifty or over in the year 2001 and approximately 80% of these people will be looking for someone to take care of their tour and travel needs. This business could be yours!!*

How the business of travel is changing

There are several factors that are changing the way people book their business and leisure travel today. The main influence, of course, is the *Internet*. The accessibility that people have to airline flight information, tour and travel itineraries, and travel information in general is phenomenal. With technology advancing at the speed of light (literally, in some instances), people are departing from the conventional way of booking travel. Instead of calling a travel agency, they can search the web, find, and book all of their travel arrangements via the Internet without leaving the comfort of their home. Personally, I'm already amazed at what can be found, bought and sold, travel-wise, over the Internet today. What we will be capable of doing on the Internet in the near future will probably not only be amazing, but will border on *"staggering"* for most of us.

Bad news, good news

What effect is the Internet having on travel agencies and the services they provide? Put simply, a profound effect. Because of the Internet, almost all of the major travel suppliers are starting to sell directly to the consumer. This includes airlines, hotels, car rental agencies, and tour operators. The travel agencies' "once-upon-a-time" travel partners are now some of their stiffest competitors! Making the situation worse is that the small, personalized "Mom and Pop" travel agencies are getting squeezed out of business by BIG corporate/tour and travel conglomerates. Also, more and more corporate executives are booking their business travel through the Internet, as are individuals who just need a simple point-to-point airline ticket. That's the bad news.

What's the good news? The leisure market business, people wanting to take a vacation, is booming! Remember the one hundred million baby boomers? *They all want to take a vacation, or two...or three!* When it comes to vacations, most people want to work with someone they know and trust, someone who is reliable and has a good reputation for personal service. Because of the demand for personalized service in the leisure market, reputable, progressive travel agencies (the survivors), and travel clubs will have a great business opportunity during the next decade.

When planning a personal vacation, most people like to sit down with a travel expert and have them explain the details of their trip, what it includes, what they are going to see and do, and in essence, *reassure them about the great time they are going to have!* Everyone wants a "perfect vacation" and the more we enter into Orwell's Big Brother era, the more a personal touch will mean to those seeking reassurance of their "perfect vacation." I don't think a voice coming from a computer that sounds like Darth Vader (Star Wars), or Hal (2001 Space Odyssey) will give them the same reassurance. Sort of scary actually. As I mentioned, since the baby boomers still remember how it used to be in the "good ol' days," most of them *really* want to talk to someone about their personal vacation. The travel agent and group travel leaders who take time to do this will not only survive, but will experience substantial, long-term growth. That's the good news!

Survival of the fittest!

A little more about travel agencies. The "Mom and Pop" agencies that flourished so well in the 1960's, 1970's and early 1980's are finding it hard to survive in the 1990's. In 1995 there were nearly 33,000 travel agencies in the U.S. By January 01, 2000, there will be 26,000 travel agencies in existence, with another 5,000 expected to be sold, merged, or just closing their doors, in the next eighteen months (source: Leisure Travel News/Dec., 1999). During the first few years of the next decade, it will truly be the survival of the fittest. High overhead, cut commissions from suppliers, and heavy price competition from the mega-travel companies and the ever-growing competition from the Internet for travel dollars, are all contributing factors. The "squeezing out" of small businesses is certainly not limited to travel agencies. You read or hear about it in the news on a daily basis as big companies begin hostile takeovers, or merge, or buy out smaller companies.

The world is changing into a global economy and the key to success for many mega-companies is to get even bigger. In the case of the mega-travel companies, they will try to be a "one stop" travel service. I am sure when it comes to corporate and individual airline ticketing, they will be efficient and competitive. Since the mega-agencies tend to be "ticket factories," how they handle the leisure side of business will probably be another matter. *On the other hand*, if someone books a tour with a service oriented travel agency (a survivor), the agent will take the time to research, package and explain the details of the tour. If they book with a travel club, the group travel leader will do the same, as well as be with them during their tour from start to finish. That is one of the group travel leader's responsibilities, not only to take the trip but to also take care of the tour participants. It all comes down to personalized service. Whoever offers the best service, before, during, and after a tour, will be the long term winner and keeper of the gold.

The trend

When one door closes ("Mom and Pop" travel agencies) another door opens, e.g., opportunities for smaller, innovative travel agencies, independent travel agents, leisure travel clubs and group travel leaders. The trend in the travel industry for the next decade will likely proceed this way:

1. Smaller travel agencies will be phased out of business, for reasons discussed earlier, by either being bought or merged into a large travel conglomerate. Or, in some cases, they will just shut their doors and walk away.

2. Travel agencies that survive will be both progressive and innovative. As discussed, they will know the value of personalized service and what it can mean to the growth of their agency. Along with great service, many also become brokers or suppliers to independent or intermediary travel agents *and group travel leaders.* The independent travel agents pay a monthly or annual fee to the travel agency, which in turn will provide a desk, telephone/fax, support service, and airline computer access. The independent agents usually have the option of working at the travel agency, out of their home, or sometimes both. More will be discussed about the independent outside travel agent opportunity in Chapter Three.

3. Many surviving agencies will become specialized and deal in higher profit travel services, such as cruise only or islands only agencies. Others will gear toward more unique travel services such as photography travel, wine and culinary tours, flower and garden tours, museum and estate tours, or adventure tours, to name a few. Specialty tour options are endless and you are only limited by your imagination. As a group travel leader, specialization is an option you may want to consider. Specialized tours make your role in the

group travel business fun, interesting and profitable. Specialized tours will be discussed in detail in Chapter Twelve.

The bottom line is the Internet and mega-travel companies will keep growing and growing and become bigger and bigger. In some cases, maybe bigger can be better. But in the case of leisure travel, which is such a personalized service, personal attention to the packaging of your tour is going to be the order of the day for most people. Because of this trend, there is going to be a great opportunity for people who have always thought about being in the travel business to *actually* do it! And, as a bonus, you are getting into the very best area of the tour and travel industry, *group leisure travel.*

Along with the surviving travel agencies that have jumped on the baby boomer wagon, small travel clubs, promoted and managed by independent group travel leaders, will be the hope of future personalized tour and travel as we used to know it. Don't let this opportunity pass you by; join in the fun and future of being a group travel leader!

A wave of opportunity awaits you...

Consider the evolving travel club and group travel leader opportunity the same way a surfer considers how to catch the "BIG WAVE." The key to their successful ride (travel club/group travel leader opportunity) is to catch the wave BEFORE it gets rolling, not three feet from the shore. Just like the surfer, you want to be in front of that wave...and you are, by several years. The indications for starting a successful group leisure travel business during the next several years is phenomenal and the time could not be more opportune for anyone having the desire to travel, meet new people, experience new cultures AND make money at the same time. What a deal! The new millennium has arrived; it is a new decade and the "wave" is just a ripple at this time. Over the next few years, a gigantic wave of opportunity will open doors for thousands of people smart enough to act now. The home-based group travel club and group travel leader wave is coming, and coming in a big way. *CATCH THE WAVE!*

CHAPTER 2

Are You Qualified to be a Group Travel Leader?

The answer is probably "Yes"!

Are you qualified to be a group travel leader? As the chapter's subtitle says; probably *YES*. But you will never know until you try. As you will see, investigating this opportunity is easy, interesting and fun! Read on and see if it is right for you.

First of all, the qualifications for a successful group travel leader are simple and few, but nevertheless essential. They are as follows:

The Three Essential Qualities of a Group Travel Leader

1. **You must be a people person:** True success in the group travel business comes from a sincere desire to show your group a fantastic time during their trip. Once you have accomplished this, they will be yours forever! It is very important that you understand that *you* are the group tour leader, and that means taking an active interest in your group participants. It starts with answering their first questions regarding your tours or cruises, watching out for

them during the trip itself, and then waving goodbye to them once you have returned home. Going that "extra mile" for your tour participants will gain you a good reputation and set your club apart from other group travel clubs.

Liking people is an important criteria for success in almost any business, but especially the travel business. You must offer a good tour at a good price, answer all questions and concerns with sincere interest, and take care of your group members while they are on your tour. These are your main functions as a group tour leader and will be the cornerstone of your travel club.

2. **Attention to detail:** This is a very important qualification but one that can be developed and learned over a period of time, if it is not already one of your strong points. If your detail strengths are a little "weak" at this time, do not fear! Worksheets to help you get quotes from travel suppliers and help you to price your tours are discussed in detail in Chapters Eight and Nine. Using the worksheets will assist you with the preliminary task of setting up tour programs and will help you avoid making many of the typical first time pricing errors that can cost you time, money, and grief. As you steadily gain knowledge of the group travel business, you can adjust and redesign the worksheets to fit the particular way you like to price your tours.

    Attention to detail also needs to be foremost in your mind when negotiating with travel suppliers. Careful notes, taken at a meeting or during telephone conversations with a potential tour operator, may be needed later to help remind them of certain concessions they made to you. There will be more about negotiating in the later chapters.

    If you are considering this venture as a way to take two or three vacations a year, the last thing you want to do is come up "short" when pricing your tours. This business is meant to be fun and exciting, not draining, emotionally or financially.

3. **Desire to Travel:** This is a very important qualification since *your desire* to travel and see the world will be the driving force behind your club. The destinations and tour packages *you* select to offer your club members need *your enthusiasm* behind them in order to get your groups to materialize and for your travel club to grow.

> *NOTE! A good group travel leader should:*
>
> *1. Like people*
>
> *2. Be attentive to details*
>
> *3. Love to travel*

A classic example

A classic example of someone who has taken full advantage of the group leader opportunity is Dr. John Schachet. If you missed reading Dr. Schachet's testimonial letter at the beginning of the book, (page V) you may want to go back and read it.

SeaVision, Inc. – Conferences at Sea

Dr. Schachet is a respected optometrist in the Denver, Colorado area where he has a thriving eye care practice. He is also a consultant to some of the major manufacturers of eye care products and, on their behalf, speaks nationally and internationally to fellow optometrists regarding advanced eye care technology.

After Dr. Schachet was made aware of the group travel opportunity a few years ago, he immediately saw himself as a potential group tour and seminar organizer. As it should be, the good doctor's first love is to his profession, followed closely by his love of golf and a penchant for cruising the oceans of the world. After analyzing the many established optometric conferences held annually, he realized there was a unique opportunity for him to carve out a niche providing continuing education through seminars...held at sea! Since there was a very successful continuing education seminar held annually during the winter called Snowvision (always at a ski resort), he took the opposite route and had his venues on a cruise ship, an island, or a coastal resort area. Thus, SeaVision, Inc., Conferences at Sea was born.

Now in its seventh year, SeaVision Conferences at Sea averages eighty to one hundred participants per sailing and continues to grow each year. Obviously, Dr. Schachet is pleased that he took action to become a group tour leader. He is now traveling for free (and playing golf), making new friends and business acquaintances (and playing more golf), *Making Money (and playing more golf)!* You get the picture.

Dr. Schachet's success can be attributed to his meeting the three main (and very important) requirements of a good group travel leader:

1. He likes meeting new people and making new friends (a people person)

2. He pays attention to details

3. He has a desire to travel

In my opinion, point one and point three need to be a "natural" for a group travel leader. Point two, *attention to details*, can be learned as well as other business related skills. Studying group travel books and guides, joining group leader organizations, subscribing to group travel publications, and most importantly, networking with other group travel leaders and tour operators will give you the business acumen you need. After reading and studying *How to Organize Group Travel for Fun and Profit*, you will have a good working knowledge of the travel business such as:

- How to structure and organize your travel club

- How to make travel supplier contacts

- How to keep your travel club growing and on the right track

- How to plan, package and market tours

- How to escort tours

Perhaps your educational and working background has already provided you with some of this knowledge. Many group travel leaders that I know have had careers that gave them a good basic business knowledge and allowed them to make an easy transition from their chosen professions to the travel business. Hopefully this will be your case as well.

Beneficial careers that complement the group travel leader

The following are some of the careers that lend themselves to a good transition to the group travel business. Many group travel leaders come from these professions:

- Teachers (active and retired)
- Military
- Corporate sales and marketing
- Corporate trainers
- Secretaries and administrative assistants
- Seminar speakers
- Medical doctors and nurses

- Writers
- Ministers and religious leaders
- Law enforcement personnel
- Athletes

It is not necessary that you have a professional background, such as the ones listed above, to become a group travel leader or start a travel club, but it does help speed the process up. Remember, anyone, from any background or profession can get into the group travel business if the motivation is there. The list of professions mentioned above is just some of the group travel leader backgrounds personally known to me.

Admittedly, in many cases, some people have a distinct advantage and can gain an additional "edge" because of their backgrounds or professions, such as these three examples:

1. Expatriates Living in America

A fantastic opportunity is knocking on the door of any expatriate who has an interest in becoming a group travel leader. Whatever your nationality, if you are living in America, you have a great advantage over most Americans by being foreign-born. Why? In general, most Americans have a genuine interest in anyone from another country. This is especially true if they know them personally as neighbors or co-workers.

I know of several expatriates who were literally "drummed" into becoming group travel leaders because their friends, neighbors and social acquaintances wanted to travel with "a local" to his/her home country. Once the ex-pat has taken a few group tours to their homeland, they automatically have a following and a nucleus for a travel club. Then, after proving themselves as quality group travel leaders, the ex-pat's travel club members will follow them anywhere. I have seen this scenario happen time and time again.

By-the-way, a suggestion to all of the future ex-pat group tour leaders; don't lose your accent! If your accent is starting to fade away, practice until you get it back. Americans are suckers for accents. *We love accents!* So play it up and use it to your best advantage.

2. Active or Retired Association Members

Many group travel leaders and travel club owners got their start by being members of a professional or fraternal association. Many associations have extensive memberships and, as a member yourself, this list of "kindred sprits" is <u>usually</u> accessible for your use.

Almost everyone likes to associate with people with whom they have something in common. So, when a retired teacher, who belongs to the National Association of Retired Teachers, promotes their group travel club and tours to the members of this particular association, the members are more likely to consider them over someone who is not a member or a former teacher. The same would work for a member of any association, alumni group, fraternity, etc. Take advantage of the common bond you have with your past or present association members whenever and wherever you can.

Remember, most people do not want to lead. They just want to be part of a tour where they know they are going to be taken care of. You already have the confidence of your professional associates, now all you have to do is show them how you excel in your group travel business!

3. Ex-Military

People with a military background seem to excel in the group travel business also. The discipline and leadership they learned during their military career is excellent training for running their travel club. If they had a leadership responsibility while in the military, then organizing groups of people (hopefully they won't make them do push-ups!) and running a good operation is just business as usual.

Once again, the contacts they have developed through their years of military service can give them a good start toward establishing a base membership for their travel club. If you are ex-military and are a member of any club, organization or association such as the VFW, Army, Navy, Air Force or Marine Corps., these will be a great resource for you. Even better would be the personal associations, if they are qualified to belong, such as the Vietnam Helicopter Pilots Association, The Flying Tigers of the 14th Air Force Association, The Association of the USS IOWA, etc. These membership rosters should be on the "A List" of your marketing plan as the camaraderie in these associations is much stronger.

The following story is an account of an extremely success-ful travel club that is run by a retired military man. It started with a few friends getting together to go skiing, and has blossomed over the years into a major, international group travel club.

The Over the Hill Gang International

Located in Colorado Springs, CO, the Executive Director of the Over the Hill Gang International is retired Air Force General, Dennis C. Beasley. The Over the Hill Gang International (OTHG) travel club is a senior adventure club with members who are fifty years or older. The OTHG epitomizes the natural transition of a small ski club into a large, dynamic membership travel club. From the original few friends getting together to go skiing in 1977, the OTHG has grown to become an international travel club of over six thousand members in fifty states and nineteen countries with thirteen chapters. Now that's a travel club!

The OTHG has also gone from exclusively promoting ski tours to selling group tour packages all over the world. Although they still average around thirty ski trips a year, the OTHG group tour programs now include bicycling, white water rafting and golf, totally tailored to the senior adventurer. The OTHG also offers discounts and other membership benefits.

The Over the Hill Gang International should be an inspiration to anyone just starting a group travel club. The vision of the leadership has guided this organization to where it is today, a first class international travel club. As a group travel leader yourself, try to emulate other travel clubs successes such as the OTHG.

Keep in mind, while having the training of an Air Force General certainly would help, leadership qualities can be found in many varied backgrounds, i.e., Boy/Girl Scout leaders, President of a PTA or social club, most corporate careers, etc., can give a person good, basic leadership skills.

NOTE! Remember, anyone, from any background or profession can get into the group travel business if the motivation is there. Motivation is the keyword!

Feel honored, they're asking you "The Question!"

After your club has been established and you have a few tours under your belt, something remarkable starts to happen. Once people start discovering your new endeavor, *you* all of a sudden become the "Guru of Travel" in your immediate social circles. People who travel the world generally fascinate their neighbors, casual acquaintances, business associates, and even complete strangers, *especially when the travel is for pleasure and is also your business*! As an established group tour leader, you should be prepared to answer...*"The Question."* Sooner or later the conversation will come around to: "How did you get started in the travel business anyway?"

This is a question you will be asked over and over again. As my dedication states, I have been asked this question hundreds and hundreds of times. I love answering this question and you will too! I guarantee that you will never get tired of discussing your latest trip, your most favorite place in the world, where are you taking your next group, and so on.

All of these people who ask "The Question" will be prime prospects for your travel club. Pass out your business cards like crazy; give them to anybody, especially family, friends, and even strangers. You will be surprised at the number of people who eventually contact you and become tour members of your club.

To conclude this chapter, I hope you will decide to give the group travel leader opportunity a try. If you do, you will find it interesting, exciting, fun and fulfilling. Travel, money, long-lasting friendships, and everlasting memories are just a few of the wonderful rewards you will reap for your efforts.

Are you qualified to be a group travel leader and operate your own travel club? If you answered yes to eight or more of the twelve questions at the beginning of the book and fit the three essential qualifications in this chapter, then "YES" is the definitive answer. In Chapter Three, find out about the great opportunities for potential group travel leaders and the many support organizations waiting to help you get started. *You're never too young or too old...now, go for the gold!*

CHAPTER 3

Group Travel Leaders Needed

Teenagers to seniors...the demand is there!

Today, the group travel leader opportunity is greater than ever. The "KEY" to getting started is having a *desire* to travel. Practically everyone has a "dream" country or city that he or she would someday love to visit. It could be China, Switzerland, Australia, Italy...London, Paris or Hong Kong. Teenager or senior, a "dream" destination probably exists somewhere.

My original dream destinations, when I first started in travel, were the capitals of Europe and exotic islands. I wanted to roam the ramparts of medieval castles and swim in blue lagoons surrounded by coconut palms. Whether London, Paris, Rome or Robinson Crusoe's island came first, I did not care, just as long as I got to all of them eventually.

Fortunately, being a group travel leader for many years has allowed me to fulfill these very specific travel dreams and many, many more...more than I ever imagined.

What's age got to do with it...?

Absolutely nothing! Young adults to grandmothers and grandfathers all have the same opportunity to excel in the group travel business. The only limitations that you may experience to succeed will be *self-imposed*. Every generation will have some advantage over others. Young adults will have youth, optimism and an "I can do anything" attitude (ignorance is bliss), plus all of their zealous friends to go along with "The Plan!" The thirty to forty year olds will have some real life experiences to play on and guide them, such as their career experiences, steadfast business acquaintances, friends and family. Seniors, on the other hand, have *all of this and more!* The seniors can call upon the memories of their youth (all of the places they dreamed of traveling to), and their career (all of the places they didn't have time or money to travel to), and all of their life experiences to guide them. Now, adventurous seniors can finally go and do what they want, when they want, and with whom they want to do it with. Essentially, this is a golden opportunity for anyone, of any age to get involved.

The subtitle to this chapter states that there is a "demand" for travel leaders of all ages. Perhaps the more appropriate word to use would be "opportunity." Proof of the growing group travel leader trend and the demand for travel leaders of all ages is apparent. There is a noticeable emergence of professional group travel organizations and publications being established and dedicated to serving this new travel community. All over the USA, group travel organizations, associations and societies are being formed to educate and help anyone who wants to become a group travel leader. The benefits for the group travel leader joining these organizations are many, for both new and established group leaders. Most beneficial, is the opportunity to meet *legitimate travel suppliers* that can help you and your business grow.

Whether you are searching for a fall foliage bus tour or an African safari, these will be the people that can help you accomplish your travel agendas. The tour operators and travel industry suppliers that belong to credible group leader organizations are insured, trustworthy and competitive. After joining some the organizations, these people, along with your fellow group leaders, are all the contacts you will need to blossom and grow your business.

Special organizations for group travel leaders

The following are a few examples of the growing number of professional group travel organizations that have been established to accommodate the emerging group travel leader, independent outside travel consultant, and personal travel club phenomenon:

- **BankTravel (dedicated to senior bank group travel planners)**
  P.O. Box 129
  Salem, OH 44460
  Tel: (330) 332-3841   Fax: (330) 337-1118
  E-mail: editorial@group travelleader.com
  Web site: http://www.banktravel.com

  Note: The BankTravel organization is nationwide

- **Group Leaders of America (GLAMER)**
  P.O. Box 129
  Salem, OH 44460
  Tel: (800) 628-0993   Fax: (330) 337-1118
  E-mail: glamernet@aol.com
  Web site: http://www.glamer.com

  Note: The GLAMER organization is nationwide

- **Heritage Club International (dedicated to senior bank group travel planners)**
  P.O. Box 1708
  Mason City, IA 50402-1708

Heritage Club International - continued

Tel: (515) 424-1600   Fax: (515) 424-7863
E-mail: geaker@firstcitizensnb.com
Web site: http://www.heritageclubs.com

Note: Heritage Club International is nationwide

- **International Group Tour Association (IGTA)**
  (Formerly known as Senior Travel Recreation & Activities Company / STRAC)
  2465 112th Avenue
  Holland, MI 49424
  Tel: (800) 767-3489   Fax: (616) 393-0085
  E-mail: ccarley@grouptour.com
  Web site: http://www.grouptour.com

  Note: The IGTA association is nationwide

- **National Association of Senior Travel Planners (NASTP)**
  P.O. Box 212
  Hingham, MA   02043
  Tel: (800) 543-9736   Fax: (781) 749-4099
  E-mail: nastp@mediaone.net
  Web site: http://www. nastp.com

  Note: The NASTP is primarily East Coast region

- **Outside Sales Support Network (OSSN – association for independent travel agents and group tour leaders)**
  1340 U.S. Highway 1, Suite 102
  Jupiter, FL   33469
  Tel: (561) 743-1900   Fax: (561) 575-4371
  E-mail: ossn@ossn.com
  Web site: http://www.ossn.com

  Note: OSSN has members in both the United States and Canada

NOTE! Applications to join organizations referred to in the book, or subscriptions to various publications mentioned can be found in the Group Tour Leaders Application section at the end of the book.

Special publications for group travel leaders

The *GREAT NEWS* is that membership in most of these organizations is either *FREE* or at a nominal cost. In addition, most group travel organizations have a publication of some type to communicate with their members. So along with your membership, you also receive that organization's newsletter, magazine or bulletins. The following are some of the group travel leader publications, which offer the latest news about the group travel industry (listed in no particular order):

- **Leisure Group Travel Magazine** (Nationwide circulation – published six times per year)
  4901 Forest Avenue
  Downers Grove, IL 60515
  Tel: (630) 964-1431   Fax: (630) 852-0414

- **The Group Travel Leader** (GLAMER's full color newspaper/ nationwide circulation – published monthly)
  401 West Main Street, Suite 222
  Lexington, KY 40507
  Tel: (606) 253-0455   Fax: (606) 253-0499

- **Travel Tips** (Western USA circulation – published six times per year)
  4901 Forest Avenue
  Downers Grove, IL 60515
  Tel: (630) 964-1431   Fax: (630) 852-0414

- **Tips on Trips** (NASTP's "specials" newsletter – Eastern USA circulation – published bi-monthly)
  P.O. Box 212
  Hingham, MA 02043
  Tel: (800) 543-9736   Fax: (781) 749-4099

- **Group Tour Magazine** (5 regional publications in a tabloid format – published four times per year)
  2465 112th Avenue
  Holland, MI 49424-9657
  Tel: (800) 767-3489   Fax: (616) 393-0085

- **SYTA's Student & Youth Traveler** (Distributed in the United States and Canada – published two times per year)
  2465 112th Avenue
  Holland, MI 49424-9657
  Tel: (800) 767-3489   Fax: (616) 393-0085

- **Bank Travel Management Magazine & Bank Shot Newsletter** (Nationwide circulation of 4,000 bank club directors– published bi-monthly)
  401 West Main Street, Suite 222
  Lexington, KY 40507
  Tel: (330) 332-3841   Fax: (606) 253-0499

The organizations and publications listed in this chapter are waiting to hear from you. They offer guidance, inspiration, and a wealth of travel supplier contacts. The information you will receive from them will be invaluable to your group leader education and success of your business.

Also, there are new associations and organizations being started specifically dedicated to the growing group travel industry and most of them will have a news and educational publication supporting them. As a member of the organizations and a subscriber to the publications listed in this book, you will most likely be included in their mailings.

Note! Immediately join one or more of the group leader organizations mentioned in this book and start receiving their publications. Reading about other group travel leaders experiences and about the travel business in general can help you decide where you want to position yourself in the group travel business.

Benefits of group travel leader organizations

Some of the benefits of belonging to a group travel leader organization are:

1. Continuing education through:
    *   Organization publications and newsletters
    *   Conferences and tradeshows
    *   Low cost familiarization & educational tours

2. Opportunities to:
    *   Learn from the experiences of others
    *   Keep informed of special travel destination deals
    *   Co-op tours with other clubs
    *   Socialize and network with established group travel leaders
    *   Meet quality tour and travel suppliers
    *   Attend industry seminars and tradeshows
    *   Travel domestically and internationally

A prime example of one of these progressive, growing organizations is Group Leaders of America. Known as GLAMER, this organization was founded in 1989 by the current President, Charlie Presley. Prior to founding GLAMER, Charlie owned and operated a motorcoach tour company called Great American Vacations, located in Pittsburgh, PA.

No stranger to the tourism industry, Charlie served seven years on the National Tour Association Board of Directors and two years on the U.S. Senate Tourism Advisory Committee. As Great American Vacations grew, Charlie realized that most of the growth his business was experiencing could be attributed to *senior group travel leaders* and their personal travel club members. Charlie also saw a lack of structured support for these people and, therefore, a need to be filled. Charlie was right! There was an ever-increasing number of small travel club leaders seeking quality travel suppliers to fulfill their club's trip requirements. Also, the opportunity for group travel leaders to network with each other was another equally important issue that had to be addressed.

Charlie went to work and the rest is history. Since GLAMER was established, the organization has enjoyed an annual growth of eight to ten percent and boasts a data base of more than sixty thousand group travel leaders and travel suppliers. Today, GLAMER stands as one of the premier nationwide organizations for group travel leaders and consistently maintains strong industry wide relationships that secure its members position as the grassroots force behind the boom in domestic travel.

Annually, in a Spring and Fall series, GLAMER sponsors over eighty conferences and trade shows throughout the United States and Canada with over four thousand travel industry companies exhibiting. National sponsors are featured at these quality programs which help bring together the best of the group travel leaders and tour operators for a day of networking, education and fun, *free* to group tour leaders. This is just one of the many "perks" that you, as a group travel leader, will enjoy as a member of this organization.

Chapter 3

Independent agents and serious group travel leaders ...rejoice!

For those of you wanting to make a serious career of the travel business, there is another group travel organization you should be aware of, the Outside Sales Support Network Association (OSSN). Established in 1990, OSSN is one of the most progressive associations that is actively involved in the education and advancement of people who sell leisure travel (group travel leaders, outside sales agents and independent travel agents). OSSN is considered by many as "the voice" of the independent travel promoter in the travel industry and is continuously improving the professionalism status of independent agents and group travel leaders.

A twenty five year veteran of the travel industry, Gary M. Fee, the Chairman and President of OSSN, has trained thousands of independent agents and group travel leaders on how to succeed in their home based travel businesses. By holding several National, International and Regional Conferences each year, OSSN offers one of the most aggressive educational opportunities available to independent sales agents and group travel leaders. OSSN also offers a wide range of familiarization tours (FAMS) and training seminars throughout the year (usually over 80), that are held nationally and internationally at resort destinations and aboard cruise ships. For serious independent outside sales agents and group travel leaders who want to build a viable travel business, OSSN is a "join now" organization. OSSN will continually provide you with important knowledge of the travel industry, help you stay on top of the ever-changing trends, and give you an opportunity to see the world at the same time!

A few of the *many* great benefits OSSN offers its members are:

- **Access to OSSN'S Website** - This extensive web site (almost

600 pages) offers online support services and assistance to its members in a variety of ways. OSSN's website will be of great assistance to anyone wanting to establish a viable travel business as an independent group travel leader.

- **Legitimate Travel Industry Identification Number** – OSSN has lobbied long and hard to gain the travel suppliers respect and recognition of independent travel agents and group travel leaders. OSSN's TRUE (Travel Retailer Universal Enumeration) identification system does just that. The universal TRUE ID numeric code allows OSSN members to book travel services with thousands of travel industry suppliers. The TRUE ID system will be very beneficial to you if you are also planning to book individual travel as well as group travel. This benefit alone is worth the cost of joining OSSN!

- **Preferred Suppliers** – OSSN has an outstanding list of preferred suppliers that you can draw from to help you with your group travel arrangements. These travel suppliers have been "qualified" by OSSN to meet the high standards expected by this top-notch association.

In my opinion, OSSN is a "must" association for anyone who truly wants to build a serious, progressive travel business. The membership fee to join OSSN is $125.00 and is well worth it. To join, find OSSN's page in the Application Section of the Reference Section. Let them know you learned about OSSN from *How to Organize Group Travel for Fun and Profit* and they will deduct $10.00 off your membership fee.

Wait...here's another great connection!

Joining the International Group Tour Association (IGTA) can help you "jump start" your group tour business in a big way. The IGTA is a membership based organization that provides group travel leaders the information they need to create and book exciting travel packages. Here is the IGTA's mission statement:

> "A marketing solutions company dedicated to act as a conduit between group friendly suppliers and group tour planners through our informational, educational, and technological services."

The mission statement says it all! As an ITGA member, you will receive informative tour and travel publications, be invited to regional trade shows and offered educational seminars. Attending these IGTA sponsored venues will help you generate ideas, create group travel packages and make significant tour and travel contacts. Starting in 2001, the IGTA will be promoting a series of regional travel trade shows around the USA which are appropriately called "Group Tour LIVE!" The innovative format that IGTA has developed breaks the mold of traditional travel trade shows by bringing group travel leaders, tour operators, travel agents and bank travel managers, along with leisure tour and travel suppliers, together in the same setting for the group tour industry's most unique, two-day networking and group travel planning event. The regions that Group Tour LIVE will appear are:

- Eastern Regional

- Midwest Regional

- Western Regional

Whether your group travel plans are regional, national or international, the IGTA can be a great help to you in planning, packaging and promoting your tours. Call 1-800-767-3489 for details.

Quality contacts important to your business

Today, more and more of these organizations are being established all over the United States. Supporting a common cause, they bring thousands of group travel leaders and tour suppliers together for the greater good of the group travel community. Not only are these organizations a wonderful benefit to established group travel leaders, but are especially invaluable to people who are just getting started. This is where you will meet your travel suppliers and fellow group travel leader contacts. As in any business, quality contacts are very important to your progress.

GLAMER, NASTP, OSSN, IGTA and other support organizations are just waiting to help you get started in the right direction. They will be the major source of your business contacts. Joining one or more of these group support organizations will give you instant insight into the exciting world of the group travel leader. Take advantage of these opportunities as soon as possible.

> *NOTE! A list of these group travel organizations, including points of contact, telephone, addresses, fax, e-mail and websites are listed in the Reference Sectuon for your convenience.*

Again, age is not a factor for ultimate success

I want to reiterate...no matter how old you are, the group travel leader opportunity awaits you. If you have the desire to travel, and the desire to be independent and go where you want to go, then you can be on your way to establishing yourself as a qualified group travel leader in no time at all.

The information provided in *How to Organize Group Travel for Fun and Profit* is meant to:

1. Inform and educate you about the ever-growing need for group travel leaders.

2. Inspire you to give the group travel leader opportunity a try.

3. Show you how to get started as a group travel leader, sell the tours and build the club.

4. Provide you with systematic procedures that they can use as a guideline for their tours.

5. Provide a list of standard potential tour package "pit falls" that the new group travel leader can easily avoid.

6. Provide you with an extensive reference section of group leader organizations, airline, cruise, destination management companies and tour operator contacts for them to use as a handy reference guide.

Opportunity's knocking!

As you will see after reading *How to Organize Group Travel for Fun and Profit*, practically anyone intrigued with the idea of traveling should investigate this inviting opportunity. Summarizing the first three chapters:

•   Chapter One, you learned of the phenomenon of the group travel leader potential and the small personal travel club *as a home-based business or hobby* that is sure to take the next decade by storm

•   Chapter Two, you learned about the three important qualifications needed to become a successful group travel leader.

•   Chapter Three, you learned of the great opportunities for anyone wanting to be in the travel business and the marvelous supporting organizations ready to help you grow and become a success.

Chapters Four through Ten are the *"how to"* chapters. In these chapters we will discuss everything from setting up your travel club business, to tax advantages of a home-based business, to who your travel suppliers are and how they can help you with your tours. This information, along with example Group Proposal Request worksheets, will show you how to qualify and use your travel suppliers to your best benefit, and at the same time, will help you work with confidence as you progress toward your group travel leader position.

CHAPTER 4

Setting-up Your Group Travel Club Business

It's easier than you think!

OK, you have answered the questions and passed the test at the beginning of the book. You know you have the three *essential* personality traits to qualify as a group travel leader. You understand the changing climate of the travel industry and how wonderful opportunities are going to <u>be in abundance for anyone with the vision and the drive to take advantage of them</u>. Congratulations! Now it's time to go to the next phase – the "how to get started" part.

Getting started

Getting in contact with the group leader organizations mentioned in the last chapter and signing up as a member is high on the list of first things to do. *But, before you do this*, there are two decisions you will need to make:

1. **Name Your Travel Club** – You need to think of a name for your travel club. Take your time and use your imagination,

but don't get too fancy or cute with the club's name. Some of the travel clubs I have dealt with over the years had names so *cutesy*, you didn't know whether it was a travel club or a pet store. Also, don't be shy about incorporating *your* name into the club name formula, like Donna's Personalized Travel or Tindell Tour & Travel. After all, your personal name and good reputation as a reliable group travel leader is what will eventually be a strong draw for people to join you on your trips.

2. **Establish Your Travel Club's Base of Operations** - Before you start joining, subscribing and requesting information from tour and travel suppliers, establish your club's official contact information. As I have mentioned before, I believe *the group leader/travel club business is one of the best, most fun-filled, **home-based** businesses in existence today.* My suggestion is that you use your home as your official base of operations and work the business out of your family room, basement or extra bedroom. I call it the one-minute commute! This way, even if you eventually move your travel club business to another location, you will always get information coming to your home. So, unless you already have a suite of corporate offices at your disposal, operate from your home.

   Important Note: I just want to mention to those of you who are already in the group travel business and who are established group travel leaders with a bank, church, community center or your own travel club, etc., that the home-based operation is just a suggestion for newcomers to the business. So, as you read this book and find me on my soapbox touting the glories of what I consider to be the best home-based business in existence today, pay no attention to my ranting (even though it's true!)

You now have an official name for your club and since you will probably be working from your home, you have a permanent address and telephone to use on those applications. *Just having an official name and address for your travel club will give you instant group leader recognition.* I am sure all requests for information from travel suppliers are filled with equal consideration as a norm, but a request for information from an "established group travel leader" will definitely get you on a company's active mailing list.

Once you have your base of operations established, you need to get your office organized to do business.

Business is business...

Whether you work your travel club as a hobby or as a money making venture, it is still a business and should be treated as such. You should seek guidance from accounting and legal professionals to assist you in structuring your club as a legal business and to cover your club's liabilities. The designation of your club as a sole proprietorship, a partnership, or a corporation, can make a big difference in the amount of tax you will pay. The following are two important steps you should take before physically setting up your office:

1. Contact a local accountant or small business accounting firm and/or attorney to advise and help you to:

    a) Legally structure your travel club to your best advantage.

    b) Set up your day-to-day accounting books.

    c) Advise you on the tax advantages and possible disadvantages of a home-based business.

2. Inquire about any city, county and state licensing that may be required. Your accountant can probably help you in this area also.

Important Note – Covering your club's liabilities: You can limit your personal and club liability by including travel insurance in your tour packages on each participant or, have them purchase it directly with the insurance company. Either way, the insurance company will pay you a commission (because you will be a registered agent for them), so this is another profit center for you. By having everyone covered with insurance, you are "killing two birds with one stone," making money and covering your club's liability. More details on other types of insurance you may want to consider, how to become a commissioned agent for a travel insurance company, and how the commission structure works will be discussed in Chapter Twelve.

If you choose to operate your travel club as a home-based business, you can take advantage of several tax breaks. Rich Owens, my accountant and an owner of Century Small Business Solutions (centurysmallbiz.com), provided the following general tax guidelines for a home-based business. This is general tax information and should be reconfirmed by your local accountant regarding your tax situation.

Tax advantages of a home-based business

One major advantage of operating a business from your home is the opportunity to deduct the costs of certain activities or luxuries as business expenses. These deductions can prove very helpful in reducing your taxes. It is very important to keep accurate records of all expenses to help substantiate them. The following are a few tax issues to be aware of while considering this or any small business:

Operating Expenses

Generally, direct expenses incurred in operating your business against income such as stationery, telephone, office supplies, postage, printing, etc., will be fully deductible.

Home Office Expenses

If you operate your travel club as a home-based business, you may be able to deduct part of your office-in-the-home expenses. At the time of this writing, the rules to qualify for the home-office deduction were recently liberalized, making it easier for people to qualify. Generally, a home office will qualify as the principle place of business if:

1) it is used for administrative or management activities.

2) there is no other location to perform the duties.

If the business use of your home qualifies under the above tests, then you may be able to deduct part of home office expenses. These are expenses that are allocable to the portion of your home that is used for your business, in addition to home mortgage interest, property taxes and casualty losses. For example, if 25% of your home is used, you could possibly deduct up to 25% of your occupancy costs. This would include gas, electricity, insurance, repairs and similar expenses, as well as 25% of your rent or depreciation expense on the tax basis of your house. Take note, however, that the amount of qualifying home office expense you can deduct is limited to the gross income from your home business, reduced by regular operating expenses.

The downside of taking home office deductions is a potential tax bite when you sell your home. For example, if 25% of your home had been used for the business and you sell your home with a gain, you will have to pay tax on 25% of the gain. This applies even if you reinvest in a new house or qualify for the Section 1231 Exclusion. Thus, a few hundred dollars of home office deductions at this time, could later result in many thousands of dollars of tax on the "business" part of your house

Chapter 4   **61**

if you sell it for a gain a few years down the road. For more information on the deductibility of home-office expenses, obtain IRS publication 587, Business Use of Your Home.

Travel, Entertainment and Meal Expenses

Business travel expenses such as airline tickets, car rentals, hotel accommodations, etc. are 100% deductible. Business-related meals are deductible, including the entertainment of your clients, however, you can only deduct 50% of qualifying business meals and entertainment. For instance, if you stay in a hotel on a business trip and charge your meals to your room, you are required to separately break out your meal expenses for tax purposes because your meal expenses are only 50% deductible.

To claim any of these deductions, you must keep daily, detailed records of such expenditures, including bills, receipts, and the following information for each expense:

- The relationship of the expenditures to business

- The time the expense was incurred

- Where the money was spent, and to whom it was paid

- The amount of the expenditure and the identities of the persons involved

It is strongly recommended that you pick up a daily expense record book or diary and enter all expenses for travel, meals and entertainment you think should be deductible and include the above information for each item. It's a little bit of a hassle, but a necessary evil I'm afraid.

Automobile Expense

If you use an automobile more than 50% of the time for business purposes, you will generally be able to deduct a percentage of the costs of owning and operating the car if you can substantiate the business mileage. For example, if it can be shown that 80% of your mileage is for business, you should be able to deduct 80% of the gas, oil, maintenance, and insurance costs relating to the car. You can also depreciate the cost of the car, less 20% for personal use.

If you drive an inexpensive economy car or an older car that is paid for, it may be simpler and more advantageous to elect to deduct a flat per mile rate. Be aware the deductible amount can change annually, so always check the allowable amount before figuring this expense. Using this method eliminates the need to track actual expenses incurred in operating your vehicle. However, you still need to keep an accurate mileage record of your business travel. You can't just say, "I put 15,000 miles on my car this year." The IRS will still require proof if you are audited.

I want to reiterate, this is <u>general tax information</u> at the time of this printing and should be confirmed by your local CPA or accountant regarding your individual tax situation.

> *NOTE! Whether you work your travel club as a hobby, or as a money making venture, it is still a business and should be treated as such. You should seek guidance from accounting and legal professionals to assist you in structuring your club as a legal business and to cover your club's liabilities.*

Chapter 4

Setting up your office

Any start-up business that wants to succeed today needs a well equipped office…especially a <u>service oriented</u> business like travel. Since you are not selling tangible merchandise, the strong points of your company need to be personal service, professional looking promotional literature, and a smooth operation. This should be the main objective of your travel club. All you need to deliver the personal service is yourself. For the smooth running operation and professional looking promotional literature, a little help from your corner office supply and equipment store may be in order.

Your smiling face and friendly, outgoing nature will take you a long way in the travel business…as long as you are standing in front of somebody. But, the literature and promotional material that gets delivered to someone's home needs to have an impact – something that says "class act!" As explained below, a few good office machines can help you accomplish this and keep you ahead of the competition. I highly recommend the following office equipment for your initial office set-up. Please consider taking advantage of these technological marvels that can make a two person operation working out of their spare bedroom look like a high-powered, multi-national conglomerate!

- **Fax Machine** - If you do not have a fax machine at this time, *buy one*. They are very inexpensive and will be a tremendous asset in helping you communicate with your travel suppliers, tour operators and club members. Once your club name gets circulated among the various travel industry circles, watch out…the faxes will start coming your way. Important note; *be sure to set the fax machine to receive messages twenty four hours a day*. With the different time zones around the world, you will continually receive various fax messages with promotional offers from domestic and international airlines, tour operators, resorts and cruise lines. Many of these offers can greatly benefit your groups and many can benefit you personally, such as familiarization and educational tours, discount airfares and more.

Also, these days, you will get as many tour registrations by fax as you will by phone or mail. The fax machine can be hooked up to your existing telephone line so you do not need to order a dedicated line for it, although if possible, I strongly recommend a dedicated line. A dedicated line shows that you are serious about your business, but more importantly, it gets a lot of action day and night, so you may not want your main telephone line tied up that much (and ringing in the middle of the night).

Note: Buy a plain paper fax. One that uses plain, standard, letter size paper (not one that uses paper by the roll). Fax machines have been improved a great deal over the past few years and now, for a very reasonable price, you can buy a machine that is a fax, a scanner (used in conjunction with your computer) and a photocopier. In your travel business, you will eventually need all of these functions to create your tour package brochures, bulletins and travel documents. I suggest you consider a multi-function fax machine for your office.

- **Computer** – I know many of you (especially <u>some</u> of the senior population) do not want to hear this, *BUT*, if you do not have a computer at this time, *I again, strongly recommend that you consider purchasing one.* If you already have a computer, *great!* You are ahead of the game and can quickly make some serious progress in developing your club and tour packages. Anyone truly wanting to have a well-organized group travel club, will need to be computerized. A computer will allow you to:

a) Have a file of all your travel club members (and potential members) names, addresses, telephone, fax and e-mail numbers at your fingertips.

b) Produce your own stationery, letters, fax sheets, bulletins, brochures, newsletters, etc.

c) Maintain an accounting of your group member's tour payments and due dates.

d) Have a daily calendar of events and a "to do" list that automatically opens up on your screen when you turn your computer on. This will help to keep you on schedule.

e) Print your group manifest (name list) for your tour operators and other travel suppliers.

f) Maintain a database of tour operators and other travel providers.

g) Produce professional looking itineraries and travel documents for your group members.

h) Maintain an accurate, day-to-day accounting system of your club's financial transactions.

i) Keep your financial records in order for tax purposes (there are many tax benefits to having a home-based office, as noted earlier).

j) Have an e-mail address.

k) Have a website advertising your travel club (more details about this in Chapter Twelve). Also, check out the Sun and Breezes travel club website at www.sunandbreezes.com).

l) Play solitaire when things are slow.

- **Laser Printer** – If you have a computer, you will need a printer to print out everything listed above. Again, the printers on the market today are all basically excellent and very reasonably priced. You will want to buy an ink jet or *laser printer*. An ink jet printer is good, but a laser printer is better. The office equipment salesperson can explain the difference to you. A laser printer will give your brochures and promotional pieces a printing press quality that you will be proud of and, at the same time, impress both your existing members and potential members.

Any brand name such as Hewlett-Packard, Brother, NEC, Xerox, offers top of the line printers in a variety of price ranges. Color printers are also in abundance and something you will probably want to consider later on after you are established. At this point they are a luxury and not totally necessary. In the beginning, purchase a good, high volume, black and white laser printer that will serve you well during your start-up period. You will be amazed how much you will use this machine! Before you buy the office equipment you need, if you do not already know what you want, consider the equipment I have recommended in this chapter. Next, talk to friends and business acquaintances you know who have computer systems, printers and fax machines. Find out what brand names and models they like and recommend, and make your decision on what to buy. *Then go power shopping!*

So now, you have selected a name for your club, you have established a base of operations (your home), and you realize the virtues of a good computer system and a well-equipped office for your travel operation. All is well!

NOTE! Check out the deals that the big office supply stores offer, such as Office Depot, OfficeMax, and Staples. These discount superstores are the place to shop for most of your office supplies, computers, printers, fax machines, etc. These stores have everything you need to outfit your office at very competitive prices. They also have great return policies!

One more note: Regarding your computer software programs:

- **For a good, overall organizational software program**, I recommend you consider the Microsoft Outlook software program for your calendar, address book (club member contacts),

Chapter 4   **67**

sending and receiving e-mail messages, making notes and keeping track of tasks. This software also works well with a Palm Pilot.

- **For the travel planner wanting to build a serious group travel business**, there are two excellent group tour management programs that I highly recommend. One is a computer software program and the other is a hosted Internet service. Both group tour management programs are specifically designed to help group travel leaders keep track of their client contacts, invoicing, receivable collections, deposits due, and much, much more. If you plan to be in the group travel business in a big way and for the long-haul, you should consider one of these great management programs. It will keep your groups on track for years to come.

The following is a brief description of the two management programs and the contact information for both companies. Each company recognizes the needs of the growing group travel leader population and have customized their programs to fit those needs.

Each company has an abundance of information to share with you, but it is far too detailed for me to list. Also, I have left out the pricing since each company has different programs to fit different needs, so their pricing varies accordingly. If your business is going to be computerized, please take some time and visit their websites listed below. For more details and information, call the respective numbers. Also, both of these companies work closely with the Outside Sales Support Network (OSSN). As a member of OSSN, you will be entitled to a discount off of the retail sales price.

WesMarc Corporation is a software company that develops and markets software to independent travel contractors, group travel leaders and small travel agencies. It was formed by individuals who have experience with independent travel contracting and group tours, as well as software development.

"As independent travel contractors we found that there was a lack of good quality software for the industry. We set out to provide that software product. By combining our experience from the travel industry with our experience in software development we have produced a product called **TravelSales**™ that meets this need at a very affordable price. As we market and sell **TravelSales**™, we recognize that our customers are very important to us. We actively seek their input on ways we can improve it. We have included and plan to include many of these changes as the product evolves."

WesMarc Corporation
P.O. Box 1185
Riverton, UT 84065

Tel: (801) 254-0464   Fax: (801) 254-2067
E-mail: WesMarc@WesMarc.com
Website: www.wesmarc.com

ITAMS, LTD. (Independent Travel Agent Management System) software was designed to help anyone in the travel industry simplify the day-to-day management, organization and marketing of their travel business. This makes ITAMS Internet software program ideal for group travel leaders, independent sellers of leisure travel and travel agencies (including multiple agencies). Whether you are just getting started or already an established provider of travel, you need to investigate the time and money saving potential of ITAMS.

Darla Graber, founder and President of ITAMS Ltd. has been in the travel business for 20 years. As the owner of a travel agency for over ten years she has been through all of the major changes in the travel industry. Besides specializing in corporate and leisure travel, Darla also worked extensively with tour groups. Seeing the future benefit of the Internet in the group travel business, Darla joined forces with her close friend (software engineer and business partner), Dana Overmyer to develop ITAMS. The end result is an outstanding Internet database program that is ideal for the travel industry, specifically the group travel industry. The software they have designed simplifies the paperwork, policies, procedures, and communications needed to operate a smooth-running travel business.

Travel management software is readily available to meet the needs of agencies or independent contractors specializing in corporate travel, but very few programs exist for the people just selling leisure and group travel. ITAMS fills that void.

ITAMS Ltd.
1339 Twp. Rd. 653
Ashland, OH 44805

Tel: (419) 681-1650   Fax: (216) 820-6439
E-mail: darla@itams.com
Website: www.itams.com

My suggestions regarding your computer software...

- Use Microsoft Publisher software for your letters, faxes, bulletins, and newsletters. Anything that has to do with desktop publishing, Publisher can handle.

- Use Intuit Quick Books or Quicken Small Business software for your accounting program.

  Note: Quality software equivalent to the Microsoft, Quick Books and Quicken programs mentioned is also available for Mac users.

- Select one of the group tour management programs to help you operate your business.

Who's going to be your Gutenberg?

Now is the time to find a printer! You have a wonderful name for your travel club and its official world headquarters has been established (your spare bedroom). It's time for action! Here are your next three steps:

Step #1

Set-up a telephone system for the travel club. *You want a dedicated line and telephone number for your travel club if possible.* Even if you have only one telephone line coming into your house at this time and cannot therefore have a dedicated line, no need to panic! Here is what to do: contact your local telephone company and order another telephone number for your travel club. Then ask for a custom ring feature to be put on your current telephone. The custom ring feature allows both of your telephone numbers (home and travel club) to use the same line, but each number will have its own distinctive ring. You will know when someone calls the travel club line because of its distinctive ring so you can answer it appropriately. This service is very inexpensive and is charged to your monthly bill. Besides, when tax time arrives, you can deduct it as a business expense! To reiterate, if possible, <u>a dedicated telephone line and number for your business is the optimum way to go</u>. If that is not possible, the custom ring feature will serve you well.

Step #2

Find a printer and have your business cards and stationery printed. <u>*Make sure you include your fax number, e-mail and website address*</u> if you have them. Because of the "one-stop, quick print" explosion, there is a good printer on almost every corner nowadays. Not only are they good, most are also fast *and* reasonable. Also, g*et to know your printer; be friends with him or her. Sometimes they can work miracles for you when you are in a bind, especially if you are a good customer and a good friend!* To start with, get quotes from two or three printers just to find out who really wants your business. Once you have selected your printer, they can assist you with customizing

Chapter 4   **71**

your business cards and stationery. Many printers have stationery packages to offer. Some are very upscale and pretty reasonable. In my opinion, company business cards, stationery and literature need to have some thought put in them as the end result needs to impressive. These are your initial front-line marketing pieces that will, in many cases, reach people before they ever get your club and tour literature. It represents you and your style of doing business. Even though you are just starting, your business cards and stationery must be professional and suggest you are already successful. First impressions are important, so don't drop the ball!

Another option, (if you are computerized and have a good laser printer), is to go to one of the specialty paper stores, like Paper Warehouse, that are becoming so popular. Just choose a paper you like from the wide selection they offer, and you can design and print your own stationery. This option would be a little more costly, but would provide you with fast service and a variety of quality stationery. If nothing else, it's an interesting and fun store to visit.

If you do not have one of these specialty paper stores in your vicinity, the following are two mail order specialty paper stores you can contact for catalogs:

- Paper Direct
  P.O. Box 2970
  Colorado Springs, CO   80901-2970
  Tel: 1-800-272-7377   Fax: 1-800-443-2973
  Web site: www.paperdirect.com

- Idea Art
  P.O. Box 291505
  Nashville, TN   37229-1505
  Tel: 1-800-433-2278   Fax: 1-800-435-2278
  Web site: www.ideaart.com

<u>**Step #3**</u>

Associate yourself with a travel agency. *Make sure you select the type of agency discussed in Chapter One.* It is very important that you align your travel club with a travel agency that prides itself in being progressive, and offers the personal service and attention to its clients as discussed in Chapter One. Hopefully, you already have a relationship with a travel agency that you have worked with in the past. If you have had good service from that particular agency, then that is the agency you should approach first. You will use this agency for three things:

- **Airline ticketing** - When you cannot, or do not (for whatever reason) want to book directly with the airlines.

- **Inclusive packaged tours for your group** - If your travel agency is competitive with other tour operators or destination management companies (DMC), and they could be, use them.

- **Commissions** - You will negotiate a commission split for the business you bring to your travel agency associate. This should include any and all business, not just your group business. As your travel club grows, your members will eventually approach you with individual travel requests. Instead of turning this business away, set them up with your associated travel agency and make a commission. The commission split you negotiate with your travel agency will be on a sliding scale.

When it comes to your group tours, the agency will either deal with you on a net basis (which means they already have their commission worked into the price) or a split-commission basis. When it comes to individuals, the commission you receive could be reduced, depending on how involved you get with the booking of the ticket or tour. Almost all travel agencies nowadays have a commission split formula in place. Sit down with the agency owner or office

Chapter 4   **73**

manager and listen to what they have to offer. Since you are possibly going to be their travel partner, don't be afraid to ask them hard questions about how their outside sales commission is structured and what exactly they expect of you.

Before you agree to align your travel club with a particular agency, make sure you thoroughly understand the proposition they are offering. If, for some reason, the travel agency you have selected does not seem to have a "This is great, we would love to work with you!" attitude, then go on down the road and find one that that does have that attitude. *Do not settle for anything less!* Like the cruise lines, most travel agencies love group travel leaders. They only have to work with one person (you) and you are giving them multiple bookings per deal. It is a win-win situation for everyone!

Get ready to open the doors!

Your office is now set-up, resplendent with shiny office equipment that is not only going to make your life a lot easier (no Bob Cratchitt life for you!) but will also position your travel club to do a great business. Your business cards and stationery are printed and no doubt impressive and award winning by anyone's standards.

Move on to Chapter 5 to learn how to get established as a bonafide group travel leader and how to start earning commissions!

CHAPTER 5

Establishing Yourself as a Group Travel Leader

Start earning commissions now!

Now that your office is set up and your business cards are ready to present to the world, the next move is to get the travel industry suppliers to recognize you as a qualified group travel leader. How do you do this? It's very easy…it's *literally* as simple as 1,2,3!

3 simple steps…

SIMPLE STEP #1

Join group travel leader organizations. As I mentioned at the beginning of Chapter Four, one of the first things you want to do is make contact with the group travel leader organizations. The object of this exercise is to get your name *and your club name* on these very important lists that the tour and travel suppliers hold so dear. Go to the *Reference Section* at the end of this book and find the Group Travel Leader Organizations & Publications sections for information on these group leader/independent agent organizations and their telephone, fax and e-mail numbers. **Next, block thirty minutes of your time to contact these people and join**

their organizations. I recommend calling; it's a free call (most have toll free numbers) and it will get you on numerous tour and travel lists fast. Once you are a member of these various organizations, your name will be swiftly passed on to the tour and travel suppliers. This will result in a stream of brochures and booklets coming to you in abundance. You can use this information to start your travel files, your tour and travel education, and set up your first tours. This is good information and will give you a lot of options to consider.

Also, many of the best "deals" nowadays are sent by fax (hopefully you have one). The faxes can range from discounts for early book-ings, to great savings for last minute bookings, to invitations to participate in familiarization and educational tours. Pay particular attention to these specials as they can be very useful to the growth of your club.

SIMPLE STEP #2

Subscribe to group travel publications. These magazines and newsletters are a wealth of information, loaded with travel supply contacts, articles on successes of group travel leaders, popular destinations to visit, which destinations are offering the best deals, wise advice in general, and much, much more. Keep in mind that many of the group leader organizations you joined (Simple Step #1) will have a publication which you will automatically start receiving, e.g., Group Leaders of America (GLAMER) publish The Group Travel Leader.

Again, go to the Group Travel Leader Organization & Publica-tion section and find the publications that are not associated with a group leader organization. **Take another thirty minutes of your time to contact these people and subscribe to their publications.** As in STEP #1, I recommend calling because it is usually free, fast and easy. Once you start receiving the publications, respond to some of the travel supplier advertisements that look intriguing and that you find interesting. The information you receive from them will serve you in two ways:

1. It will be the start of your travel and tour reference files.

2. It will initiate a relationship with the tour and travel people who will help you develop your tours and make your travel club a success.

These first two steps will get you recognized as a bonafide group travel leader and will set you up to receive commissions from many of the travel and tour suppliers. A great start! SIMPLE STEP #3 will do the same *and more*. You are about to become an agent for one of the hottest growing areas of the travel industry… the cruise lines!

In Chapter Ten, I will go into great detail as to why you should strongly consider promoting cruise vacations to your groups and what makes cruising such a wonderful deal for you, your travel club, and your members. Meanwhile, have faith in what I say and go on to…

SIMPLE STEP #3

Cruising…instant agent, instant commissions!

Join the Cruise Line Industry Association (CLIA). Being a CLIA appointed agency in itself could provide you with a very nice lifestyle and income. Plus, cruising is fun, fun, fun! If you have not been on a cruise yet, you are in for a treat. If you have already taken a cruise, I am sure that you will agree with me, that it's great fun!

There are two ways to get your application to become a CLIA agent; by fax or by mail. Obviously, using the fax will be a lot faster than "snail" mail. For those of you who do not own a fax machine or do not have access to one, you can call CLIA's headquarters in New York at 212-921-0066 and request that an application be mailed to you. CLIA's offices are open from 9:00 AM to 5:00 PM EST, Monday through Friday. If you do have a fax machine, or can get access to one (your friendly print shop for instance), this is how you should proceed:

1. **Call the CLIA Fax Response Service** - The toll-free telephone number is 1-800-372-2542 (CLIA). You will get a recorded message that will give you several prompts.

2. **Select prompt #1** - New Member Information and Applications.

3. **Note:** Since this service and information is free, for your files and future information, you may also want to select:

   - Prompt #2 - CLIA Training Seminars & Schedules
   - Prompt #5 - Outside Sales Kit & Order Form
   - Prompt #7 - Product Information & order Form
   - At the time of this printing, there were nine prompts. If any of the other prompts sound interesting or of possible assistance to you, order them also.

4. **After you receive the New Member Application** - answer all of the twenty-one questions honestly and to the best of your knowledge. Along with that and a little guidance on the question and answers listed below, you can be a <u>CLIA appointed agent</u> in the very near future.

   Note: The Affiliation Application will refer to your travel club as your "agency," which to CLIA, is the same.

   The following is a question and answer overview of the CLIA Affiliation Application form for you to use as a guideline:

78   **Chapter 5**

Question #1

AgencyName/Address/Tel/Fax/E-mail information

Answer #1

List travel club name & address (no P.O. Box number), telephone and, if applicable, your fax & e-mail address

Question #2

Please enter existing ARC/IATA number if applicable

Answer #2

Not applicable

Question #3

Type of ownership / MUST BE COMPLETED

Answer #3

State the type of ownership of your travel club; Individual, partnership or corporation (refer to Chapter Four)

Question #4

Is your business location also a residence?

Answer #4

Yes or No

Question #5

Name(s) of owner, partners, or officers, as appropriate

Answer #5

Answer accordingly

Question #6

Does your agency have one of the following insurance's – Errors & Omissions insurance (E & O), a Bond?

Answer #6

List any travel club business related insurance you have (refer to Chapter Twelve for information on E & O insurance and how to obtain it)

Question #7

Do you:
a) Have business letterhead?
b) Actively promote your agency via direct mail advertiing?
c) Have a designated & promoted telephone number?

Answer #7

a) Yes (Chapter Four)
b) Yes (Chapter Four)
c) Yes (Chapter Four)

Question #8

Is your office a:

a) Single entity?
b) Branch office?
c) Home office location?

Answer #8

Answer accordingly

Question #9

If applicable, furnish the name and location of home office with which affiliated:

Answer #9

Not Applicable (unless otherwise)

Question #10

Key agency contact for fast distribution of important cruise industry news:

Answer #10

List your name and title or the person you want to receive this important information

Question #11

Year started in business

Answer #11

Answer accordingly (Don't worry that you are just starting in the travel business and do not have a track record at this time. Everybody has to start from the beginning and that includes you. But after you have a few tours under your belt, it won't be long before the travel suppliers will be beating on your door to compete for your business).

Question #12

Number of employees

Answer #12

Answer accordingly (Don't be afraid to list just one employee. Because your travel suppliers act, in many cases, as your travel partner, lots of individually owned and operated club owners are "power houses" in the travel business)

Question #13

Your agency is / You are:

a) **A full service agency**
b) **A cruise division of a full service agency**
c) **A cruise only agency**
d) **Outside sales agent**
e) **Independent contractor**

Answer #13

Independent Contractor (unless otherwise)

Question #14

How many of your employees focus their sales efforts primarily on cruise vacations?

Answer #14

Answer accordingly (If your travel club consists at this time of just you or your spouse or partner, list one. Once you see what a great opportunity the cruise business has to offer, I'm betting cruise tours and vacations will be a primary part of your business).

Question #15

Total agency sales:

Answer #15

a)   Less than $500,000 (unless otherwise)

Question #16

What is your approximate percentage of:
a)   Leisure business
b)   Corporate business

Answer #16

a)   Leisure business / 100% (unless otherwise)

Question #17

Number of individual cruise passengers booked in the past year:

Answer #17

None / just opened agency (unless otherwise)

Question #18

Cruises are what percentage of your agency's total business?

Answer #18

Projected - 50%

Question #19

What is the approximate percentage of cruises booked through your agency in each of the price ranges listed below?

a) Under $200 per day

b) $200 - $399 per day

c) $400 or more per day

Answer #19

a) Under $200 per day – 60%

b) $200 - $399 per day – 35%

c) $400 or more per day – 5%

Question #20

To what destinations do you routinely sell cruises?

Answer #20

Answer: Projected – then check five of the most interesting to you from their list

Question #21

CLIA's MOST IMPORTANT QUESTION: Method of payment:

Answer #21

Answer accordingly – Check, Mastercard, Visa or American Express (Don't you just love America?)

The fee to become a CLIA affiliated agent is $299.00 plus a one-time application fee of $90.00. To cover this, you only have to sell <u>one couple</u> on a cruise to <u>more</u> than pay for CLIA's fee!

Chapter 5   **83**

Also, included in CLIA's application fee is a nice bonus: as an a affiliated travel agent, you are entitled to a FREE listing in the Travel Agency Locator section of CLIA's website. And remember, as a CLIA agent, you are allowed, in fact encouraged, to sell individuals as well as groups. It's all good, fun business and money in the bank!

You're off and running!

At this point, you're off and running! Your name and the name of your travel club are being circulated among the tour and travel suppliers of the world. Very soon you will start receiving important information from these suppliers that will help you to create your tour programs.

When you start receiving this information, it is essential that you have a good filing system in place. You will want to have ready access to certain information *and nothing is worse* than going through stacks of brochures and papers and *still* not finding what you need. Listed below are several categories of files that you should incorporate into your filing system. I suggest you use *Hanging File* folders for your lead files and *1/3 Cut* file folders for your sub-files. The following outline will help you in your initial set-up:

United States Information

- States
- Cities

These files will contain information on states and cities that you are interested in and to where you may want to promote a tour eventually. You will get the information for your files from tour and travel suppliers (by mail), from your personal research, and from requesting information from various Bureaus of Tourism and Chambers of Commerce (see reference section).

International Information

- Countries
- Cities

These files will contain information on countries and cities that you are interested in. The information to fill the files will come from the same sources as above.

Tour Operator Information

- Domestic
- International

These files will contain contact information on various tour operators that you have personally been in contact with or received information from. Always keep at least two copies of each brochure in these files.

DMC Information

- Countries

These files are for your direct international contacts. (DMC - Destination Management Company)

Cruise Line Information

These files are for each individual cruise line.

The file categories I have listed above are just a beginning. All of the files listed can be further sub-divided, e.g., railroads, motorcoach companies, museums, restaurants, sights-to-see, castles, islands, regions and on-and-on. There are no limits to how detailed you can get. So jump into that stack of brochures and file away! If you want to go "over the top," you can color coordinate the file folders and tabs (very 2001).

Decisions, decisions, decisions...

All you have to do now is to decide where you want to go, set up a tour program, sell out the tour, and be on your way. To you, that may sound like quite a project. But if you approach it using these step-by-step procedures, it can be a walk-in-the-park! However, there are just a few more decisions to be made before you jump in with both feet. Oddly enough, that's what Chapter Six is about. Read on!

CHAPTER 6

Where in the World Do <u>You</u> Want To Go?

It's your decision

You are now the proud owner of one of the most exciting and fun businesses that exists today (in my humble opinion). Your office is established, organized and ready to do business. You are a CLIA appointed agency and are in the process of being placed on some very important travel industry supplier lists that will eventually open many new avenues for you to travel the world. All you need now is a place to go and a few people to take with you. No problem!

How hard do you <u>really</u> want to work?

The next decision has to do with how active you want your travel club to be (how busy do <u>you</u> want to be?) and what tours you want to promote (where do <u>you</u> want to go?) Your decision on your level of activity will dictate how aggressively you promote your club and market your tours.

Consider these questions...

Again, it is a step-by-step procedure, so these are the next three steps for you to take:

STEP #1

Consider how you want to structure your travel club. Before you select and promote your first tour, you need to make several decisions and each one should be given careful consideration. After doing a little "soul searching" and answering the questions listed below, you should be able to make some confident choices about how involved you want to be, how hard you want to work, and which direction you want your club to go.

Answering the following questions will help guide you in the right direction. I suggest highlighting or drawing a circle around the options that you choose, incorporating your answers at a later date into an initial business plan with specific objectives and goals.

Question #1

How do you see this opportunity?

- As a hobby?
- As a part-time business?
- As a full-time business?

Now that you know *how* you want to work your travel club, the next question is:

Question #2

How do you want to benefit from your travel club?

- Free travel, a couple of trips a year?
- Free travel, three or more trips a year, and make a little money?
- Free travel, several trips a year, and make *good* money?

Now that you know *what* benefits you want out of your travel club, answer the following question:

Question #3

Regarding your tours:

- How many trips do you want to take per year?

- How long do you want your trips to be? One week, ten days, two or three weeks?

- What are the maximum group participants (pax) that you would like to work with per tour (30, 40, 80-100 or more?)

- Which time of the year would you like to travel? Ordinarily, in the winter, if you live in the northern states you will probably head to sunshine and blue skies. In the summer, if you live in the southern states, finding someplace cool and relaxing is probably in order. Since your travel club business is a year-round business, you can go anywhere at anytime, depending on your scheduling. Remember, since it is your travel club, it's OK to "stack the deck" in favor of your preferences. **A word of caution:** In order to take care of your club's daily business and keep caught up with deposits, final payments, registrations, getting tour documents finalized, etc., you should keep at least thirty days or more between tours. Unless you have a full office staff to take care of the business for you while you are touring, this is an important policy to follow.

With these questions answered, your travel club now has a purpose and objectives. You know at *what pace* you want to work

Chapter 6   **89**

your travel club, *what* benefits you want out of it, and *how hard* you want to work (*or not*) to get those benefits.

> *NOTE! I personally believe most people buying this book will fall into the free travel, several trips a year, and make good money category. If I assumed wrong, and you have decided to do this as a hobby, beware! I can guarantee that once you have organized a few successful group tours, your reputation as a great group tour leader will spread, and your "hobby" can easily turn into a business. Just thought I would warn you!*

Pick a place...any place

STEP #2

Decide on the first tour destinations that you want to promote. While waiting for your printing to be done and the group travel leader information and tour and travel publications to arrive, start making a list of the places *you* want to travel to over the next few years. These destinations should be the first tours you want to promote through your new travel club. Why? Because you *really, really,* want to go there yourself! One of your lifelong dreams is going to be realized and because of this, your enthusiasm for this trip will become infectious as you talk to potential tour participants!

Select your "dream destinations," places you have always wanted to see but never had the time, money or opportunity. Also list places that you have already visited that truly "knocked your socks off." As an example, on our honeymoon, my wife and I spent three weeks in Switzerland, Germany, Austria, and Italy. Absolutely all of the places we visited were magical; Lucerne, Innsbruck, Salzburg,

Cortina d' Ampezzo, Portofino, Rome, Venice…all fantastic. Then there was the *little village of Bellagio*, located on the banks of Lago de Como (Lake Como) in Northern Italy. Bellagio "knocked our socks off!" Since our honeymoon, my wife and I have returned several times, sometimes by ourselves and sometimes with a small group of friends. One thing is for certain; we never tire of visiting Bellagio, talking about Bellagio, or recommending Bellagio to our friends. Even a new luxury resort in Las Vegas has been named after this little village in Northern Italy!

This is the kind of place I want you to include on your "dream destination" list. If you have experienced a "Bellagio" during your travels and would love to show it to your friends, by all means consider packaging a tour around it. Your love and enthusiasm of this destination will create excitement among your club members and, consequently, help your tour to sell.

Now that you have your "dream destination" list prepared, it's time to set up and package your first tour. Feel at ease, because you have a virtual army of support personnel in the form of tour operators and destination management companies (DMC) ready to take your call.

Whatever destination you have selected for Tour #1, there is a tour operator, somewhere, who has a tour package ready for you to sell to your group. On top of that, there are DMC's in practically every city, state and country that are ready to customize a group program for you, should you prefer a very personalized itinerary.

The main point to understand is almost <u>anywhere</u> in the world you want to visit, these travel professionals are ready to help you package the perfect program. So, if you are a little anxious about planning and packaging your first tours, don't be…your army awaits you!

Chapter 6   **91**

See the USA...or the UK?

The following is Step #3 and an outline for a three-year plan of action. It should be explained that in this outline, I have used mostly international destinations and cruises as examples. My background in the group travel business has been extensively global and I tend to assume that everyone else wants to travel the world, *the whole world*, like I do. To my surprise this is not necessarily so! During my travels, I have met people...

- Who do not want to leave the U.S.A. (some didn't want to leave their state).

- Who do not like to fly...period (especially 9 hours).

- Who do not want to go abroad ("The problem with Europe is there are too many foreigners").

- Who, if they can't drive to it, they don't go.

Even though I've had wanderlust since I was a young man and ended up traveling around the world, I still believe the best country in the world is the USA. In order to really appreciate this great land (and by great I mean both its size and beauty), America needs be toured, visited, and explored. The greatest benefit of traveling abroad is coming home. Every time I return from an international trip, it makes me appreciate America even more.

So, take all of my international examples with "a grain of salt" and lay out *your* dream destinations, which very well may be the Grand Canyon, Orlando, New Orleans, Branson, San Francisco, or Las Vegas. There was an old ad that said "See America first" and there's nothing wrong with that!

Whether you are traveling domestically or internationally, the main point is that you're traveling!

Three year plan of action

STEP #3

Develop a plan of action. Next, you need to prepare a three-year plan by incorporating the places you listed as your dream destinations in **Step #2**. Start with the first destination on your "dream" list and go right down the line. Just think...in the next three years you will probably visit at least six of your lifelong dream destinations. Now that's an accomplishment!

Prioritize your first year's tour programs by your strongest desire to visit these places. Make a more detailed list of the states, islands or countries you want to visit and the cities or regions you want to see while there. If you have always wanted to go to Austria, and you love the waltz music of Strauss, then Vienna is your first stop. However, if you are a Mozart aficionado, you need to make Salzburg your first city to visit (then go to Vienna). *Live your dream*...go where your desire leads you! Again, this will be a major key to your travel club's success.

When outlining your three-year travel plan, make two drafts. On the first draft, the main heading should list only the destinations *you* want to visit with your groups. Maybe Paris is high on your "dream destination" list. If it is, research Paris and the surrounding area for things to see and do (if you haven't already). After you have listed your primary destinations, then do the second draft and create sub-headings that define what you want to see and do while you are there. As an example, if your goal is to take three major trips a year, then your plan should look something like this:

Note: In Draft #1, list only main destinations e.g., states, countries, regions, islands, major cities, etc., you are interested in visiting.

THREE YEAR TRAVEL PLAN - DRAFT #1

YEAR ONE

- ***TOUR #1*** - **Holland & Belgium – 10 days**
  Holland: Cities – Amsterdam
  Belgium: Cities – Brussels, Ghent & Bruges

- ***TOUR #2*** - **England & Scotland – 10 days**
  England: Cities – London
  Scotland: Cities – Edinburgh & Glasgow

- ***TOUR #3*** - **Cruise / Panama Canal – 14 days**

YEAR TWO

- ***TOUR #1*** - **France – 8 days**
  City: – Paris

- ***TOUR #2*** - **Cruise / Western Caribbean – 7 days**

- ***TOUR #3*** - **Portugal – 10 days**
  Cities: Lisbon, Estoril, Cascais & Sintra
  Cities: (the Algarve) – Faro & Portimao

YEAR THREE

- ***TOUR #1*** - **Hawaii – 10 days**
  Islands of Hawaii, Maui & Kauai

- ***TOUR #2*** - **Switzerland & Austria – 14 days**

Austria: Cities – Innsbruck, Salzburg & Vienna
Switzerland: Cities – Zurich, Interlaken, Montreux, Lucerne

■ *TOUR #3* - **Australia & New Zealand – 21 days**

Australia: Cities – Sydney, Cairns & Port Douglas
New Zealand: Cities – Auckland (North Island) & Queenstown (South Island)

Note: In Draft #2, go into the details of your trip. Under sub-headings, list exactly where you want to go and what you want to see and do when you are there. Also list any hotels you would like to use along with restaurants, specialty shops, museums, etc. that have been recommended to you or that you personally know of. If you don't know of any, use your personal travel reference guides (the World Travel Guide is especially helpful), and other reference material you can gather from the travel industry suppliers e.g., Travel and Tourism Bureaus, tour operators, and Chambers of Commerce. Be as detailed as possible; the more detailed the better.

This exercise serves four purposes:

1. The research you do to complete this list will make you more knowledgeable about these particular destinations.

2. Because of your research, and because you are going to one of your "dream destinations," your enthusiasm for this tour will be apparent when you talk with potential tour participants. And enthusiasm is infectious!

3. The details you list in this draft can be used in your promotional marketing material. Writing and creating your brochures will be a breeze!

4. Draft #2 will end up being the outline you will use to package your tours (if you piece them together yourself) or give to your tour operator or DMC as a guideline for them to use.

The following is an example of the first tour of Year One in your Plan of Action. This example will show you *exactly* how to do an initial outline of the tours you are considering. This is a solid, standard procedure that works well and gets more effective each time you do it. Once you have done this exercise a few times, it will become second nature for you. *Since the procedure is the same for every tour, I am going to outline only the first tour. The other tours can be outlined using my example. The procedure is exactly the same, only the destinations and various components (hotels, sightseeing, etc.) change.*

The key element of Draft #2 is research. If this draft is complete enough, it will take very little time and effort to "cost out" your tour and finalize the tour package. So, do serious research on your proposed destinations from the start. Use all the reference material you can get your hands on, including input from friends, family and acquaintances who have traveled to any of the places on your Three Year Plan.

If you have already had the pleasure of traveling to some of the chosen places, great! The input of your personal knowledge can definitely benefit your tour package.

In the next chapter, we will incorporate Draft #2 into a costing sheet. This is a simple transition and an easy way to cost your tour program. **Note**: In Draft #2, you need to add the number of nights you want to spend in each city taking into the consideration the sightseeing you want to do.

THREE YEAR TRAVEL PLAN - DRAFT #2

YEAR ONE

▪ *TOUR #1* - HOLLAND & BELGIUM −10 days

COUNTRY - Holland

COUNTRY - Holland...continued

City: Amsterdam
Number of nights: 4 nights

HOTEL - **Holland**

Amsterdam: Amsterdam Marriott or the Golden Tulip Barbizon Centre (on the fifth canal ring & both close to the Rijksmuseum).

SIGHTSEEING - **Holland**

Amsterdam: City tour / Rijksmuseum (Van Gogh's Night Watch) / Van Gogh Museum / canal cruise / Anne Frank's house (go early to avoid crowds) / diamond factory / Maritime Museum / Floating Flower Market / Royal Palace, the Mint Tower / definitely explore the town by streetcar.

South Holland: Alsmeer Flower Auction (largest flower auction in the world - go early to avoid crowds) / The Hague (Peace Palace) / Delft / Keukenhof Gardens.

North Holland: Zaanse Schans (open air museum with working windmills, wooden shoe maker and historic Dutch community) / Volendam / Edam

RESTAURANTS - **Holland**
Amsterdam: De Kelderhof / Indrapura / Café Restaurant Suisse / d'Vijff Vlieghen (Five Flies) / 't Swarte Schaep (the Black Sheep)

COUNTRY - **Belgium**

Cities: Brussels & Bruges
Number of nights: Brussels - 4

COUNTRY - Belgium...continued

Number of nights: Bruges - 2

HOTEL - **Brussels**

Hilton Brussels or Le Meridien Bruxelles (close to the Grand'Place)

HOTEL - **Bruges**

Golden Tulip Hotel de Medici (town center)

SIGHTSEEING - **Belgium**

Brussels: Grand'Place / St. Michael's Cathedral / Place Royal / Manneken-pis / Waterloo (outskirts – 11 miles)

Bruges: Town Hall / Cathedral of the Holy Savior / Canal Cruise / Grote Markt

Ghent: Castle of the Counts / St. Bavo's Cathedral (has the Van Eyck masterpiece *The Adoration of the Mystical Lamb*) / Town Hall / Three Abby's

RESTAURANTS - **Belgium**

Brussels: Chez Flo / Aux Armes De Bruxelles / Le Saint-Germain / Auberge De Boendael

Bruges: De Gulden Spoor / Oud Brugge / Sint-Joris / La Taverne Brugeoise

Ghent: Amadeus / De Koperem Pomp

TO RE-CAP, FOLLOW THESE THREE STEPS:

STEP #1 - Structure your travel club to fit your future plans i.e., how hard you want to work, how much you want to travel, etc.

<u>STEP #2</u> - Make an extensive list of both domestic and international destinations that you want to visit in the next three years.

<u>STEP #3</u> - Lay out your Three Year Plan of Action based on Steps 1 and 2.

It's good to be the group travel leader

You are now recognized as a legitimate group travel leader with a viable travel club. Someone to be taken seriously by all who wholesale travel arrangements and tour programs. You are making your own contacts and, in turn, being contacted almost daily by tour operators, cruise lines, cities and even countries. You know where and when you want to take your tours and how long you want to be gone. The next step is to decide which type of travel supplier will best fill your needs and requirements. Careful decisions need to be made because these will be the first tour packages you will promote to friends, family and social acquaintances, *your future travel club members.*

In Chapter Seven, discover the differences between the major travel suppliers from which to choose. Once you understand your travel supplier options, it will be easy for you to make the right decision. Chapter Seven will set you on the right path toward making these decisions.

Riches Through Knowledge...
        Knowledge Through Travel

The Pleasant Travel & Tourism Institute

CHAPTER 7

Developing and Qualifying your Contacts

How to choose and who to use!

Now that you have your travel club's tours outlined for the next three years, it's time to cost out your first year's tours so that you can start promoting them. Before you do this however, it is *very important* that you have a good understanding of who the different travel suppliers are, their specific roles in the travel industry, and what they can do for you (*especially* what they can do for you)!

Once you have an understanding of the roles that each tour and travel supplier plays in the industry, you will be able to make an informed decision as to which you think will do the best job for you on a particular tour.

Developing your tour and travel supplier contacts will be one the most important agendas that you set for yourself. After reading this chapter, you will know your travel supplier options and how each one can serve you best when setting up a particular tour.

The next two chapters will give you details on *How to Cost and Price Your Tours.* The knowledge gained from chapters 7, 8, and 9 will give you all the information you need to select the appropriate travel supplier, get quotes, and set a price for your tours with confidence.

But first, I will explain the principal differences between the tour and travel categories from which you have to choose:

1. A travel agency

2. A tour operator (U.S.A. based)

3. A destination management company or "DMC," as they are known in the industry (internationally based, some with U.S. representation)

4. Booking arrangements directly with the supply source e.g., airlines, hotels, motorcoaches, etc.

One out of four – pick your option

As a group travel planner you have the above four options to select from to package your tours. Depending on how active you want to be (hobby vs. full-time business), some options will be more advantageous than others. After learning the differences, you should be able to select which option will serve you best. Eventually, you may use all four options because as your tours vary, so will your tour and travel requirements.

OPTION #1 - TRAVEL AGENCY

As you probably know, travel agencies offer a full range of services such as airline ticketing, hotel accommodations, car rentals, cruise vacations, etc. They work on a commission basis with the respective travel suppliers and they work hard to get you the best fares and prices available for your time frame of travel.

As I discussed in Chapter One, travel agencies are fighting harder for smaller commissions and their fair share of the travel market than ever before. Also, today, many people can buy travel services directly from the suppliers, even as individuals. Because, cut commissions and heavy competition from seemingly every direction, many travel agencies are becoming more creative and competitive than ever before. As a group travel leader, you will want to associate yourself with one of these creative and competitive local travel agencies, as they can be of great service to you.

As mentioned in Chapter Four, a travel agency can do airline ticketing for you; they can work with you on inclusive packaged tours; and they can be a source of revenue for you by paying you a commission for the business you bring to them. Once you have found the agency you want as your "travel ally," meet with them and negotiate a commission split. The commission split can range between 25% to 50% (or higher) of the *commission,* which is based on the net amount of the ticket sale, not including tax. The percentage you receive will depend on how active a part you take in the booking and ticketing process. The more you do, the higher your percentage.

Until you establish a relationship with some of the various tour and travel suppliers, work closely with the travel agency with whom you have aligned yourself. Use them as a sounding board and for advice. Let them bid on your proposed tour(s). Since it doesn't cost you to have an agency price a group tour for you, give them a chance to provide a competitive bid. Many travel agencies can be very competitive. So, get a bid from your travel agent and compare it with your other bids and make your choice. If they give you an attractive bid, use them. If they are not competitive, then use one of your other three options.

Since you have a travel club which deals only with groups, your concern is getting the best deal for yourself and your members. Consider your options carefully.

Chapter 7   **103**

When to Use a Travel Agency

- For airline ticketing (individuals and groups, or when you are unable to secure airline ticketing directly with the airlines)
- For tour package bids (competitive comparisons)
- For a source of brochures and information
- For direct access to the airlines reservation system (if you are a home-based business and are knowledgeable about computers and booking reservations)

OPTION #2 - U.S.A. TOUR OPERATOR

Tour operators provide an all-inclusive group tour package program for you at a net rate. You simply add your mark-up to their net price and your complete tour package is ready to promote!

Depending on what you want, their package can include airline transportation, motorcoach tours, cruise line arrangements (cruises incorporated in their tour package), arrival meet and greet services, guides and escorts, sightseeing, meals, etc. Also in their pricing, they will include the free trips you require. For example, if you have a group of thirty or more people, you may want one free trip for every ten or fifteen full-paying participants. You then use these free tickets for you and one or two of your assistants (like your spouse, best friends, children, etc.) to escort the group. It takes just one call to a tour operator and you will have an attractive total package to offer your group!

Note: Today, group oriented tour operators are also willing to work with you in customizing your tour by "tweaking" one of their packaged programs to fit your requirements. Keep this in mind should you want to offer a specialized tour to your club members.

When to Use a Tour Operator

- For convenience of time and effort

- For proven, successful tour packages
- For competitive bidding
- For a source of brochures and information

OPTION #3 – INTERNATIONAL DMC

There is very little difference between an international DMC and a USA tour operator. The DMC is just a little further away! There are several reasons you may want to deal with a DMC *after you have been in business a while.* I say, *after you've been in business a while* because you need some good educational travel experiences running your tours before jumping into international negotiations.

Basically, a DMC offers the same services as a U.S.A. tour operator with a couple of exceptions. Like the tour operator, they will provide you with an all-inclusive group tour package program for you at a net rate. Simply add your mark-up to their net price (as you would with a tour operator) and your complete tour package is ready to be announced on the travel club hot line. Most DMC's are native to the country you want to visit and have their base of operations in that country. Along with providing an all-inclusive group tour package program for you at a net rate, you are also getting advice and guidance from someone who was born and raised in that particular country. This is a definite PLUS in terms of guidance regarding what you should, or should not include in your program.

A DMC's tour package will (usually) include *ground arrangements* only. These include meet and greet services upon your group's arrival, motorcoach and rail transportation, hotel accommodations, meals, special group functions, sightseeing, professional drivers and guides, etc.

Note: Many of the DMC's belong to various DMC marketing

organizations, which provide a U.S.A. based office for you to work with. This makes working with a DMC *almost* as convenient as working with a U.S. tour operator.

The following are two points that differentiate a tour operator from a DMC:

1. **Airlines** - Most DMC's (as a rule) do not get involved with providing air transportation for your group. It will be up to you to handle the air arrangements.

2. **Deposits & Payments** - The deposits and payments to your DMC will (usually) need to be in the currency of that country. If your group is traveling to Great Britain, you will need to pay in English pounds (GBP); if to Australia, you will need to pay in Australian dollars (AUD), etc. However, there is good news on the horizon for European destinations. Effective in the year 2002, money exchanging in Europe will be simplified when the Euro Dollar comes on the open market. Once in circulation, the "Euro" will be the common currency for most of Europe's most popular countries. This should be a stabilizing factor regarding the Euro/US Dollar fluctuation, thus eliminating the worry of the US dollar weakening against a foreign currency.

If these two points seem like a drawback to you, *they're not*. This is why:

- **Airlines** – If you have a group of ten or more people from one gateway city (leaving from the same airport), most airlines will work directly with you to do the ticketing. As long as you have a group for them, they usually treat you the same as any travel agent or large group operator. They will normally quote you a net airfare and you then add the profit you want to make. On net group airfares, you can usually add at least ten percent to the ticket for your profit, and still be considerably less expensive than the published airfares that are advertised in magazines and newspapers.

Note: When doing your final calculations, be certain that you are aware of all airport and departure taxes in effect at the time of travel. The airline reservationists you book with or the travel agency or tour provider you use should provide you with this information.

If the airline will not work directly with you, then go to your travel agency or an airline discount ticketing agency, commonly known in the as a "consolidator." Either will be happy to do the ticketing for your group. Consolidators are travel companies that reserve blocks of seats on various airlines at a deep discount. They choose popular routes (New York to Los Angeles or New York to London, Chicago to Hawaii, Los Angeles to Sydney, etc) that are in demand by the public in general. The consolidators get a considerable discount because they guarantee a particular airline that they will sell those seats or pay for them if they don't. Business is good (thanks to the growing group travel leader movement) and many consolidators are adding more routes almost daily, making their service to the group travel leader community a valued commodity.

Eventually, *you will need* a good consolitor connection! To help you, one of the best sources for consolidator connections is the Moffit's Consolidators Guide. This detailed guide, which sells for $39.95 is a great value for the money and features over 200 consolidator profiles listing business hours, trade affiliations, years in business, insurance/bonding, number of employees and annual sales. It also includes important information on commission/net fare payment policies and complete contact details including telephone, fax, e-mail and website.

You can contact OSSN at 800-771-7327 to purchase a copy

or log on to **www.ossn.com** to order it over the Internet (If you are an OSSN menber you will get a $10.00 discount).

When I find a supplier that does a good job for me, I am more than happy to recommended them to my fellow group travel leaders. One of the consolators I use frequently is Travel Professionals, Inc. They consistantly have very competitive airfares and are extremely efficient with their ticketing process and delivery. Travel Professionals President, Mark Gordon, runs a smooth operation and does a good job of staying on top of the ever-changing world of discount air fares. If you need a quote for a group, you can contact Travel Professionals at:

Travel Professionals, Inc.
401 N. Michigan Ave, Suite 200
Chicago, IL 60611

Tel: (800) 654-1583   Fax: (312) 321-0501

Most air consolidators use major, regularly scheduled national and international air carriers. As mentioned in Option #1, when working with a travel agency, you need to negotiate a commission split. Dealing with a consolidator, you work with a net ticket price and then add your mark-up. Besides the low ticket prices that a consolidator usually offers, another good benefit is that there is ordinarily no fare amount written in the fare box on the airline ticket; it just says *bulk fare*. This gives you a lot of monetary latitude between the low net fare you paid and the much higher published fare people would have paid.

- **Deposits & Payments** – Some international DMC's have U.S. bank accounts and will let you pay deposits and the balance in US dollars. Most DMC's require that you pay in their currency through a bank-to-bank wire transfer. Wire transferring money is easy; your local bank representative can provide assistance on how to do this.

Dealing with money transactions in another currency can seem a bit complicated at first, but once you have done it a few times, it will be easier, even interesting. When costing your program in a foreign currency, it *is very IMPORTANT* that you use a conservative U.S. dollar-to-foreign currency exchange rate. For example: If you have a group to Australia, the exchange rate may be 1.87 Australian Dollars (AUD) to $1.00 USD. When calculat-ing the cost of the tour package your DMC has quoted you in AUD, you would want to use a little more conservative exchange, such as 1.80 AUD to the $1.00 USD.

The reason you do this is to protect yourself in case of a fluctuation against the US dollar to a foreign currency exchange rate. Then, if the US dollar weakens against the foreign currency, you may make a little less profit, but you should not have to take a major loss. On the other side of the coin, if the foreign currency weakens against the U.S. dollar, you could end up with a nice windfall profit! When this happens, and it happens more often than not, you can put the money in your pocket, *or,* I suggest, spread some of the wealth by surprising your group with an extra reception, sightseeing tour, or dinner. They are always grateful and will remember your kind deed by telling everyone back home about your wonderful travel club and how great your tours are. Once again, when the Euro currency takes effect in 2002, working with a DMC in a foreign country will be greatly simplified.

When to Use a DMC

- For tour packages you want specialized or customized

- For higher profit margins (usually)

- For local advice and guidance from a travel professional and resident of that country

- For competitive bidding
- For a direct source of brochures and information

OPTION #4 - BOOKING ARRANGEMENTS DIRECTLY

Normally in business, dealing directly with a supply source and eliminating as many middlemen as possible is the optimum way to conduct business. Upon occasion, however, this is not necessarily so, and the group tour business is a classic example. So, it is important that you understand which option will benefit you and your tour members the most, and then use that option.

As an example, if you are operating your group travel club for the fun and benefits, and as more of a hobby than a money making enterprise, then a travel agent or tour operator would be a great way for you to run your tours. On the other hand, if a good profit is your number one goal, and the fun and travel benefits are secondary, then packaging your own tours by contacting the airlines, hotels, motorcoach companies, restaurants, sightseeing, museums, etc., directly may be the option to choose.

Even though you could potentially have a larger profit margin, keep in mind that booking arrangements directly with travel suppliers can be very time consuming. In addition to that, because of all of the contracts you make with multiple entities, *you must* be a detail oriented person. As an example, if you have a group of forty people on a typical seven-day, all-inclusive tour (to anywhere), you will book and commit to pay for:

- 40 roundtrip airline tickets
- 20 hotel rooms per night (based on double occupancy)
- 1,120 meals (21 breakfasts, 3 lunches & 4 dinners per person times 40 pax)
- 49 passenger deluxe motorcoach for 7 days

- entrance fees to sightseeing attractions

- motorcoach driver and guide fees and gratuities

- and more

After proper research, booking the group is fairly easy. Taking care of the contract details (deposits and payment schedule, cancellation deadlines, invoicing and collecting money, etc.) is where the work really starts and it takes a very detailed and disciplined person to handle this. There are many group travel leaders who work this way and are very good at it. They love both the challenge and the detail work, and most of all, they love to see the group program come together. The accomplishment and extra profit is their reward...and of course they also go on the tour!

My point is, if your time is limited, this may not be the route you want to take, especially in the beginning. On the other hand, if you like a challenge and can rise to the occasion, the opportunities are certainly there for you to pursue.

When to Book Direct with Travel Suppliers

- For greater profits (domestic tours / short overnight trips)

- For the challenge

- For the accomplishment

Those are your four group travel supplier options. Depending on what you decided your level of activity is going to be, take the tours from your Three Year Plan of Action (Chapter Six) and match them with the travel supplier that will best fit your tour and travel criteria. As with any new venture, it may take some trial and error for you to get your system down to the way you want to operate your travel club. You may start out thinking that booking direct is perfect for what you want to accomplish but eventually the travel agent or tour operator will win you over because of the ease of doing business with them.

As a group travel planner and incentive operator myself, I use all four options, because each have their advantages. My decision is based on certain criteria, such as: where is the tour going? Do I know the area well enough to book directly? Do I have a good tour operator or DMC contact for that area? How limited is my time schedule to work on the program? As a rule of thumb, I make my decisions about which option to use based on what type of group it is. The following is an example of how I use the different travel suppliers:

Leisure Groups

Domestic (U.S.A.) / One or two city tour / same state – I *book directly* with the travel supply sources (airlines, hotels, sightseeing, etc). utilizing the various state and city tourism boards for information. I might also use a local tour company for all of the motorcoach tours, sightseeing and transfers.

Domestic (U.S.A.) / One to two week motorcoach tour – I use a *tour operator*. However, this is certainly an opportunity to *book direct*. If you really like figuring, planning and coordinating cross country trips and are good at it (and many people are good at it), t hen go for it! The reason I choose a *tour operator* is because my time is very limited and a tour operator provides a great service to me.

International – I use a *DMC* probably sixty percent of the time and a *tour operator* the other forty percent, even though, a well established, group oriented *tour operator* is pretty hard to beat for competitive price, fast response, and good service. I can see the percentages eventually ending up at a 50%-50% split within the next few years.

Incentive Groups

Domestic – I *book direct* (airlines, hotels, sightseeing, etc).

Incentive Groups ...continued

International – I use a *DMC.*

Conferences & Conventions

Domestic – I *book direct,* heavily supported by State Tourism Boards and local Convention and Visitors Bureaus (CVB).

International – I use a *DMC.*

Cruises

Domestic or International – *You are a registered CLIA agent; ALWAYS book directly with the cruise line.*

> *NOTE! For those group tour leaders who are looking at this travel opportunity as a hobby, your best option is to book only with USA based* <u>*group*</u> *tour operators or international destination management companies (DMC) that have a representative in the USA.*

And in the beginning...

Since many of you are just starting your career in the group travel business, I want to emphasize the advantages of a tour operator or a U.S. based DMC. I believe that using either one of these two options, in the beginning, will be the easiest way for you to start your travel club with minimum risk.

Advantages of using a U.S. based tour operator are:

• Utilizing their buying power. Because of the high volume of business they do with travel suppliers around the world, their

Chapter 7   **113**

buying power is extremely strong and the benefit of this buying power is passed on to you in the form of a competitive price for your tour group.

- Negotiating power. Again, because of the volume of travel services they demand, they negotiate very good rates and terms.

- Since they only provide travel services for groups, their travel experiences and guidance can be of great help to you.

- Their target market is the group travel leader. Just like Uncle Sam – *"They want you!"*

- Your contact is located in the U.S.A. and is accessible by e-mail and toll-free telephone and fax numbers.

- You will deal in U.S. dollars.

- You only need to make deposits and payments to one company.

Advantages of using an International DMC are:

- Being a native of a particular country, and a resident as well, definitely gives the local DMC an edge over most outside competition.

- The same as the U.S.A. tour operator: Utilize their buying power.

- The same as the U.S.A. tour operator: Utilize their negotiating power.

- The same as the U.S.A. tour operator: Since they work primarily with tour groups, their travel experiences and guidance can be a great help to you.

More about U.S.A. tour operators...

In general, tour operators in the U.S.A. offer a variety of

specialties. Some specialize in domestic motorcoach tour packages and others in European itineraries. There are tour operators that have only tour programs to the Holy Land, to Asia, to the Mediterranean islands, or to specific regions of the world.

Tour operators that have a specific area of expertise are wonderful to work with. If you want a fall foliage tour to the East Coast for your group or a tour of California's wine country, there is a tour operator ready to help you package it. Depending on the size of your group, most tour operators will be happy to customize a program to fit any special requests you may have, such as including a particular place to visit or a special venue to have a meal function.

The advertisement on the prior page and the one shown below are a sample of two prominent tour operators who know, help and and support the advancement of group travel leaders. Keep in mind, however, that these are just two of many, quality tour operators ready to help you with your tour needs (see the Reference Section / Tour Operators).

Travel for free with 10 friends!*

Organize a group and travel for free on your next Go Ahead Vacations tour! Bring as few as 10 passengers in your group and you travel absolutely free! Once you've earned a free vacation, you can apply additional passengers toward a second free place or receive a cash bonus.

goahead vacations

Call for your free Group Leader Packet
1-800-438-7672

* Applies to fully escorted tours only. For information on cruises and city stays, please call.

Most of these tour companies have group travel leader programs in place, which range from helping a new, inexperienced, group travel leader get started, to guiding an established group travel leader on how to reach their maximum potential. Many of the tour operators have their "how to" group travel leader programs printed in a booklet form. These marketing materials are very informative and explain how the two of you can work hand-in-hand to accomplish your group travel goals.

Tour operators are group travel leader friendly! Many of the U.S. tour operators have realized the group travel leader/group travel club movement (more like explosion) is just beginning, and have developed special programs catered to these special sellers of leisure travel. They understand what group travel leaders want, and what it takes to make their tours a success.

Have some conversations with a few tour operators (usually a sales representative for your area) and get to know them. Ask them if they have a group travel leader program, and, if they do, have them send you the material so you can look it over before you ask for them for a group proposal quote. Get material from a few tour operators and analyze who offers what, and then make a decision on who to use based on that information and the rapport you had with the sales representative.

More about international DMC's...

To me, DMC's are very special people. Once you have built a solid business relationship with a particular DMC, They eventually become more of an "extended family" member than a business partner. After this transition happens, every time you have a group to their particular country, it's like a family reunion! Traveling the globe during my thirty year career in travel, I have seen some of the most beautiful and exotic places in existence. But much more meaningful to me is the friendships I have made during that sojourn. I cherish this part of my travel career more than any other. After you develop a few of these relationships over the next few years, I know you will feel the same way.

"Who do you use?"

When I talk with other group travel planners, the subject always comes around to what destinations you have been selling lately and "who is offering the best deals?" The next subject that always follows is "Who's your DMC?" So, everyone starts talking about their ground operators and, in many cases, we find we are using the same DMC in a particular country. If the DMC's are different, then the conversation goes into a "Let me tell you how great my DMC is" mode. Usually in fun, we then try to get the other group planner to change over to our DMC. If the DMC they have been using has always done a good job for them, there is no reason for them to change and they remain loyal to their DMC, as they should.

Loyalty is the key word here. To reiterate what I said above, a good relationship with a DMC will be invaluable to you and, after you have taken a few groups to their particular destination, they will become part of your "travel family." Once this happens, you have an ally who will work very hard to meet your group requirements, tour package expectations and price range. For their loyalty and hard negotiating efforts on your behalf, all you have to do is deliver the number of group tour participants you projected (or close to it) and make your deposit and payments on a timely basis as per the DMC's schedule. In turn, your DMC will fulfill their obligation by giving your group the best guides, drivers and motorcoaches, sightseeing tours and group functions that will be remembered forever, and much more. In general, you will receive top-notch service and a 110% effort.

The Reference Section in *How to Organize Group Travel for and Fun and Profit* is loaded with respectable tour operators for you to consider. It is up to you to select which one you wish to work with.

Which tour operators or DMC's are right for you? That's the million dollar question! As with any business, a personal recommendation is always the best. Talking with other group travel leaders who have been in business for a while will be one of your best options to help get you started.

After joining some of the various group leader organizations mentioned in Chapter Three, you will meet other group travel leaders while attending local trade shows and conferences. Ask them which DMC's and tour operators they use, and then compare notes. Whether you ask about tour operators, DMC's, or favorite destinations, your fellow group travel planners will be more than willing to help you any way possible.

Who do I use?

Since my wife and I have owned and operated our group travel company, ETC Services, Inc., for the past sixteen years, we have our tour operators and DMC's pretty well in place. We take great pride in the quality of service we provide for our group tour participants, and we put 110 % effort into each one. This type of effort is what I also expect from any travel suppliers, tour operators or DMC's that I use.

I have several favorite destinations and countries that I love, and never get tired of visiting. In these countries, I am happy to say, I have found the DMC's that provide the quality of service that should be expected. If you have not had a group to the following destinations, I highly recommend that you add them to your "places to go" list.

The following is a partial list of the tour operators and DMC's that I enjoy working with and use for my group tours. I know the owners of most of these companies and have dealt with some of them for over twenty years. I consider them close personal friends and personally invite you to consider these destinations and operators for your future group tours. For ETC Services, Inc., the DMC's listed below, and the destinations they represent, have proven to be a very wise and profitable combination. I am sure it will be the same for you and your groups also!

■ *Australia / New Zealand*

Pan Pacific Incentives
6 Glen Street, Suite 7
Milsons Point,
Sydney NSW 2061, Australia
Tel: 011-61-2-9957-1355   Fax: 011-61-2-9929-4826
E-mail: incentives@tourcontractors.com.au

It's a long way from the good ol' USA but I can assure you that it's well worth your time and effort to package a tour to Australia and New Zealand. You can be that sure your group will have a wonderful time and return home "singing praises" of the friendly Aussie's and Kiwi's (New Zealander's) they met during the tour.

Because there is so much to see and do in Australia and New Zealand, your goal will be to cover as much territory as possible during your stay without making it an "If it's Tuesday it must be Belgium" tour. To help you accomplish this mission, I suggest that you contact Narelle Falting, the Divisional Manager for Pan Pacific in Sydney and my DMC for these two great countries.

Narelle and her staff of "mate's" will work their magic for you and tailor-make a tour package that will maximize your budget to its fullest potential. The last tour I had "down under" was a group of 117 people in August of 2000 and, as usual, Pan Pacific excelled with their service. Moving this number of people from point A to point B on this big Continent is a challange to say the least, but Pan Pacific made the transition for the group smooth and interesting. So call Narelle (soon), say "G'day" and give her an idea of what you want to do. She will do the rest.

Also, everyone really does say "G'day" and "No worries Mate!"

■ *France*

Holt Paris Welcome Service
12 Rue du Helder
75 009 Paris, France
Tel: 011-33-1-45 23 08 14   Fax: 011-33-1-42 47 19 89
E-mail: france@euromic.com

Strangely enough, my "French Connection" is a couple from Great Britain (go figure)...but it's true! The owners, Susan and Alan Holt, have lived in France for over 40 years and run an operation that would make Napoleon jealous. As energetic as they are entertaining, this "take charge" couple work hard on the group tour leaders behalf to assure the group gets the most "bang for their tour buck." What makes them special is that they understand the American tourist (as well as anyone can anyway) and know how to work hand-in-hand with American group tour leaders.

The Holt's home office is in Paris but they handle business for the whole of France. Whether you have a large conference or small leisure group, you can be sure the Holt's will treat you with the same consideration, respect and their usual great service. Also, forget the myth that all French people hate the Americans (with the exception of a few Parisian waiters). My trips to France over the past few years have been nothing short of fantastic and extremely enjoyable. *Vive la France and Vive la Holt Paris Welcome Service!*

■ *Greece, Turkey & the Mediterranean*

Cruise Club Holidays
85 Vouliagmenis Ave.
Athens 166 75, Greece
Tel: 011-30-1-960-4250   Fax: 011-30-1-964-4943
E-mail: sales@cruiseclub.gr

I have been working with the two owners of Cruise Club

Holidays (CCH) since 1980, and while I still have a hard time pronouncing their names, I don't have a hard time deciding who to use for my Greece, Turkey and Mediterranean tours. When I first met Pavlos Holevas and Christos Sahinoglou (say that 3 times fast!), they were young Greek entrepreneurs and now they are two distinguished Greek businessmen whose tour operation is one of the best in the Mediterranean.

My first group to Greece with Cruise Club Holidays was in 1980 and I have not used anyone else since then. The most impressive quality about CCH is that "nothing is impossible!" As a young boy I was always intrigued by Greece and vowed that one day I would go there (I was young and nothing was impossible). When I met Pavlos and Christos for the first time, I told them that I *really* wanted to go to Greece but did not have much money. Pavlos said "Whatever you have, I can get you to Greece." And he did! The rest is history and Greece to this day is one of my favorite countries to visit.

Well connected throughout Greece, Turkey and the Mediterranean, CCH's prices are unbeatable. Whether it's a land only tour (they have a great 18 day "In the Steps of Paul" program), Mediterranean cruise and land package, or a cruise only package, nobody will beat their prices...and I mean NOBODY! If you have ever dreamed of going to Greece (like I did), now's your chance!

■ *Netherlands (Holland) & Belgium*

I.T.B. Amsterdam
"Travel by Design"
Olympisch Stadion 14
1076 DE Amsterdam
Netherlands
Tel: 011-31-20-3051358   Fax: 011-31-20-6758651
E-mail: jaap@itbams.nl

When the DMC's name is Jaap Snijders, you sort of wonder

if you will even be able to communicate. I soon found out that his English was a whole lot better than mine! For the most part, the whole of Holland's population and a substantial part of Belgium's speak English very well. One BIG plus for taking a group there! Jaap became my permanent DMC, and a close friend, when he helped revive two groups (200 participants) that were almost lost because of the lack of service of another local DMC. Jaap stepped in, made things happen, and both groups were a great success.

I cannot begin to tell you what a winning combination you have with I.T.B. Incentives as your DMC, and Holland and Belgium as your destination. Also, they love Americans...how's that for a change? And if you want your group participants to *love* you, take them to Holland. When you do go, be sure the group visits the Alsmeer Flower Auction, the largest flower auction in the world. They sell between fifteen and seventeen million flowers a day at Alsmeer. This is truly a sight to see and will be a great experience for everyone! To get the full impact of how truly magnificent the tulips of Holland are, you need to schedule your groups starting in late April or May. This is when the tulip season is in full bloom and most enjoyable.

■ *Portugal*

Especialtur
Av. Santos Dumont, 63 – 8. B
1050-202 Lisboa
Portugal
Tel: 011-351-1-793- 7420   Fax: 011-351-1-793-7419
E-mail: portugal@especialtur.mailpac.pt

The good news is that Portugal is a fantastic country. The *really good news*, for group travel planners anyway, is that very few Americans know about Portugal! So, for us wise, "in the know" travel planners, we have a beautiful, Old World country as a "new" group destination. And because the rest of the world vacations in Portugal, the country is loaded with first class hotels and resorts, golf courses, restaurants and nightclubs. My Portugal DMC, Fernando Coelho, and his family have successfully owned and operated Especialtur for seventeen years.

Their enthusiasm shows in everything they do for your groups, as they take great pride in the quality of service they provide. For group travel planners just starting to take your groups international, Portugal is a very inexpensive destination, especially considering the quality of the hotels, food, dining venues, sightseeing, etc. Take advantage of this great group destination at a great price while you can. More and more Americans will be discovering Portugal in the next few years. Beat the rush...go now! By the way, Portugal is not a part of Spain (contrary to what the Spaniards tell you).

■ *Spain*

Lib/Go
69 Spring Street
Ramsey, NJ 07446
Tel: (800) 899-9800   Fax: (201) 934-3821
E-mail: crespoe@libgotravel.com

Contrary to what the Portuguese say, Spain is not still ruled by the Moors! Emilio Crespo, my good friend and DMC for Spain for over sixteen years. Years ago, Emilio educated me about the many benefits that Spain had to offer groups, and challenged me to bring a group over and see for myself. I took a group, and the rest is history!

My first group to Spain, American Investors Life Insurance Company, was a huge success, thanks to Emilio's help and guidance. I have had many groups to Spain since, and all have had an excellent outcome, and at an excellent price to boot! Culturally, Spain has so much to offer that it's almost overwhelming. The names of the cities alone stir the imagination; Madrid, Barcelona, Cadiz, Seville and Grenada. Then there is the Costa del Sol, the Spanish Riviera, a stones throw from North Africa and Tangier, Morocco. And speaking of stones (big ones), the Rock of Gibraltar is just a few miles away. As popular as Spain is today, it is still a good value for the dollar and a super destination for groups. *Bravo!*

■ *Switzerland*

SM Travel Ltd
Ringstrasse 14
CH – 8057 Zurich
Switzerland
Tel: 011-41-1-311-3500   Fax: 011-41-1-312-3129
E-mail: smtravel@bluewin.ch

Talk about your dream destination! Just the thought of going to Switzerland makes me want to start packing my suitcase and jump on a plane! Although Switzerland is not the most inexpensive destination to take your groups to today, remember, *it only costs a little more to go First Class!* But what an easy destination to sell! Put together a tour program to Switzerland, print a brochure, and you've got a group! On top of that, I have a miracle worker of a DMC who can put together a program that will usually fit your budget. Extremely creative, Ralph Schwaller and his team of experts have been in business since "Heidi" was a baby. Starting as a motorcoach company back in the 1960's, the DMC company, SM Travel Ltd, was established in 1977 and has been one of the leaders in Swiss tourism ever since. The business is now in the hands of his daughter, Ursula, who has never ceased to impress me, time and time again, with her ability to "make things happen."

Every group I have taken to Switzerland has been impressed by the people, the hotels, and the food. They are equally impressed (in awe actually) of the countryside and the alpine villages they visit. I encourage you to package a tour to Switzerland as soon as it is possible. You will love it, your group will love it, the people of Heidi's village will love it, and Ursula will love it! Also, keep in mind the train system in Switzerland is convenient and very economical. By incorporating a Swissrail pass into your group tour program you can accomplish two things:

1) It will help lower your per person budget.

2) It gives your people some freedom to really see the country at their own pace on their free days.

When you consider Switzerland for one of your tours, think of SM Travel. You can't go wrong using SM Travel as your Swiss DMC.

USA Based DMC / Group Tours & Airline Ticketing

The next three listings are in a category of their own because two of these companies are USA based tour operators/DMC's with multiple international destinations to offer group travel planners and one is a combination international tourist organization/DMC.

■ **Conferences International**
(A division of Associated Incentive Travel)
1101 Worcester Road, Suite 401,
Framingham, MA 01701-5249
Tel: 800-221-8747 (TRIP)   Fax: 508-842-5566
E-mail: conferences@conferencesintl.com

Conferences International and its parent company, Associated Incentive Travel, established by Dick Kisker and Brian Pollock respectively, are exceptions I make when it comes to using a USA based DMC. These two companies have a lot to offer group travel planners and I take advantage of their services whenever I can.

Ordinarily, when it comes to the booking and ticketing of my groups, I deal directly with the airlines and negotiate the airfares myself. On many occasions, however, Dick has been able to beat my ticket price. Now I often use Conferences International to do the ticketing for some of my groups. Because Dick works closely with several major International Air Carriers, his influence is substantial and can possibly benefit your group travel package. If an airline is not giving you the airfare you need, check with Conferences International...they may have just the fare you are looking for.

Also, as a DMC, Dick represents several destinations in Europe and Asia and is adding more all the time. For your next group, contact Conferences International, and find out about the many services they have to offer.

■ *United Kingdom, Spain, Turkey, New Zealand, China, Hong Kong, Singapore, Thailand, Malaysia & Bali*

World Marketing Group, Ltd.
4444 W. Lake Harriet Parkway, Suite 10
Minneapolis, MN 55410
Tel: (612) 925-4432   Fax: (612) 925-0955
E-mail: jane_shuldt@wmgpw.com
Web site: www.worldmarketinggroup.com

The countries that World Marketing Group, Ltd. represent are some of the best group destinations in the world. A very sharp lady runs this company, and she runs it right (with help from her very efficient staff)! Ordinarily, when booking a group internationally, I prefer to use a DMC located in that country and deal as directly as possible. However, there are a few USA based companies that offer outstanding service and very competitive prices to their specialized destinations. The World Marketing Group, Ltd. is one of them, and the President of the company, Jane Schuldt, CITE, goes the "extra mile" to make things happen for your group.

As destination marketing specialists, the multi-faceted World Marketing Group, Ltd., is a one-stop-shop for several *primo* international destinations. The exotic countries she represents in

Asia are rising stars on the travel horizon, and booming as group destinations, so there are great deals to be had! If anyone can get you a deal it will be Jane!

▰ Montreux & Swiss/French Region

Montreux Tourist Organization
P.O. Box 1557
Burnsville, MN 55337
Tel: 800-590-4686   Fax: 952-892-1639
E-mail: montreux-usa@fishnet.com
Website: montreux.ch

The Montreux Tourist Organization (MTO) is, literally, in a category of its own because it is a tourism bureau and a DMC! This type of operation is particular to Switzerland, where regional tourism bureaus and a DMC operation are often combined. By specializing in specific Swiss regions (French, German and Italian), these two-in-one operations can be "one-stop shops" for group travel leaders interested in this beautiful part of the world.

Denny Migletz, the Sales Director for the MTO in the U.S.A., balances both jobs admirably and continually has some of the best deals to be found for groups to Switzerland. Montreux is a city of festivals and the annual International Montreux Jazz Festival ranks as one of the best in the world. Because Montreux is one the most visited cities in Switzerland, the city has an abundance of great restaurants and nightclubs, with a wide variety of hotels that will fit almost any group's requirements.

The great asset of the MTO is this; When using Denny as your main point of contact, he can supply you with brochures and all of the hotel and regional sightseeing information that you need PLUS customize a tour package for you at the same time. If you already have a Swiss DMC that does a good job for you, then certainly use them. If this is your first venture into this part of Switzerland, then give Denny and the MTO Montreux Tourist Organization a try!

Can you tell I love my DMC's?

There are thousands of wonderful tour operators and DMC's around the world, and many of them, I am sure, are as great as the DMC's I use. But, I don't know them and as long as I keep getting the competitive prices and great service that I have over the years from the DMC's I have mentioned, there is no reason for me to know them. If you have a DMC you are happy with, by all means, stay with them! If another group planner raves about their tour operator or DMC, get their name and keep it on file, you never know when you may need it. If you don't use my contacts, I hope you have as much good luck with who you do use as I have!

What you know and Who you know are equally important!

Actually, the *Who* part is really, *really* important. A big portion of the *What* part (knowledge), can be gained by having conversations and working with other group travel planners, airline and hotel representatives, tour operators and DMC's, etc. This interaction will automatically advance your travel knowledge by osmosis. Soon, other group planners will be asking for your advice. That's always a great day!

Now that you have a good idea of who to use for your travel supplier, you are ready to start making contact. If you are going to book directly, get on the telephone and fax and start getting prices and availability. If you decide to use a travel agency, tour operator or DMC, all you have to do is give them your tour requirements and have them give you a quote.

In Chapter Eight, learn about what exactly the tour and travel suppliers need from you in order to give you a quote on your tour, and how to request a group proposal.

NOTE! When packaging your international tour, use:

1. *A travel agency that you have a good working relationship with and who is equally competitive with U.S. tour operators.*

2. *A U.S. tour operator who already has programs to the area(s) you are interested in...or*

3. *A DMC that is located in the country or region you are interested in.*

4. *Anyone of these travel providers will save you time, money, aggravation, and make you look good at the same time!*

CHAPTER 8

Getting Group Tour Quotes

How much was that again?

Chapter Eight is a "how to" chapter and will include worksheets for you to use as guidelines for tour quotes. These worksheets help get your tour priorities in order so that you know exactly what to ask for from the tour suppliers that you contact. Once you are comfortable with the system, feel free to revise these sheets to meet the needs of a particular group or a particular way of doing business.

Since you have completed your Three Year Plan of Action, you know which tours you want to develop and promote through your travel club. You also understand the differences between the various travel suppliers and what each one can do for you. The next step is to price your tours and get them ready to advertise and promote. Start by working with the first three tours that you listed for Year One in the Three Year Plan of Action (Chapter Six).

Prior to contacting the various travel suppliers to negotiate a net cost, you will need to have a very detailed idea of what is to be included in each tour. No matter who you contact (a travel agency, tour operator or DMC), they will all need this information in order to give you a valid tour quote. The more your tour is defined and the more organized you are, the faster you will get your quote. As a result of "having your act together," you will be appreciated as a professional by the travel suppliers. Also, you won't be wasting their time by giving them only a vague idea of what kind of tour you *think* you may want to do. With your Group Proposal Request worksheet in hand, you'll come to the table ready to do business!

Group Proposal Request Form

Alas, the *"worksheets."* I suspect you knew you were going to have to write something down eventually and the time has come. In order to work cooperatively with the travel suppliers who will be giving you quotes, you must answer some of the important questions on the Group Proposal Request worksheet. The Group Proposal Request worksheet will help you formalize your tours by listing everything to be included in your tour…you just fill in the blanks.

The following is an explanation of the different categories listed on the Group Proposal Request worksheet. Before you pick up a telephone to make a call, type a fax, or mail a piece of correspondence, you should have at least the following information completed on the Group Proposal Request worksheet:

GROUP PROPOSAL REQUEST - EXPLANATION

- **Tour Supplier (travel agency, tour operator, DMC)** - *List all of the pertinent information on the company.* The *Contact* is the person with whom you will be negotiating and ultimately, if you select them, booking the tour. This person can be very important to you, so you need to get to know them, because they are the ones who will fight for you regarding departure dates, space availability, upgrades, etc. List their telephone numbers (it will save you time if you can get their direct numbers), fax number, and e-mail address. Go ahead and get their e-mail address for your files even if you do not have a computer at this time. If you are serious about this business, you may have one in the near future. Also, make sure that you have the correct spelling of their name.

Tour Name & Tour Package #: After you select the tour on which you want to get a quote, list the tour name and tour identification number on the worksheet. As an example, the tour may be *The Canyon Lands and National Parks* tour. Somewhere close by will be the ID number, *CNP0699.*

Brochure/Page #: Most major tour operators have several brochures listing their tours. They may have one brochure dedicated to Europe, one for Asia and the Orient, and one for America. You will soon notice that many tour operators' brochures look similar and many names of the tours themselves are even similar to each other (there are only so many ways you can say *fall foliage*). So, in order to prevent confusion with another company's tour, list the exact name of the brochure and the page number your tour is listed on.

Destination(s): List the states or countries you will be visiting.

Length of Tour: List the total number of days your group will be gone including flight days.

Airline Routing: List your group's departure airport(s) and the destination airport. The destination airport is usually in the city where your tour will begin and end.

- **Travel Dates** - *List the exact dates of the tour, (i.e., the* departure date and return date). Have three sets of optional dates available in case your first choice, or *preferred dates,* are not available. On the worksheet itself, the dates are listed as #1 (preferred), #2 (second choice) and #3 (third choice).

- **Group Size** - *List the approximate number of tour participants* *you expect to sign-up.* Use a conservative figure to negotiate with the group travel suppliers. As an example: if you think you will have 35 to 40 passengers (pax), then base the group size on 30 pax. It is *always* better to exceed your projected numbers than to reduce them. The travel suppliers (and people in general) expect you to produce what you say you are going to do and they like it when you do. But when you actually do more, *they love you!*

- **Tour Conductor Tickets** - *List the number of free tour conductor tickets (TC) you need to escort your group.* In the quotes from the travel suppliers, have them include TC's for you and anyone else you want or need to help you escort the tour. As an example, if you are expecting a minimum of 20 pax, you may want to have one free for every 10 full paying pax (this means the eleventh person travels for free). One free for every 10, 15 or 20 full paying pax is the norm. Anything less than one free for 10 is a little greedy and will reflect in a tour price that will not be competitive.

  Important note to remember! *There is **no magic** in how this system works.* Basically the travel suppliers will take their net cost and divide it by the number of TC's you want, and add that amount to the bottom-line of their quote. So, in the travel business, there are *literally* no "free rides" to be had. The more TC's you demand, the higher your net price will be, pure and simple.

  Having said that, one free for every 10 to 20 pax or more is perfectly acceptable and your travel supplier's quote should still be competitive and a good deal for your tour participants. Also, because you are getting a free trip, *do not* think you are taking advantage of your tour participants. The free trips are a part of this business and you deserve every one you take. Believe me, you'll earn them!

  Note: *Most per person tour quotes are based on double* *occupancy per room with single, triple and quad prices listed separately. It is important to understand that the one-free-for-every (number of pax you require) that you negotiate with your travel supplier is based on double occupancy, or one half of a room or cabin. In order to secure a room or cabin for yourself, you will either need to earn two frees from the travel supplier or, if you know you will be going as a single, negotiate a single room/cabin up front. An example would be if you negotiated one free for every fifteen full paying passengers based on a group of thirty paying pax, and then only produced eighteen pax, you will have earned only one half of a double occupancy room/cabin. If someone were to accompany you and share your room/cabin, they would have to pay the per person equivalent of one half of that room/cabin. Having a single room or cabin is totally in the realm of good negotiations. If you normally travel as a single, then by all means, let the travel supplier know that you want single accommodations included for in their quote.*

- **Hotel Accommodations** - *List the type of hotel accommodations you want for your group.* On the worksheet, the class of hotels is listed as: Budget/2 Star, Moderate/3 Star, First Class/4 Star, and Deluxe/ 5 Star.

  When dealing internationally, the "Star" hotel rating system can be a little deceiving, so ask for your DMC or tour operator's opinions and recommendations. They will help you make the right decision.

- **Hotel Location** - *List the preference of your hotel(s) location.* On the worksheet, the selection list is: city center, city proximity, suburb, country, or resort.

- **Hotel Rooms** - *List the type of room accommodations the majority of your group will require.* On the worksheet, doubles, singles, triples and quad rooms are listed. Also, something else to consider is the number of smoking/non-smoking

Chapter 8 **135**

and handicap accessible rooms you may need.

- **Meals** - *List the meals to be included in your tour.* The list on the worksheet includes; continental breakfast, full breakfast, lunch and dinner. In the travel business the meal plans are referred to and designated as:

  - EP - European Plan: Continental breakfast (sometimes called CP: Continental Plan)

  - Full Breakfast: Usually a buffet, these can be a full American breakfast, a full Irish breakfast, a full Israeli breakfast, etc.

  - MAP - Modified American Plan: Breakfast and dinner

  - FAP or AP - American Plan: Breakfast, lunch and dinner.

In the 1960's, '70's and '80's, the MAP and the AP were very popular with Americans traveling abroad ("If it's Tuesday, it must be Belgium"). Today, Americans are much more adventurous and like more freedom to roam, explore and dine out on their own. The days of the tour guide in a baseball cap with a whistle yelling, "OK...everybody in the pool" are over. Depending on how long the tour is, a nice package today will usually include a full buffet breakfast daily, American or otherwise, a lunch or two, a few dinners, and maybe a welcome and/or farewell reception and dinner.

Many senior groups still like a tour with a fairly full meal program because they would rather pay up front before they travel. Also, dining with a group is perceived to be more convenient, simple, and safe. However, the senior scene is definitely changing because today seniors are healthier, wealthier and more active than ever before. I believe the popular tours of the future will be the ones that will have *some* free time worked into them.

Give this some thought when it comes to planning your inclusive meals. Maybe having a little flexibility in your program will please your participants and will cut some of the cost of the tour at the same time. After a few tours, you will learn to know the preferences of your club members and what they like and don't like. Again, listen to your tour operator's advice when it comes to this.

- **Special Functions / Theme Dinners** - *If you are in a unique part of the USA, or the world, and you want a very special evening for your group, consider a theme party.* I can tell you, there is nothing more fun than being in the South of France and having a "Mexican Night" theme party. Just kidding! On the other hand, being in France and having a private candlelight dinner in an old stone warehouse at a winery is not only fun, it's also classy and something most memorable for your tour participants. So, whether you are in Arizona and have a steak cookout at a ranch under the stars, or in Australia having a private dinner on a secluded island in the Great Barrier Reef, it's all great fun.

  Something to remember; your tour operators and DMC's are quick to recommend all of these wonderful options to you, *but they all cost money!* So consider their theme party suggestions and *if* it fits into your budget, include it. If it is too expensive, ask them about Plan B or what else can be done that would be less expensive. They always have a Plan B! *On the other hand,* if your travel club evolves into a membership of up-scale travelers who really want unique experiences incorporated into their tour, then theme parties are definitely in order. Just remember, *the only place* to have a Mexican Night theme party is in Mexico!

- **Sightseeing** - *List the sightseeing you would like included in your tour (you will know this from your research).* Wherever your tour is going, the travel suppliers will give you their recommendations on what there is to see and do, and their suggestions are usually right on target. If, however, you

Chapter 8   **137**

have found something special in your research that you want your group to see or do, then let the tour supplier know. Ninety nine percent of the time, they will work it out for you. Also, reconfirm that items such as entrance fees are included in the tours. They *usually* are but you don't want any surprises.

- **Receptions** - *List special receptions you want included in your tour.* Both welcome and farewell receptions are a nice touch to include in their tour. In the past, these receptions were more corporate and incentive travel oriented, but now leisure groups, especially the independent travel clubs, are adding these special events to their tour programs. A welcome and farewell reception serves the group well by:

  - Giving the tour participants a chance to meet and get to know each other in a more relaxed atmosphere.

  - Giving the group travel leader an opportunity to mingle and get to know the travel club members better.

  - Giving the group travel leader an opportunity to speak to the group in a controlled setting, welcome them to wherever they are (city, state, country) and thank them personally for their participation and support of your travel club. You will be surprised how this can turn into a good question and answer session about the current tour and the travel club in general.

- **Orientation Meetings** - *Let the travel supplier know that you want an orientation meeting for your group* (these are usually held in conjunction with the welcome reception). At the orientation meeting, the group travel leader usually says a few words in general about the background of the local tour operator and then introduce the local representative. The tour representative speaks about the tour in detail, answering any questions and, if the group has any free time during the tour, they will talk about optional tours being offered. Remember *optional tours*...these are good! Why? Because they give your tour participants a chance to see and do a few things of specific interest **and** they are usually *commissionable* to you. It's all part of the negotiations with the travel supplier.

- **Optional Tours** - *Negotiate a commissionable rate for the optional tours sold to your group.* Most tour operators and DMC's know that this is part of the program and it is normally assumed that they will make these optional tours commission-able to you. Since the commission amounts vary from tour to tour, discuss this in advance to get a clear understanding of exactly what commission is expected.

- **Hospitality Desk** - *Let the travel supplier know you want a hospitality desk included in the quote.* The hospitality desk will be manned by your travel supplier's personnel but is, in essence, an extension of your travel club. The hospitality desk professionals will answer questions regarding local sites and what to see and do during their stay, recommend dinner and shopping options, sell optional tours, and make reservations. The hospitality desk always provides a good benefit to your tour.

  Note: Many tour operators have a hospitality desk included in their escorted tours. There will usually be a charge when working with an international DMC.

- **Baggage Handling** - *Let the travel supplier know that you want all baggage handling at all hotels, airports, piers, train stations, etc.*

- **Gratuities** - *Let the travel supplier know that you want <u>all gratuities included for the motorcoach drivers and guides</u>.* Let your tour participants know they are not going to have to "reach in their pockets" for gratuities, because it has been included in the tour cost. For the drivers and guides of motorcoach tours, a daily gratuity amount is expected from the passengers or the group travel leader. The amount varies from city to city and country to country, but the end result is the same...they look forward to that tip! The **best** way to handle this situation is to include the gratuity amount in your tour package. Then, everyone's happy and your tour participants don't have to dig in their pockets on a daily basis. Plus, you don't have to worry if your group is going to rise to the occasion and tip properly. *Whatever you do, **do not** leave this up to the individual group participants.

- **All Applicable Taxes** - *Let the travel supplier know you want all applicable taxes and surcharges included.* The last thing you want to hear is "Oh, by the way..." You want all taxes taken care of and no surprises.

These are the *basic, minimum* questions you need to answer to complete the Tour Program Worksheet. More details from your research can, and should, be added to enhance the list such as; specific transportation (e.g., boat rides, trams, cog wheel railroads, etc.), specific sightseeing, (e.g., museums, cathedrals, parks, castles, shrines, etc). and even restaurant requests. Again, the more details you can provide to your travel supplier contact, the better, more complete the proposal will be.

Group Proposal Request Worksheet

The Group Proposal Request is the form you will complete and use when you contact your travel suppliers. This work-sheet can easily be duplicated by computer, word processor or typewriter, or even hand written if necessary. It should be enlarged to 8 ½ inches x 11 inches (a standard size stationery sheet). After it has been duplicated to the larger size, have several photocopies made. Use one of these worksheets for each tour for which you need a quote.

The following is an example of a completed worksheet you will use when using either a *travel agency or tour operator*.

Note: This particular example is for a quote from a travel agency. You will need to complete the worksheet for a travel agency with much more detail than for that of a tour operator. When you are filling out the worksheet for a tour operator, many of the item listings to be completed are already answered for you in the tour operator's package description. Most of these items can be answered "as per tour package." As an example, most of the following items are usually included in an all-inclusive tour and therefore can be answered "as per tour package:"

- *Hotel Accommodations*

- *Hotel Location*

- *Meals*

- *Special Functions*

- *Sightseeing*

- *Receptions*

- *Orientation Meetings – Hospitality Desk*

- *Baggage Handling*

- *All Applicable Taxes*

The exception to this, of course, is if you want to customize or add anything special to the program. If this is the case, just write your notes in the space provided and the tour operator will deal with it accordingly.

NOTE: The following is just an example of one worksheet format. If you have a better system, use it. The main point is that you should provide as much detailed information as possible to your travel suppliers about the tour on which you want to get a quote.

Chapter 8   **141**

GROUP PROPOSAL REQUEST

☑ Travel Agency
☐ Tour Operator / DMC

TOUR SUPPLIER

COMPANY: MTS TRAVEL

ADDRESS: 124 E. MAIN ST.
EPHRATA, PA 17522

CONTACT: CINDI BRODHECKER

TEL 1: 800·418·2929   TEL 2: 717·721·7383
CINDI'S DIRECT LINE

FAX: 717·733·1009

E-MAIL: CINDI@MTSTRAVEL.COM

WEB PAGE: WWW.MTSTRAVEL.COM

TOUR NAME / #: NORTHERN ITALY/MAGNIFICO

BROCHURE: TOUR PKG. # 3208·M   PAGE # 24

DESTINATION(S): MILAN · COMO · BELLAGIO ·
LUGANO · VENICE · SAN GIMIGNANO ·
PISA · FLORENCE

LENGTH OF TOUR: 11 NIGHTS / 12 DAYS
(10 NIGHTS ITALY PLUS ONE NIGHT
ON FLIGHT)

AIRLINE ROUTING: ATLANTA / MILAN / ATLANTA

GROUP DEPARTURE CITY: _ATLANTA_

TOUR DEPARTURE CITY: _MILAN_

TRAVEL DATES – Year _2002_

#1 Dates: Depart: _JUNE 01_ Return: _JUNE 12_

#2 Dates: Depart: _JUNE 02_ Return: _JUNE 13_

#3 Dates: Depart: _MAY 31_ Return: _JUNE 11_

GROUP SIZE (projected number of participants)

_35_ pax

TOUR CONDUCTOR TICKETS (TC'S)

One free for every _15_ full paying pax

HOTEL ACCOMMODATIONS

☐ Budget / 2 Star   ☐ Moderate / 3 star

☑ First Class / 4 star   ☐ Deluxe / 5 star
    AS PER PACKAGE

HOTEL LOCATION

☑ City Center   ☐ Suburb

☐ Country   ☑ Resort
    AS PER PACKAGE

HOTEL ROOMS

☑ Doubles – King / Queen   ☐ Single

☐ Triple   ☐ Quad

☐ Smoking   ☑ Non-smoking   ☐ Handicapped accessible

MEALS

☑ Daily Breakfast   ☐ Continental   ☑ Full buffet
AS PER PACKAGE

☑ Lunch
FULL DAY TOURS ONLY

☑ Dinner
WELCOME & FAREWELL - AS PER PACKAGE

☐ Theme Dinners
— O —

SPECIAL FUNCTIONS
— O —

SIGHTSEEING
FULL DAY TOURS: MILAN & LAKE COMO.
VENICE · FLORENCE · AS PER PKG.

RECEPTIONS

☑ Welcome   ☑ Farewell
WELCOME AT HOTEL FIRST NIGHT
FAREWELL AT CASTLE DE GARDA
LAST NIGHT

ORIENTATION MEETINGS – HOSPITALITY DESK

ORIENTATION AT THE END OF WELCOME RECEPTION / Hosp. DESK IN EVENINGS ONLY

BAGGAGE HANDLING

☑ Airport   ☑ Hotel

☐ Pier   ☐ Train

SEPARATE LUGGAGE TRUCK

GRATUITIES

☑ Motorcoach drivers   ☑ Guides   ☐ Miscellaneous

ALL APPLICABLE TAXES

☑ Airport   ☑ Hotel   ☐ Port

Getting a quote

Now that you have seen a completed worksheet, it should be simple for you to duplicate this process. The key to getting *what you want* from your tour suppliers is to <u>know</u> *what you want* before you make the call. Knowing what you want is a matter of your desire to visit a destination and doing your research. Before you pick up the telephone to start getting quotes, you should:

- know when you want to travel (3 sets of dates)

- know the destination(s) you want to visit

- know what kind of accommodations you want

- know what special sights you want to see and visit

- know the approximate group size (conservative number)

- know how many free trips you want to escort the tour

- know what meals, receptions and special dinners you want included

Armed with this information, you can get the quotes you need to make a decision about which travel supplier you want to use.

Who to use, or not to use...that is the question!

Even though all of your travel suppliers from whom you will be getting a group proposal quote, need basically the same information, they do have different types of operations. To re-cap the beginning of Chapter Seven, the main differences between a travel agent, a tour operator, a DMC, and booking direct with the travel supplier source:

- **A Travel Agency** – Depending on the nature of your tour, travel agencies, in most cases, will probably use one of their *preferred group tour operators* with whom they have a strong working relationship. Because of the amount of volume that some agencies do with their preferred tour operators and travel suppliers, many agencies have exceptional buying power. If you have associated yourself with one of these agencies, they could possibly be your lowest quote. Also, since many agents are well traveled (that's one of the great "perks" of their business!) they can give you seasoned advice and personal tips on the tour you are planning. In most agencies, if the person you are working with has not been to the destination you are planning to visit, someone else in the agency probably has. On the other hand, if you already know where you want to go and what you want your group to see and do, travel agencies are especially useful. If you have selected a destination that you have previously visited or if you have gained enough knowledge from your research, combine that knowledge with the wisdom of a good agent, the buying power of the agency, and a travel agency can be a very good option.

- **The Tour Operator** has established tours developed to various cities, states and countries that you can buy into. Because an *established* tour operator will move big numbers of clients annually through their operation, you benefit from their substantial buying power. What is most beneficial to a group travel leader is that the tour operator will usually have several brochures, loaded with a variety of itineraries, from which you can choose. These are packaged tours that you can purchase or, if you want your group to have an exclusive tour (their own motorcoach, private guide, meal functions, etc), you can negotiate that option with the tour operator. All it takes is money!

- **The International DMC** – A international DMC is a tour operator living in another country (how's that for a simple explanation!) Most of what a U.S. tour operator can do for you, the DMC can do also. Like the U.S. tour operator, the DMC will also move big numbers of clients annually through their operation. The main differences between the two is that the U.S. tour operator may operate its tours around the world, where as the DMC will concentrate on doing business only in the area of their expertise. The area of their expertise is usually their homeland and maybe a few surrounding countries.

The other difference is that a DMC can create a tour for you. You give them the details (from the Group Proposal Worksheet) and they will make it happen. The DMC lives to create different programs; that's what they do best. Since U.S. tour operators go after both individuals and groups, they put their creativity into set tour programs that can be marketed to both entities through their brochures. Most DMC's deal with groups only, unless they own a travel agency which is incorporated into their business. If you have a group, and you can't find exactly what you are looking for from one of the U.S. tour operator's set tour programs, then a DMC is the way to go.

- **Booking Directly** - The comparisons used for the travel agency, the U.S. tour operator, and the international DMC were based on an extended domestic or international tour. If you are planning an extended trip (2 to 3 weeks) for your group, you may want to re-think about booking direct. Unless you personally do a *phenomenal* amount of business with the tour and travel providers in the area you want to visit, I can pretty much guarantee that a travel agency, U.S. tour operator, or DMC will be able to outbid you.

The only way booking direct pays off for a group travel leader nowadays is for setting up short excursions. Nowadays, booking direct is most effective for day trips, or short three or four day excursions. Hiring motorcoaches, booking hotel rooms, arranging sightseeing, etc., is very much in the realm of a detail oriented group travel leader for these kinds of trips. Travel agencies, tour operators, or a DMC should all be considered for any tour on a grand scale or to a foreign destination.

Why use a travel agency when I can book direct with a tour operator or DMC?

When you ask a travel agency for a group proposal, depending on what you have listed for your tour criteria, most agents will start their research using tour operator brochures. Many agencies have a strong relationship with certain tour operators they have worked with in the past. These tour operators are called "preferred suppliers." The agents know the standards of these operators and the quality of their tours and therefore, will readily use them when a group opportunity arises.

Some travel agencies, like tour operators, have buying power because of the volume of business they do with a particular supplier. A travel agent that does substantial business with a *preferred* tour operator could possibly have some extra "clout" over another travel agency or a group travel leader not doing as much volume. The "clout" can be in the form of a higher commission rate (or lower net rate), getting their preferred tour dates, more free tour conductor passes, etc. So, even though you, a group travel leader, can book direct with the same tour suppliers as a travel agency, the travel agency may still be able to offer you a lower price for the same package. The best rule to follow for getting a competitive quote is: Do not prejudge who *you think* will or will not give you the best quote. Until you have established your own special relationship with various travel suppliers, always check all of the options available to you.

Now that you know who to use for your different tours and how to get a competitive quote, you need to price it out and start the marketing. In Chapter Nine, find out how to do this. SELL, SELL...SELL!

The journey is the reward.

Tao saying

Chapter 8

CHAPTER 9

Making Money and Selling Tours

The name of the game!

You now have your first year's tour schedule outlined and quotes for tours to three of your <u>dream destinations</u>. *Pack your bags, you're almost there!* The quote price you received will be on a per person basis. *Always do your calculations based on per person pricing.* Why? For a couple of reasons:

1. The travel industry, in general, (travel agencies, tour operators, DMC's, cruise lines) calculates and quotes on a per person basis.

2. It is easier to figure total costs per person, and then multiply by the number of participants (pax) in the group to reach the figures of what you owe and how much you are going to make.

The quotes you received will be priced per person and based on single, double, and triple occupancy. *The double occupancy rate is the one you will want to use for your calculations.* Unless you are specializing in singles groups, 90% of your group will be on a double occupancy basis.

How much can I put in the bank?

Next, take the quotes for the three tours and break them down into a net cost. If you were quoted net rates, then you are set to calculate the selling price of your tour. If you were quoted commissionable rates, you will need to break the price down to a net rate. For example, let's say the quote you received was for an eight day, air, land, and cruise package to Greece and the Mediterranean Islands (that sounds like a great trip!) The price quoted to you was $1,800.00 per person, double occupancy and is commissionable to you at 15%. Deduct 15% ($270.00) from the $1800.00 commissionable rate and you will have a net cost to you of $1,530.00 per person.

Simply put; if you end up with a group of 30 pax, you will owe the tour supplier $45,900.00 ($1,530.00 x 30 pax) and you will make (gross) $8,100.00 ($270.00 x 30 pax). Besides the $8,100.00 you've made, you also negotiated two free trips to escort the group (1 free for every 15 full paying pax). So, in reality, the dollar value you are getting for your efforts (getting 15 couples together to take a fantastic trip) is $8,100.00 in cash and $3,600.00 ($1,800.00 x 2 pax) in travel benefits. A grand total of *11,700.00*! *And this is just your first group...I'm impressed!*

Just to clarify, *the net price is the money you will owe to the tour supplier for the tour package.* After you add your mark-up to the net price, that will give you your selling price, or gross price. In this particular example, the price quoted was commissionable, so your mark-up was automatically 15%, or $270.00 per person.

Using the same example from above, the $8,100.00 gross profit you made is just that, *gross profit* - before expenses. In order to know your *net profit*, the actual amount of money you can put in your bank account, you will need to deduct any expenses that were incurred putting this group together. The following are standard fixed expenses that every group promotion incurs to some degree. These expenses are estimated and are hypothetical, but will do for this exercise. Also, this money will be spent over a nine to twelve month promotion period, not all at once. The expenses are:

- Printing / $800.00 - This would include brochures, travel documents, promotional material, catalog envelopes, etc.

- Postage / $300.00

- Advertising / $200.00

- Entertainment / $500.00 - Group meetings to promote tour

- Telephone & Fax / $200.00 – Long distance only

The total expenses for the promotion of this particular tour is $2,000.00. After deducting these expenses from your gross profit figure of $8,100.00, you will have a net profit of $6,100.00, PLUS the two free trips. This won't exactly get you a yacht in the harbor, but it's only your first group, right?

Making money

Are you ready for more good news? The above scenario was based on a group of 30 pax. The average group size for most established travel clubs is between 40 and 60 pax. If we take our Greece tour and figure it at 50 pax you will have earned $13,500.00 PLUS 3 free trips (1 free for 15 pax / at 45 pax you have earned another free trip). Now, since you only need two free trips to escort the group, you still have one free to use at your discretion. What to do? *You sell it* (great idea)! Let's add this up again, but we'll just do the good part…how much you will make! You have 50 pax at a gross profit of $270.00 per person. That's $13,500.00. Plus you have an extra free trip to sell. That's another $1,800.00. Add these together and you are making a *gross* profit of

$15,300.00...*plus two free trips!* The actual dollar value you will be getting for finding, let's say 22 couples and 6 singles, will be $18,900.00 ($15,300.00 + $3,600.00). *I'm close to tears.*

How do these successful group travel leaders accomplish this? By continually being on a learning quest, joining and supporting the group leader organizations mentioned in this book, networking with other group travel leaders, attending national and regional conferences and training seminars. By doing all of these things (correctly and aggressively), they have learned how to market their tours, promote their travel clubs, and negotiate good deals on behalf of their members. They know what they want, and they have the desire and the drive to make it happen.

Because you can directly promote your business through your travel club, regular advertising avenues that a travel agency, or other types of businesses open to the public might use, does not necessarily apply to you. The key to your success for promoting your tours is *direct marketing and word of mouth advertising,* of which one is reasonable, and the other is free. Since you will use direct marketing to promote your tours, your overall expenses will be much lower than those who use traditional marketing avenues, e.g., newspapers, magazines, radio and TV.

Spending money

The following are your basic expenses for promoting your travel club and tours:

- PRINTING - You will spend more on printing than any other expense you will have pertaining to a tour. But you will still spend less than most leisure travel companies. Here is why:

  Brochures: Once you have your tour itinerary finalized

and the sell price set, you will print an information sheet to promote the tour. This information is usually printed on a brochure shell that gives all of the details about the tour, enough details for someone to make a decision. Brochure shells can come in many shapes and sizes. The most common is 11 inches x 17 inches and, when folded, gives you four 8½ inch x 11 inch pages for you to put tour information on.

Ninety nine percent of the time you can find these brochures for free. The two main sources for these shells are the airlines you will be using to fly the group to their destination, and the destinations tourism board. Just call their respective numbers (see the Reference Section) and ask them for their current brochure shell. They are usually willing to send you 200 to 500 shells at no cost. You can put a lot of tour information on four pages (less the pretty, full color pictures located in various areas). So, the brochure shell is your main promotional piece, and it's free. All you have to do is get your printer to put ink on paper!

Travel documents: Very inexpensive. If you use a travel agency or a tour operator to handle your tour, the travel documents will come nicely packaged in a special travel document folder. However, these travel folders will have the travel agencies or tour operators name all over them, which does not do a whole lot to promote *your* travel club. The solution to this is to have your own travel document folders printed with your travel club's name and logo on them. When you receive the travel documents from the tour supplier, just re-package and add your personal touch to them. The point of re-packaging is to have *your travel club's* name as the main focus of who organized the tour. Travel documents and what to put in them, where to purchase them, etc., will be discussed in much more detail in Chapter Twelve.

Promotional material: Most of your promotional material will be in the form of large and small brochures (which you can usually get free of charge), and single letter size or legal size sheets printed on one or both sides. The main promotional piece that will be used in your initial mailing or presentation will be the large brochure shell printed on four sides mentioned above.

Other promotional material, such as small brochures and marketing pieces on cities, states, countries, sightseeing, historical and cultural events, maps, and much more, are available from the various tourism boards, convention and visitors bureaus, and chambers of commerce. These promotional pieces can vary widely in their content, but are usually very nicely done (four-color, glossy paper, lots of nice pictures). The printing of the brochure shells and the regular letter and legal size promotional pieces is relatively inexpensive. Most of the time you will use black ink on a colored paper stock and this is where most quick print shops excel.

Catalog Envelopes: For your main mailing piece, (the large 4 page brochure shell), I suggest you use a white, 9 inch x 12 inch, catalog envelope. At the top left hand corner (as usual) will be your travel club's logo, name and address. Somewhere on the right side of the envelope, put:

FIRST CLASS MAIL (in capital letters)

At the bottom left or right hand corner, put:

PLEASE OPEN IMMEDIATELY – DATED INFORMATION ENCLOSED

The statement at the bottom should really stand out and convey *"OPEN THIS ENVELOPE NOW AND READ ME!"* You can accomplish this effect by having your printer do a solid block of color and reverse the print of the message. I usually use a rectangle box or a bar angled across one of the corners for my message blocks. Color-wise, red or dark blue is always effective. Your printer will give you more ideas on how to create the "perfect promo envelope."

- **Postage** – Use first class postage to mail all of your promotional pieces. People receive so much junk mail today that many just look at the top right hand corner to check the amount of postage on it. If it is anything less than first class, much of it's tossed and never opened and read…and you don't want that to happen to your piece of important information! That's one reason to use first class mail. More importantly, your travel club is a First Class operation and everything you do should reflect that image. Most of your postage expense will be in the initial mailing announcing your tour(s) and one or two follow-up mailings after that. The final travel documents should be personally given to your tour members and not mailed if possible. More about this in Chapter Twelve.

- **Advertising** – The bulk of your advertising money will be spent on a direct mail campaign. The direct mail campaign will be targeting your "A List" and "B List" of potential tour prospects and, eventually, club members (more about direct mail marketing and prospect lists in Chapter Twelve). A big part of your advertising will be by word-of-mouth (the best form of advertising you can get). This will happen after you do your initial direct mail promotion and have one or two group meetings, touting the virtues of your upcoming tour(s).

There is no need to spend big dollars advertising in newspapers, magazines or any other print media. The most effective way to reach the type of people you are looking for is by directly contacting your potential tour prospect by mail, by fax, by telephone, or by face-to-face meetings. If you are "into computers" and can afford it, a web page site for marketing your travel club can be beneficial to you in many ways. Check with your local computer experts for their advice. If you cannot find someone locally to help you, give the person who designed, setup, and is hosting the web site for this book (www.etcpub.com) a call. His name is Mike Gilbert and he does a fantastic job at a reasonable price. You can contact Mike at:

Clee.com, Inc.
253 Watkins Road
Stoneville, NC 27048

Tel: (336) 573-9722
Fax:(336) 573-2588
E-mail: msg@clee.com

- **Entertainment** - One of the best ways to promote your tour(s) is to have a tour and travel get-together at your home, or some other convenient meeting place. These informal gatherings of potential tour participants will help get the word out about your travel club and the tours you are offering. Nothing will give your travel club more credibility than to have a group of people circulating among their friends "talking it up" for you. The tour and travel meeting will help spread your tour information faster than almost anything else you can do promotionally.

  If your home is not convenient for these meetings, then check into using a clubhouse at an apartment complex or town home community, or a room at your church. Do whatever it takes to find a nice meeting room for your attendees. *The tour and travel information meetings are a must!* Once you have your meeting place, you will send out invitations to the people on your "A List."

At these meetings you will want to have some refreshments for those attending. This expense can be a lot, or a little, depending on what you decide to serve. Use the KIS system (keep it simple) and serve coffee, tea, soft drinks, and nowadays, small bottles of water are a nice touch. Stay away from hard liquor, beer and wine. It's expensive; it can make people groggy or drowsy, and you want them to remember the next day what information you gave them about your travel club and upcoming tours.

- **Telephone & Fax** – This expense will be mainly long distance calls that you make by telephone and fax. Most of your tour participants will be local, but because a few of them will get some of their out-of-state friends or family to join your tour, there will be a certain amount of long distance activity. Your friends will get their friends to join the tour, and so on. This is how the system works. After a few tours, your mailing list will grow like crazy because of this pass-a-long system. *Remember the Over the Hill Gang International;* they started as a small group of friends going skiing in the Colorado Rockies and now have over six thousand members in fifty states and nineteen countries with thirteen chapters!

Now that you have an idea of what you can make on an average group tour and what you can expect in the way of expenses, let's analyze an item-by-item quote and how much you want to mark-up your tours.

What did I leave out?

Since I like Greece and the Mediterranean, we'll stay with the Greece scenario as our example, the eight day, air, land, and cruise program. To change it just a little bit, we'll use a quote from a travel agency. The travel agency has given you a price of

$900.00 *net* per person, double occupancy basis, for the land and cruise portion of the tour. They have quoted the round trip group airfare from your home city (Atlanta) separately, at $600.00 per person *net*. The price is NET, which means, at this point, there is no money in it for you and no free trips to escort the tour. We can fix that! First, we need to add to the net quote the following:

- Air transportation – Roundtrip for two escorts

- Site inspection expenses - if applicable (I will explain more about site inspections and how they work in Chapter Twelve).

- Escort fee – two escorts

- Profit

These are the initial expenses that you will want to add to the net quote.

After we have a subtotal, we will "fine tune" the overall quote before coming to a final selling price. The Greece tour and cruise quote from the travel agency, *as per your Group Proposal Request*, includes the following:

- Meet & greet upon arrival at Athens Internationl airport

- Roundtrip transfers between Athens airport, hotel & pier

- Baggage handling at airport, hotel & pier - 2 bags per person plus carry on

- Porterage gratuities at airport, hotel & pier

- Hotel taxes and service gratuities

- Four nights Deluxe hotel accommodations in Athens at the deluxe Grande Britagne or Athens Plaza Hotel

- 4 day cruise on Royal Olympic's cruise ship *Triton* - outside cabins

- Shore excursion of Ephessus (at Kusadasi)

- Welcome cocktail reception first night in Athens with orientation briefing followed by dinner at the hotel

- Athens city tour (1/2 day)

- Full buffet breakfast daily at hotel

The net price for the above is $900.00 per person, without airfare. Basing the group on a minimum of 30 pax, the following is an example of how you would factor in your projected expenses and profit:

Land/cruise program .... $900.00 net p/p
Roundtrip airfare from Atlanta .... 600.00 net p/p
Total .... $1,500.00 net p/p

**Total land/cruise/air program,
net per person from Atlanta $1,500.00**

**Escort & Profit Calculations – Add these amounts to the
net price to arrive at your selling price**

Land/cruise for tour escorts: $60.00
($900.00 p/p ÷ 30 pax = $30.00 P/P x 2 escorts = $60.00 p/p)

Air transportation for tour escorts: $40.00
($600.00 p/p ÷ 30 pax = $20.00 P/P x 2 escorts = $40.00 p/p)

Site inspection fees: No site inspection necessary   -0-
Profit: $225.00 (15%)
($1,500.00 p/p x 15 % = $225.00 p/p)

Total escort fees (2) plus 15% profit ..... $325.00 p/p

Selling Price Calculations – Add these amounts to arrive at your selling price

Total land/cruise/air program,
net per person from Atlanta $1,500.00

Total escort fees (2) plus 15% profit .... $325.00 p/p
($60.00 p/p + 40.00 p/p + 225.00 p/p= $325.00 p/p)

Grand total (gross): $1,825.00 p/p
($1,500.00 p/p net cost + $325.00 p/p escort fees & profit)

Selling Price: $1,825.00 p/p based on double occupancy

Finally!

Once you have received a quote, use the calculation system above to arrive at your selling price. This is a proven, tried and true method of calculating the selling price for your tours. As with tours and cruises, many of the components remain the same, only the destinations and itineraries change. With calculations, the figures change, but the method to get to the ultimate figure remains the same.

When calculating your figures, check and re-check to make sure you have left nothing out. There's nothing that will break you out into a cold sweat faster than a financial miscalculation!

You now have most of the information to get you started on your way to becoming a successful group travel leader and the owner of a leisure travel business. The next three chapters are very, very, important for you to read and understand. Once you have read them thoroughly, read them again. They are extremely important to your new travel career, how fast you can get started in the leisure travel business, and how to avoid some very typical travel industry pitfalls that can be detrimental to a new group travel leader.

Go on to Chapter Ten and discover what I consider to be the best travel opportunity going for group travel leaders today…cruise vacations! In fact, Chapter Ten's so good, I'm even going to read it again!

We all have two choices:

We can make a living or we can design a life.

Jim Rohn

CHAPTER 10

Sailing The Oceans Blue

"The best of the best"

You can have a piece of the pie, a piece of the action, and even a piece of "The Rock," but none of those will come close to what you can gain from having a piece of the *cruise line business!*

This part of the travel industry is *sooo good* that I am devoting an entire chapter to it. In my opinion, of all the travel business opportunities available to you, this is the best!

To help prove my point, the following is a reprint of the Cruise Line International Association's (CLIA) cruise industry overview (Marketing Edition - August 1999). This fascinating, forty three page report is filled with solid statistics, graphs, and charts which show that the cruise line business is on an ever increasing rise and will continue this upward direction for many years to come. The total over-view report was too much to reprint in this book, but it is well worth reading in full. Once you are a certified CLIA affiliate agent, request a copy of the Cruise Industry Overview Report to read and study. It will give you a good insight into this very special area of the travel industry as well as some great statistics that you can use in marketing your cruise tours.

I'm not big on statistics, *but occasionally* some statistics have such an impact that they get my attention. This is what CLIA's report did. The following is only page one of the Executive Summary report.

EXECUTIVE SUMMARY

- **The cruise line industry is the most exciting growth category in the entire leisure market.** Since 1980, the industry has an average annual growth rate of 7.9% per annum.

- **The cruise industry is young**. Since 1970, an estimated 67 million passengers have taken a deep-water cruise (2+ days). Of this number, 63% of the total passengers have been generated in the past 10 years. Thirty five percent of total passengers have been generated in the past 5 years alone. Of those who have cruised in the past 5 years, the average number of cruises per person has been 2.4 in this same time frame *or* one every 2 years.

- **The cruise market potential is huge.** Over the next 5 years, the cumulative market potential for the cruise industry is $54 - $97 *billion*. By the year 2000, we project that *6.5 - 7 million passengers* per year will cruise. Taking a cruise is a dream of 56% of all adults with the highest interest being exhibited by the *emerging baby-boomer* category. *To date, only 11% of the U.S. population have ever cruised.*

- **The cruise product is incredibly diversified with literally a cruise vacation for everyone.** Over the past 10 years, the industry has responded to extensive market and consumer research; research that has guided the addition of new destinations, new ship design concepts, new on-board/ on-shore activities, new themes and new cruise lengths to reflect the changing vacation patterns of today's market.

- **The cruise industry's product delivers unparalleled customer satisfaction.** Whether a frequent or first-time cruiser, the cruise experience consistently exceeds expectations on a wide range of important vacation attributes. On a comparative basis versus other vacation categories, cruising consistently receives top marks. The on-going challenge for the cruise industry is to convert cruise *prospects* into new cruisers.

- **Cruising is an important vehicle for sampling destination areas to which passengers may return.** Over 85% of cruise passengers agree with this statement. Nearly 50% fully expect to return to the same geographical area/destination for another type of vacation. Cruisers are not exclusively cruisers; rather they are frequent vacationers who cruise as part of their vacation mix.

- **The North American cruise market is strong across all 50 states and Canada.** Today's built-in air fares and stream-lined port processing have opened up cruising as a vacation alternative to more and more individuals.

- **CLIA Member Lines represent 96% of North American-marketed berths.** From a capacity stand-point, utilization is around 90%. The Caribbean represents the number one destination with almost 50% of all passengers and 43% of capacity placement. The Caribbean is followed in popularity by Europe (Northern Europe and the Mediterranean), Alaska, Trans-canal, Western Mexico, Bermuda, South America and the Trans-Atlantic.

- **CLIA has become one of the largest and most influential industry associations.** Today, it has 23 member lines and approximately 21,000 travel agency affiliates. It's the largest association in terms of North American travel agency affiliate representation.

- **Finally, the cruise industry has a very close working relationship with the travel agency community.** Almost all passengers are booked through travel agents. Cruises are profitable to sell and generate a high repeat rate. The most successful and productive agencies are those that place a premium on selling cruises and training their personnel.

Note: In this report, North American market designates only U.S. and Canada.

The one statistic that is extremely exciting to me is the fact that *to date, only 11% of the U.S. population have ever cruised.* This means that the people who have cruised so far are just (pardon me) the tip of the *cruise potential iceberg!* What this also means is that *89%* of the U.S. population *have not taken a cruise!* This makes cruising a massive market which many group travel leaders are not only going to embrace, but go after with a passion. *I predict that those who do make a concerted effort to establish a solid cruise business will be rewarded with a wonderful career in the travel industry, travel the world in fine style, and make a very good living at the same time.*

Another positive indicator that the cruise market potential is long term, is that many travel agencies are converting to *cruise only* agencies or establishing dedicated cruise departments to cater to the growing number of cruise oriented clients. You don't make business decisions like that unless you have studied and analyzed the potential market, which obviously they have.

Become a cruise expert

If you are one of the unfortunate 89% of the U.S. population that has not been on a cruise yet, take one! If you have been on a cruise, then you are already sold on cruising and know why I am so excited!

Like any profession, the key to being successful is to become an expert in a particular field, and this is equally true of the cruise business. The more knowledgeable you are about all of the different aspects of cruising, the quicker people will join you on one of the many cruises you will be offering through your travel club. The *very good news* is, *with a concentrated effort on your part*, you can become a knowledgeable cruise agent in a very short period of time. Of all the travel industry areas you could be involved in, the cruise line industry has probably the most extensive educational training opportunities available.

Anyone that sincerely wants to excel in the cruise line business can certainly do so. All you have to do is take advantage of the numerous training seminars and conferences that are constantly being offered around the country by the cruise lines themselves, or cruise line organizations such as Cruise Lines International Association (CLIA) and the National Association of Cruise Oriented Agencies (NACOA). As an example, CLIA holds 200 classroom training seminars annually in various U.S. and Canadian cities throughout the year. They have three full-time cruise counselor trainers on the road at all times! You can also attend the CLIA Institute in Miami for two and three day training sessions offered on specific dates throughout the year. At the end of the seminar, you are invited to go on site inspections of the many cruise ships mooring in Miami. There are also many home study courses available that you may want to consider. CLIA also has a on-line study course you may want to take a look at if you are into studying by computer. The web site is: http://www.theacademy.com.

If your goal is to become a cruise expert in the shortest period of time (and it should be), you will need to do the following:

1. **Join CLIA** (Call 212-921-0066 / see Chapter Five) - If you have not done this yet, *now is the time to do it!* Being a CLIA member will do two <u>major</u> things for you:

    a) It will get you in the group travel leader main-stream (information flow) faster than anything else you can do. Cruise lines and tour suppliers will immediately start sending you valuable information by mail and fax (especially fax), regarding everything from the inaugural sailing of a new ship, to deeply discounted late booking opportunities.

b) As an active member of CLIA, you can start working immediately toward your Accredited Cruise Counselor (ACC) degree, which should be one of your primary goals. Also, you are now eligible to start taking advantage of the training CLIA offers (seminars and online training) as well as the familiarization and seminars at sea cruises specially developed by CLIA for affiliated agents.

c) As a member of CLIA, you will receive their annual Cruise Manual. *This book is an unbelievable wealth of information!* The manual is power-packed with over 600 pages of cruise ship profiles, deck plans, passenger services, descriptions of ports of call by regions, and valuable information in general. Seriously studying this manual alone could make you a cruise "Guru!" I know this statement is overused, but it is truly worth the cost of joining CLIA just to get your hands on this excellent educational material.

2. **Study, study, and study some more** - If you *have to* go back to school, this is the way to go! One of the best ways to get familiar with the intricacies of cruising is to start studying the cruise brochures of the different cruise lines. Note, I said *study*, not just read or look at the pretty pictures! If you have joined CLIA, the brochures will be on their way to you. In the meantime, go to the travel agency you have aligned yourself with (if you haven't done that yet, this would be a good time) and talk them out of as many cruise line brochures as they can spare. Take them home and study them from front to back. It is very important that you learn to read and understand how these cruise line

brochures are written and laid out. Most cruise line brochures are similar in their lay out. So, once you have thoroughly studied several brochures, you should have a good understanding of the standard format and how to find specific information.

Study the deck plans, learn where to find the statistics of the ship (tonnage, number of passengers, registry, etc), and get a good understanding of the cabin category system that the cruise lines use. Also, if you need an explanation of something you don't understand, (such as the deposit requirement, cancellation fees, or whether the life boats are blocking the view of the outside cabins on a particular deck, etc.), call the cruise line reservations and get answers to your questions. It's all part of the learning process. The more questions you ask, the more you learn. Eventually, because of your in-depth knowledge of the cruise business, booking groups, paying deposits, arranging air reservations, arranging special parties for your group, etc., will be second nature to you.

Just as you found similarities with the layout of cruise line brochures, you will also discover that most cruise ships have many components in common as well, such as:

- Restaurants

- Meals - Six to eight meals and snacks per day

- Midnight buffet

- Bars and lounges

- Discos

- Floor show – main and late seating

- Various nightly entertainment

- Swimming pools / whirlpools

- Gym

- Casino

- Movie theatre

- Conference room (some of the newer ships)

- Library / card room

- Activities (everything from wine tasting to skeet shooting, art auctions to dance lessons, singles parties to children's programs, and much more)

The *main differences* between most cruise ships are:

- Age

- Size

- Shape (configuration)

- Ports of call

Once you learn what the standard amenities for most cruise ships are, then it becomes easy to talk in generalities about cruising. Most offer the same amenities, and only the name, age and size of the ship, the décor, and ports of call change. However, as with any business or attraction, some ships and cruise lines will be better than others. As a cruise counselor, you will need to know, and be able to explain to your clients or members, the differences of style between the various cruise lines and their ships, and why one cruise line or ship is considered to be better than another. This is where all of the studying, research, attending training seminars, networking with other group travel leaders, and the actual cruises you will have taken will pay off for you.

Today, the differences between the various class of ships servicing the cruise market is greater than ever before, especially with the new *mega* ships entering the picture.

As an example, there's a world of difference between <u>almost any cruise ship</u> afloat today and Royal Caribbean International's new, 142,000 ton/3,114 passenger, *Voyager of the Seas*. Today, the *Voyager of the Seas* is 30% bigger than the next largest cruise ship afloat! As big as it is, however, *it is still made up of the common components that most cruise ships have, e.g. restaurants, casinos, entertainment, bars, swimming pools, etc.* But because of its size, everything is on a grander scale and they have room for a few more unique amenities, like an <u>ice rink</u>, <u>rock climbing wall</u>, <u>golfcourse</u> (I'm not making this up), <u>in-line skating track</u> and <u>jogging track</u>. Having said that, I also need to point out that, in the cruise business, bigger does not necessarily equate to better. Some of the finest ships afloat are small, but very luxurious, such as Crystal Cruises' *Crystal Harmony* (49,400 tons / 940 passengers).

NOTE: When selling to individuals, sell the cruise based on your client's personality and what they want to see and do, not what they can afford.

This brings us to a very important point: Even though your main focus is on group travel, when it comes to cruising, *selling individuals is too good to pass up!* So, when family members, friends, or anybody you know wants to skip the group program to do their "own cruise thing," you're just the person who can fix them up! The people joining your group cruise vacations are already sold on the package you have put together and need very little advice and guidance. Individuals need to be handled a little bit differently.

When working with individuals, you should sell cruises based mainly on the client's personality, where they want to go, and what they want to do...not how much money they can afford. A classic example would be if someone wanted to take a cruise to contemplate the meaning of life; you wouldn't want to book them on the *Voyager of the Seas*. However, a nice, leisurely, riverboat cruise through Burgundy, Provence, and the South of France may be just what they were looking for. On the other hand, if a couple were "looking for the nightlife" and unlimited rock'n roll, the *Voyager of the Seas* would be right on target.

So, spend some time with your client, get some insight into their personality, learn what kind of experiences they are looking for, and book the appropriate ship and cruise vacation for them. If you keep this little formula in mind, you can count on a majority of your cruise clients being pleased and satisfied, and becoming repeat clients.

3. **Take a cruise** - Whether it's a 3, 4, 7, or 10 day cruise doesn't matter, *you need to have the experience of a cruise.* It is important that when you talk to people about cruising, you do it with enthusiasm, and nothing will give you that enthusiasm better than experiencing a cruise yourself. In those few days at sea, you will learn more about cruising and that particular ship, than you will by doing a month of research from books and training seminars. The first-hand knowledge you will get from visiting the different ports of call, talking with the different cruise personnel (including the Captain), and just roaming the ship in general, will be invaluable to you the next time you talk to your members about this particular cruise and ship.

Go to school by taking a cruise

As soon as possible, sign up for one of the many cruise line sponsored seminars at sea cruises that will be available to you as a CLIA affiliated agent. For example, I recently received an invitation from a cruise line to join their District Sales Manager (DSM) for a three night/four day seminar at sea cruise to the Bahamas. The cruise is set for late January, 2000. The invitation read; *"Join us for three nights of fun, relaxation, and education. You will discover why people of all ages find this experience so refreshing and memorable. This is a profit focused seminar with an emphasis on our unique market niche."* During the cruise, the DSM will conduct a two hour seminar which will be power packed with valuable information on how to sell and market cruises. By attending this seminar at sea, the knowledge and experience you will have gained during this short period of time will be remarkable. So, what will you have to pay for this experience and knowledge? I'll tell you, but first you need to know what the cruise includes:

- Three night /four day cruise in outside cabins

- Port charges

- Gratuities

- Private welcome and farewell parties

- One traveling companion (agent or guest) at same rate

The cost: *$129.00 per person*

This is just one example of the many great opportunities taking place annually for you to experience different ships and destinations, while at the same time, advance your education and gain valuable information and insight into the cruise line industry.

If you have been on a cruise before, but it has been quite

awhile, *take another cruise*. If you get on one of the newer ships, I am sure you will be amazed at the changes that have taken place over the last few years. On your next cruise, because you are now in the cruise business, you will probably be more aware of the cruise experience than before and look at things differently. After all, *now it's your job!* Also, during your cruise, as you are lying by the pool (you are still allowed to have fun), take in the scope of what is going on around you and I am sure you will start to realize the true potential of the cruise business and how exciting cruising is.

Compared to the "days of old" (let's say five years ago), many of the ships sailing the oceans today are both *phenomenal* in their size and the amenities they offer. The competition is very aggressive amoung the cruise lines (that's good for you) and getting more so everyday (that's even better) as each goes after the gigantic cruise market potential. Even though individuals can book with the cruise lines by calling them directly or using the Internet, the cruise lines really like doing business with group travel planners. How nice (for them) when someone calls and books 10, 20, or 50 cabins. They only have to deal with one person and they are filling numerous cabins. *They are in cruise booking heaven!*

The cruise business is very fast paced and changing almost daily with new ships being built, older ships continually being refurbished, new itineraries to more unique and exotic destinations being offered, and much more. Considering the multitude of cruise lines, cruise ships and variety of itineraries for you to learn about in great detail, this probably looks a bit overwhelming to you at this point. I admit, there is a lot to learn, but you <u>can</u> become an expert cruise counselor in a reasonably short period of time by taking the steps I have outlined for you. Not only can you accomplish this goal, you can have a whole lot of fun while you're learning!

Note: You don't have to know everything about a particular city, country, island, or ship. Because the way the world is constantly changing, you can't know everything. All you really need to know is how and where to find the information. Build-up a good reference library over a period of time as it will be invaluable to you!

How to "jump start" your cruise counselor career

To re-cap, the best way to "jump start" your cruise counselor career is to:

- Join CLIA – (212) 921-0066

- Order the *2000 CLIA Outside Sales Kit* ($115 value for only $69.00. A dynamite sales tool package!)

- Start working on becoming a CLIA Accredited Cruise Counselor (ACC)

- Start studying cruise brochures and reference books

- Attend as many training seminars as possible

- Take a home study course sponsored by one of the accredited cruise organizations

- Take a cruise yourself (soon)

- After you return, start working immediately on your next cruise group!

To become an expert cruise counselor for the long-term, you will constantly need to keep up with what's going on in the cruise industry. The professional organizations you belong to, the publications you read, the seminars and conferences you attend, and the networking you do with fellow group travel leaders will all

Chapter 10   **177**

contribute to your continuing education. This will be the key to your success.

Come aboard!

After you are established as a CLIA affiliated travel agency, there is another cruise oriented association you should know about that is ready to help guide and educate you. This association's main objective is to help *you sell more cruises!* It is the National Association of Cruise Oriented Agencies (NACOA). NACOA is the only trade association dedicated solely to the cruise vacation product and the cruise professionals who sell it. As a CLIA affilliated member (I assume you've joined by now), and seller of leisure cruise vacations, you are eligible to join NACOA. A few of NACOA's programs are:

- Sales training

- Educational Programs

- Ship inspections

- Conferences

- Errors and Omissions insurance

- Bi-monthly newsletter

For more information contact NACOA at:

NACOA
7600 Red Road, Suite 128
Miami, FL 33143
Tel: 305-663-5626
Fax: 303-663-5625
E-mail: NACOAFL@aol.com
Web site: http://www.nacoa.com

Yo ho ho and let's have a martini

The days of peg legged sea captains standing at the helm of a leaky ship with a parrot on their shoulder shouting…(whatever they used to shout), have long been replaced by suave, internationally educated sea captains. Today, the captains stand at the helm of highly sophisticated and technologically advanced ocean-going cruise vessels (and the only thing on their shoulders nowadays is gold braid). My point is, the world of cruising has changed dramatically over the years, and because of the growing number of vacationers discovering cruises, it will continue to change, and for the better. The cruise lines are on a quest to become the best vacation option for the enormous leisure travel market. Because of this, the cruise lines will continue to improve their vacation product, which is already outstanding, to the point of perfection in many cases.

For me, the bottom-line is this: If someone had saved their money over the years for a vacation, and asks me "where can we get the most value for our money," I would tell them to take a cruise. Depending on where their interest lies, the benefits of a cruise over a land tour package can be many. Obviously, if they want to ride camels in the Wadi Rum, a cruise is probably not going to "fly their kite." *But*, if they want to visit several destinations without spending half of their time packing and unpacking, getting on and off motorcoaches, checking in and out of hotels, then a cruise could be the answer. The following are a few benefits of taking a cruise vacation:

- Statistics show that taking a cruise vacation is less expensive on a per diem basis than taking a standard land tour package.

- The quality and variety of meals onboard ships are usually very good to exceptional. The problem is you can only eat about eight times a day (nine or ten if you are "pushy).

- Entertainment is in abundance and, like the food, the variety and quality is usually exceptional.

Chapter 10

- The accommodations on most ships today are very good with most outside cabins on the newer ships having windows instead of portholes and, as I mentioned earlier, you unpack once and that's it!

- The destinations that you can visit by cruise ships cover the globe. Ancient, historic, and exciting ports of call are waiting for you to explore.

Cruising the Great Rivers of the World

Before I close this chapter, I have to tell you about a new segment of the cruise industry that is getting ready to absolutely explode! And you, as a new cruise specialist, should be very excited about this! I am speaking of cruising the great rivers of the world. Cruising the rivers of the world is certainly nothing new (I believe the Druids, Vikings and Visigoths had a head-start with this concept) and clever "in the know" people have been river cruising for decades.

Taking a riverboat cruise has always been a great way to vacation, but the boats, for the most part, have been more like ferry boats with cabins instead of nice, river cruisers with the amenities that most cruise aficionados expect today. All of that is changing now and changing fast. Luxury, state-of-the-art riverboats are being built in record numbers to accommodate the growing demand of people discovering a new way to "see the world" in style. Instead of me going on about this, following is a reprint of an article I wrote for the May issue of Leisure Group Travel magazine. Even though this particular article was written specifically about the grand rivers of Europe, when you think about river cruises, don't limit yourself to just Europe or just one continent. Think the world! I believe you will have a better understanding of what the potential river cruise market is holding in store for you after reading this article. Although the Baby Boomer generation will drive this market, river cruising is great for anyone, of any age, wanting a relaxing, historical vacation.

Small Boats are Making BIG Waves in Europe - Cruising the grand rivers of Europe...what a way to go!

Most people will agree that cruising is a great way to travel and a great way to see the world. Climb aboard, unpack for the duration of your cruise and you're set to start "chilling-out." Whether it's meandering down the Mississippi on a steamer, cruising the Caribbean on a mega-ship or living the life of luxury on a chartered yacht while sailing the Mediterranean, you're getting a taste of the good life.

For the past few years, the leisure cruise business has been the fastest growing segment of the travel industry and it is showing no signs of a slow down. In fact, it keeps getting better. Because of the boom in cruising, there has been more demand for bigger ships, for more amenities and for more diverse itineraries. And to the cruising public's good fortune, the captains of the cruise industry have risen to the occasion. In recent years, larger ships have been the rage, especially for first time cruisers. These new mega ships are big, beautiful, active and exciting. So active and exciting however, that when the cruise is over, many times you return home exhausted and you feel like you need another vacation just to rest up! What's a cruise lover to do for a relaxing vacation? "Scale down" would be my suggestion.

Cruise lovers, take heart...the riverboats and barges of Europe await you! In the wonderful world of cruising, bigger does not necessarily equate to better and the riverboats cruising the great rivers of Europe prove that in a grand way. On your last cruise you were probably with 2,000 (or more) fellow passengers. On your future riverboat cruise, you will probably be with no more than 150 happy cruisers. Imagine...getting on a ship, meeting some people, and then actually seeing them again before the cruise is over. What a joy! This is just one of the many advantages riverboat cruises have to offer people who want to have a leisurely, luxury cruise vacation.

Riverboats and barges come in all shapes and sizes (literally) and are configured to carry anywhere from 20 to 200 passengers. Most of the newer riverboats being built (and there are many) will have an average capacity of 100 to 150 passengers. Riverboats of this capacity

Chapter 10   **181**

seem to be the perfect size for maneuvering the rivers while still offering spacious cabins, a great dining room, lounges and public areas.

Please Note: this article is not just about riverboats cruising the great rivers of Europe but also about the many hotel/barges cruising Europe's wonderful canals and waterways. The main difference between the two cruise categories is that riverboats carry more passengers (50 to 200) and cruise the major rivers while the hotel/barges accommodate a lesser number of passengers (6 to 50) and specialize in cruising the canals and smaller rivers. During this article, when I just refer to riverboats, I mean both riverboats and hotel/barge companies.

Is that King Arthur? Sometimes your imagination can get away from you while you are slowly cruising past historic fairytale castles, picturesque medieval villages and rolling hills of vineyards... and it's not necessarily that second glass of wine causing it. The beauty and history that abounds along the rivers of Europe *can be* staggering. To give your imagination a reality check, your riverboat will stop for a leisurely visit at many of these wonderful places and will usually dock and overnight at a place of historical significance like Avignon, Vienna, Budapest or St. Petersburg. When you over-night at one of these magical cities, you usually have several options of how to spend your evening. Many times the cruise line will bring local musicians and entertainers on board for your pleasure or they may have a planned event in the city itself. Regardless of the social events, there will usually be time for you to roam and explore the city on your own before departing on the next day's adventure.

A room with a view please. No problem! First of all, a majority of the riverboats have only outside cabins, so everyone will have a view. No one wants to miss the splendid scenery that your river cruise is providing, but you can't be on the open deck 24 hours a day. Most of the outside cabins have large windows (some floor to ceiling) that give you a panoramic view of the river and shoreline. In fact, many of the newer ships have windows that actually open (a novelty for most ships) and a few riverboats are starting to have cabins with sliding doors and small balconies. A typical riverboat cabin is usually spacious and a majority of the cabins on riverboats sailing today have beds that convert into sofas during the day giving you more space to lounge in. Many of the newer ships boast larger cabins with hotel-style beds and amenities similar to big ocean-going cruise ships. Speaking of rooms with a view, the dining rooms and lounge areas on most riverboats have wonderful panoramic windows (if not glass walls). This allows you to take in the beauty of the idyllic countryside while you are dining or enjoying that second glass of wine that I was talking about earlier.

American group travel leaders, rejoice! One of the great realizations that the riverboat companies have had recently is that the potential market for American clientele is massive. Because of this, many of the riverboat companies are starting to cater to the English speaking (American) market. On many riverboats now, English is the only language spoken on board the ship and on the shore excursions. What a pleasure this is! This eliminates having to listen to announcements in several different languages, which after a short while, are annoying at best. If you have ever been on a sightseeing tour where the guide translated the points of interest in three or four languages you know what I mean. Another plus for many Americans on riverboat cruises is that many of these ships are adopting a non-smoking policy. In order to accommodate smokers, most ships will have a designated smoking area in the public rooms (usually located around the bar) and of course, smoking is allowed on any of the outside decks. So now, your group participants can have non-smoking outside cabins with great views, plus the announcements that they hear in their cabins about dinner being served will be in English! Speaking of dinner...

Pass the fois gras, s'il vous plaît. A word about dining on a riverboat. Dining on almost any cruise ship, no matter what its size, can be a special experience with regards to the food quality and presentation, but the dining experience on a riverboat is usually exceptional. Don't get me wrong, the executive chef and their staff on the large cruise ships do a fantastic job feeding the large numbers of people they are required to serve. The fact that the riverboat chef and his or her staff is only preparing food for 150 people (or less), not 2,500 people is one of the main reasons that the dining on a riverboat excels. Also, if you are a wine connoisseur (or if you just like wine), you can add

Chapter 10   **183**

another PLUS for riverboats because most include quality wine with dinner. Since many of these cruises will take you to some of the most famous wine growing regions of the world, the dinners are usually served with local regional wines to accompany entrees of regional specialties. Of course, as with the larger cruise ships, on riverboats you get more food than you really need but hey, that's why we drink diet soft drinks!

Rolling on the river(s). If you like diversity, you're in luck! Riverboats are cruising from Moscow to Marseilles and everywhere in between. Plying the rivers of the Rhine, Rhône, Danube, Moselle, Douro, Elbe, Po, Saône and Seine allows visits to more historic cities, medieval castles, quaint riverside villages, churches, and museums than you could ever imagine. On a river cruise you are always in view of land and the majestic scenery along the way will provide more photo opportunities than you would ever have on other types of vessels. Each of the rivers offer their own unique ports of call along the way; Amsterdam, Basel, Budapest, Vienna, Prague, Berlin, Paris, Strasbourg, Lyon and on and on. With each stop you are transported back in time, standing on the same cobblestone streets that the great leaders of bygone days used to lead their legions of armies to victory in some far away place. Wherever your historical interest lies, you can be sure there is a cruise on one of these beautiful rivers that will be of special interest to you.

Riverboat - Hotel/Barge cruises are tailor made for group travel leaders who operate small, personalized travel clubs. Many group travel leaders don't leave town with 150 people every time they put together a trip. In fact, many group travel leaders *don't want 150 people* on their trips! What they do want is a quality tour or cruise for 15, 20, 30, maybe 50 people. Riverboat companies *love* these groups and they are especially receptive to working with group travel leaders. You represent the market they are looking for; one person they can work with who has the potential to book several cabins. On the other hand, these specialized cruise lines do an extraordinary job accommodating passengers. When you have a group on a river or canal cruise (and that can be as few as 6 passengers on a canal cruise), your people will *love* you because of the wonderful trip you have put together for them. It's a win-win program! Many people today are looking for unique, out of the ordinary trips that are a good value for their money. The riverboat and hotel/barge experience fills that bill. So make some *Big Waves* with your club members by booking a river or hotel/barge cruise soon. Not only will you have a great trip, but you will also impress your group with a top quality tour that they will long remember.

To help you get started – The following is a list of reputable riverboat and hotel/barge companies that I can highly recommend. Contact them for information on their various products. Many of these companies represent several river/canal cruise lines while others may only sell their own ships exclusively. So call or fax the toll free 800 numbers, request their brochures, and start a file on riverboat and hotel/barge cruises. Even better, look up their web sites if possible. This gives you instant, detailed information on what each company has to offer, how they operate, and how booking with them can benefit you. Here are some connections to help you get started:

Riverboat & Hotel/Barge Companies

Euro Cruises
33 Little West 12th St., Suite 106
New York, NY 10014-1314
Tel: 800-688-3876
Fax: 212-366-4747
E-mail: info@eurocruises.com
Web Site: www.eurocruises.com

E Waterways
140 E 56th Street, Suite 4C
New York, NY 10022
Tel: 800-546-4777
Fax: 212-688-9467
E-mail: sales@bvassociates.com
Web Site: www.ewaterways.com

Far & Wide
80 SW 8th Street, Suite 2601
Miami, FL 33130-3047
Tel: 800-FARWIDE (327-9433)
Fax: 305-908-7535
Web Site: www.farandwide.com

Grand Circle Travel
347 Congress Street
Boston, MA 02210
Tel: 800-221-2610
Fax: 617-346-6700
Web Site: www.gct.com

JFO Cruise Service Corp.
2500 Westchester Avenue
Purchase, New York 10577
Tel: 800-346-6525
Fax: 914-696-0833
Web Site: www.rivercruises.com

Peter Deilmann Cruises
1800 Diagonal Road, Suite 170
Alexandria, VA 22314
Tel: 800-348-8287
Fax: 703-549-7924
Web Site: www.deilmann-cruises.com

Chapter 10   **185**

Riverboat & Hotel/Barge Companies - continued

Premier Selections
342 Madison Avenue, Suite 916
New York, NY 10173
Tel: 800-234-4000
Fax: 646-658-0343
Web Site: www.premierselections.com

The Barge Broker
342 Madison Avenue, Suite 916
New York, NY 10173
Tel: 800-234-4000
Fax: 646-658-0343
Web Site: www.bargebroker.com

Uniworld
17323 Ventura
Encino, CA 91316
Tel: 800-360-9550
Fax: 818-461-1770
Web Site: www.uniworldcruises.com

Value World Tours
17222 Newhope St., Suite 203
Fountain Valley, CA 92708
Tel: 800-795-1633
Fax: 714-556-6125
Web Site: www.vwtours.com

Vantage Deluxe World Travel
90 Canal Street
Boston, MA 02114
Tel: 800-322-6677
Fax: 617-878-6142
Web Site: www.vantagetravel.com

Viking River Cruises
21829 Burbank Blvd.
Woodland Hills, CA 91316
Tel: 877-668-4546
Fax: 818-227-1237
Web Site: www.uniworldcruises.com

Note: These riverboat - hotel/barge companies are only listed in this chapter and not in the reference section.

You're probably saying by now *"Enough about cruising already!"* That's why I'm going to stop. *BUT,* if you have ever *truly* wanted in the travel business, this is your opportunity of a life time to make it happen. Now I'm finished.

By the way...

If you are cruising with one of the major cruise lines, you are sailing on a ship, not a boat. A boat is what you take when the ship sinks!

CHAPTER 11

Learning the Globe, the Trade, and Escorting

"Say, where exactly is Khartoum anyway?"

This is a learning chapter. It is meant to give you some direction about learning the travel trade and some insight into working with people in travel. In group travel, there are two main groups of people you will be dealing with: 1) your travel club members and 2) the tour and travel professionals who will fulfill your group travel needs. Working with these two group types can take some finesse on your part, so you need two different mindsets when dealing with these people.

Whether you package your group tours personally by booking directly with tour and travel suppliers, or use a travel agency, tour operator, or DMC, you still need to be knowledgeable about how the travel industry operates. Different business industries have their own methods of how to buy, sell and market their various products and the travel business is no different. This is especially true in the area of sales and marketing. When you are in the travel and tour business, *the world* is the "product" you sell, and that's a lot of product! In sales and marketing, the more knowledgeable you are about your product, the easier it will be for you to convince people to purchase what you are selling. But because you are selling *the world*, it is impossible for you to know everything, and eventually, you will be asked some questions that you cannot answer. So what is the solution? How can you get the knowledge you need to answer these questions? The answer is: *You do not need to know everything about every city, state or country...you just need to know where to find the information to get the answers*.

There are many sources of information for you to draw from. All of the answers to your questions are just a telephone call, fax, e-mail, or a click of the mouse away (the Internet). One of the best sources for you will be the tourism bureaus of various cities, states and countries. An abundance of information bureaus are just waiting for your call, so take advantage of this wealth of information and use it to your benefit. An extensive list of these bureaus is found in the Reference Section of this book along with addresses, telephone and fax numbers, as well as e-mail and web site addresses. More on other tour information resources is listed in the next few pages.

It's not only what you know...it's who you know!

The old axiom, "It's not who you know, *it's what you know*" has a great amount of truth in it. I think it was in the 1980's (the *me* decade), that it was changed to; "it's *not* what you know, *it's who you know*." While each has its merits, the winning combination seems to be both - *what and who* you know.

What you know – How do you gain knowledge about the travel industry and get the answers you need?

- **Read:** Read everything from travel books and brochures to encyclopedias. Subscribe to as many travel publications as you can keep up with. On that note, here is a great travel trade subscription service for you:

Travel Subscriptions For Less - This company has represented the top travel trade publications for over 15 years. Their goal is to help sellers of travel (group travel leaders, travel agents, independent contractors, etc.) find the right subscriptions to meet their needs and Travel Subscriptions For Less guarantees the lowest rates. You can contact Travel Subscriptions For Less and request a list of their specialized publications at:

Travel Subscriptions For Less
P.O. Box 916452
Longwood, FL   32791

Tel: 800-665-9067   Fax: 407-786-3689
E-mail: travelpubs@aol.com

Also, as I mentioned in an earlier chapter, after you have joined some of the professional group travel associations, you will receive travel literature from tour operators, resorts, airlines, cruise lines, etc. almost daily, so read, read, and read some more!

- **Study maps:** Your knowledge of geography is very important and studying maps can help you gain that knowledge. This is especially important in this day and age, because the borders of many countries change constantly. Also, you want to avoid one of life's little embarrassing moments, *like* not being able to point to where Hong Kong or Vienna is located on a map if someone should ask you.

- **Tour & Travel Courses:** Many travel industry associations, universities, private trade schools and community colleges now offer courses on travel and tourism. If you have one of these facilities in your area, it would certainly be worth your while to check them out. Remember, however, your interest is in organizing group tours, so at this point, you do not want to sign up for any major travel agent or travel management courses. Another avenue you can take to learn about the travel business would be to sign up for one of the many home study courses that are available. Since I published the first edition of *How to Organize Group Travel for Fun and Profit*, I have discovered a couple of very good travel schools for you to consider. One is an excellent online school (Internet) offering a complete range of travel industry courses and the other is a series of travel seminars held in various major cities in the U.S.A. and Canada. Call for information or check out their websites for more details. Meanwhile, here is a brief description of each school:

Career Quest Training Center, Inc.
Tel: 800-452-3198
Fax: 815-723-9486
Website: www.careerquesttraining.com

The following predictions have been taken from Career Quest Training Center's website regarding future growth of the travel industry (which I totally agree with but have slightly modified), and the part that group travel leaders and outside sellers of leisure travel will play during this growth period. This is what the experts say...

Travel Industry Predictions for the next Decade

- Numerous restrictions, lousy flight connections and poor service have made internet bookings loose their appeal.

- The number of home-based group travel clubs and outside travel agents will explode.

- Group travel leaders and outside agents focusing on selling cruises will continue to capture the vacation market.

- The hotel industry will really discover the business potential that group travel leaders and outside agents can bring to the table.

- Group travel leaders and outside agents that develop a niche market will not only succeed but will excel.

- Consumers (especially "baby boomers") will demand quality tours and good service...AND they will be willing to pay the price to guarantee this service.

Founded in 1999, Career Quest Training Center, Inc. was developed to provide online distance education programs to individuals seeking a career in the travel industry. Complete programs of study have helped hundreds of people start their own home-based travel businesses by offering them a 24 hour travel and tour curriculum. By the time you complete this online training program, you can begin a money-making (full or part-time) travel career planning vacations around the world for your own tour groups, family and friends. The following are the courses you will study at Career Quest Training Center's online school:

Course of Study

- Unit 1 - The Travel Industry

- Unit 2 - Domestic and International Travel

- Unit 3 - Ground Transportation and Accommodations

- Unit 4 - Selling Cruises and Tours

- Unit 5 - Researching Destinations

- Unit 6 - Making a Sale / CLIA Video
    - Winning Sales Techniques
    - Starting a Home-Based Agency

- Unit 7 - Creating a Business Plan

- Unit 8 - Setting-up Your Business

- Unit 9 - Niche Marketing and Your Client

- Unit 10 - The Legalities of a Home-Based Travel Business

After completing Career Quest Training Center's tour and travel program, you will be more than ready than ever to launch that career in travel you've always wanted!

Hibiscus Tours International Ltd.
Tel: 800-486-9881
Fax: 416-537-1975
E-mail: info@hibiscus.ca
Website: www.hibiscus.ca

Hibiscus International Ltd. is a Canadian based travel and tour organization that offers a course called "Mananging Your Own Tours." They recognize the tourism industry is growing rapidly and, as a result, there is an urgent need for qualified and well trained tour and travel personnel. This is especially true for anyone interested in the small group travel business, speciality niche markets and adventure tours.

Hibiscus Tours International offers a nine day industry accredited certificateprogram which prepares graduates on how to design, package, sell and lead small group tours both domestically and internationally. The program is made up of three courses which can be taken individually or as a series. As of this printing, the cours etitles are:

- Leading Small Group Tours
- Tour Design and Development
- Marketing, Sales & Operations

The courses are taught in sessions over a 3 day period. Currently the courses are being offered in Vancouver, Victoria and Toronto, Canada, and Chicago and Boston. Realizing the growing need for their tour and travel program in the America, Hibiscus Tours International has plans to expand to more U.S. cities in the near future.

After completing the Hibiscus Tours International program,

people will have a good grasp of small business practices specially targeted to the travel industry, licensing and legalities, developing business and marketing plans and effective selling techniques.

The Hibiscus International program is ideal for anyone ranging from college students to active seniors who has a desire to travel and an entrepreneur spirit!

NOTE: Also, you have never been in business for yourself, you may want to consider taking a Business 101 course at a local community college to learn the basics of setting up and running a business.

- **Library:** I know that I have mentioned this before, but please take advantage of your local library. Most libraries today have an extensive travel section of books, travel trade publications and videos on various domestic and international destinations. This is travel knowledge for the asking and it's free! This is also the place where you can find up-to-date maps and any special geography information you may need.

- **Tourism Bureaus:** Most states in the U.S.A. have great tourism bureaus or boards that are very accommodating and will provide you information on their major cities, parks and recreational areas, historical sites and major attractions. These bureaus can also provide additional information about seasons, average temperatures, opening and closing dates of parks and attractions, etc. The bureaus of foreign countries, with a few Third World exceptions, are very eager to provide similar information about their destinations. Usually, one telephone call to a tourism bureau will get you enough information to fill a file drawer.

- **Convention and Visitors Bureaus (CVB):** If you are interested in pursuing a larger group business, such as convention and conference meeting planning or reunion groups (alumni, military or other large groups), a CVB is your best option to call. A city's CVB can offer you an abundance of information and services to help plan your conference or reunion. You can find out availability of hotel accommodations, conference and meeting space, dining options, and much more. Most CVB's can usually provide local personnel (at a price) to assist you with your conference and registration staffing. Every major city worldwide that solicits large groups will have a Convention and Visitors Bureau.

- **Chamber of Commerce:** If you are looking for information on a smaller city, town or village, which would probably not have a Convention and Visitors Bureau, then the local Chamber of Commerce will be your best bet for the information you need. Domestically or internationally, the local area Chamber of Commerce is very civic minded and generally loves to play a part in getting groups of tourists to their little corner of the world.

- **The Internet:** This is an amazing source for travel information and for those of you with a computer system in place, the internet is an information source that can supply you with 98% of anything you want to know. Twenty four hours a day, seven days a week, information about a country, a city, a resort, what to see and do in that city or resort, a cruise line or cruise ship, etc., is at your fingertips! Tourism bureaus of almost every state and country have web sites that you can access anytime of the day or night providing information galore and immediate answers to your questions. It's all on the Internet!

- **Travel Agencies, Tour Operators and DMC's:** Besides the other sources listed above, a very large contingency of travel agencies, tour operators, and DMC's are standing by to help answer your questions. Many of these tour and travel suppliers specialize in certain areas of the world and can be very helpful by providing you "inside" information and details about your destination that may not be in the generic brochures.

Who you know – These are the people you _need_ to know:

- **Sales Representatives:** The sales representatives for the various tour and travel suppliers will be high on the list of *who* you will want to know. These include the representatives of:

- Airlines
- Cruise lines
- Hotels and resorts
- Car rental agencies
- Motorcoach companies
- Convention & Visitors Bureaus

The reasons you want to have a close business relationship with these sales representatives are:

1. They can give you guidance on the best way to work with their company. Most reps can supply you with specific literature and brochures to help promote your groups. They keep you informed of the occasional *special deals* being offered to group travel leaders. These are good people to know!

2. After an agreement has been reached with your representative, should you experience problems with the company's operations, service, etc., your first call should be to him/her. If he/she is a good rep, they will fight to make things right for you. Most of the time they can cut through the red tape and get to the heart of the problem. But in order to retain a solid working relationship, go over your representative's head only as a last resort.

Escorting tours

This is where your real people skills come into play! Escorting tours, especially your own, is a very challenging, but fulfilling experience. To travel with a group of people that you brought together, have a great tour, and return with a unique, once-in-a-lifetime experience is a joy.

I can assure you that most of your tours, if you have packaged them correctly and paid attention to the details, will come off like clockwork. Always strive for 100% satisfaction from your tour participants, but you can feel very happy with a 98% "happy factor."

As with any tour, yours or a long established tour company's, outside influences can enter into the picture which can sometime affect the outcome of your trip. A delayed flight or train departure, a malfunctioning air conditioner, or a lost piece of luggage, are all common travel occurrences. As silly as it sounds, you can bet that someone will take it personally. When this happens, just remember that your tour *is a great tour* and it is nothing personal from the person complaining, it's just the "nature of the beast" (I use this term in the kindest way, of course). Understand that it is just some peoples' nature to always say " I had a wonderful time, *but....*" Any negative comments that you receive from these people may be unjustified and could have been out of your control anyway. However, always sincerely listen to what these people have to say, because it could be something you may be able to correct on the next tour.

I will also predict that the one or two standard complainers will usually end up as avid members of your club. They will also be some of the first people to sign up for your next trip...so learn to love 'em!

As I mentioned, escorting is a real people skill and the way group travel leaders use these skills to manage their groups varies from personality to personality. Some run their program like your mother, and others will run it like a Marine drill instructor *(give me Mom any day!)* Over a period of time, based on your personality and people skills, you will also develop your own style of escorting.

As I mentioned in Chapter Two, the number one trait of a good group travel leader is that he or she *must be a people person.* Many people who join your tours will do so because of you, because you are a people person, not just because you have put together a great tour package to an interesting place. They can probably buy a similar tour from a hundred different travel sources, but they are going to join your tour. Why? Because of your personality; you're a very nice person, you're interesting, you're funny, you're knowledgeable about your business, they believe that you will take care them, and most of all, they like you. *Remember, people do business with people they like!*

There's no magic to escorting

There is no magic in escorting group tours. For the most part it's just using common sense in how to deal with people and situations. Mostly it is being a good host. You are hosting a party…it's just in another city or in another state (or country). The goal of your party is the same; make sure that everyone has a good time!

To start learning about escorting, read articles in the group travel leader publications that you have subscribed to. Escorting is a topical subject and is frequently covered. Another way to gain valuable knowledge is to have discussions with some of your fellow group travel leaders while attending one of the travel conferences, seminars, or tradeshows occurring in your area.

For those of you interested in developing an extensive motorcoach business, I would recommend you purchase a book by Anita L. Fielder called *Managing Group Tours*. It is a basic "how to" book that covers a great deal of detail about managing and escorting tours. Overall, it has some good, basic group travel information that I am sure anyone just getting into the group travel business would appreciate. Since much of the book pertains to setting-up and operating motorcoach tours, I highly recommend this to anyone who has a special interest in motorcoach tours. The book is $14.95 (plus shipping) and is available through Group Tour Magazine. To order a copy call 1-800-767-3489.

Remember, the business of running a travel club is the same as any other business. You have a product to sell (tours), you advertise the product (direct mailings, promotional meetings, word-of-mouth), you sell the product and deliver the goods (take the group on the tour and make sure they have a good time). The difference between a regular type of retail business and your travel club business is that most retailers don't spend one or two weeks with their customers talking about the product they sold them. You do!

Here are a few words of wisdom regarding escorting, and the travel business in general, for you to consider:

- There's *always* a solution to a problem situation (some are just better than others).

- *Never* settle for less than you were promised (but you can always accept more)!

- This is one business where the old saying "*The squeaky wheel gets the oil*" rings very true.

- If it rains on your group for a week, *you are not personally responsible*, no matter what anybody says.

- *"What goes around comes around."* This is especially true in the travel business. Always keep that in mind.

Work with people you like!

What a pleasure that is! First of all, the tour and travel business is a fun business and it's up to you to keep it that way…and you have the power to do it! The key is work and associate only with people you like. You are probably saying "A little easier said than done, my friend!" Think about this. In the group travel business, for the most part, there are only two groups of people that you have to contend with:

1. Your travel club members and…

2. Your tour and travel suppliers.

Group #1 / Club Members - Since this is a fun and upbeat business, your travel club members and tour participants will be pleasant to work with because they are going to finally take what is probably one of their *dream vacations*. You are the person who is going to make this vacation happen for them, so, in a way, you are special to them. You are now their personal travel counselor and their overall travel Guru. Prior to the trip, you are answering all of their questions and concerns, and have them excited about the tour. During the tour, you will see that they have a wonderful time, and that the tour comes off without a hitch! After the tour, because you have taken such good care of them, they are now staunch club members and will look forward to your next tour.

Now reality tells us that this is *not exactly* how things are going to work, and it's true, there could be unforeseen complications. But that is exactly what the complications will be, *unforeseen!* As I mentioned earlier, you cannot control a delayed flight, snowstorm or power failure. But as the group travel leader, you can make a 110% effort to take care of your tour group if some situation does arise, adjust the schedule or itinerary if you *have to*, and keep the tour on track. If you have selected a good tour partner (and I know you will), they will make the same effort to correct any problems on their side as fast as they can. Between the two of you and your gallant efforts to keep the tour running smoothly, the tour participants will not fault you for minor complications (maybe they were actually major, but you made them minor) during the tour. Your reputation as group travel leader will soar, and you will be held in high regard by your loyal travel club supporters! I know…this sounds like the ending of a Disney movie, but it's true!

Good complications?

Before we move on, and for the sake of argument, let's analyze "complications." Complications can run the gamut from minor inconveniences to major foul-ups. Ninety nine percent of the time they will fall into the minor category. But not all complications besetting you during the tour are necessarily bad. Many times, a complication can actually work in your favor. As an example, because of an overbooking at the Four Star hotel you originally had on your itinerary, you are now in a Deluxe Five Star hotel at no extra charge. That's a minor complication. What's even better, the tour group thinks you're great! Since you actually are a great group travel leader, feel free to take the credit. You can handle that, can't you? So, as these minor complications occur, you correct them, sometimes to a better deal, but always to a satisfactory conclusion. Most of the time, the complications are happening behind the scenes and you and your tour partner work out the details without your tour participants ever knowing there were any changes.

When it really gets down to it, if there were not any complications during your tours, how will you become a "champion of the tour group" if you don't have anything to solve for them? That's how you build your reputation, problems arise, you fix them, and then add another feather to your cap!

One more thing about the *merits* of complications. Some of the best stories told at dinner parties are about the terrible thing that happened to someone while they were traveling. After all of the "That's terrible!", "You poor thing!" and the "Oh my God's…" are over, everybody's laughing about it, including the person it happened to. They are the hit of the party because they fell off the ski lift in Montreux and broke their leg, and had to be rescued by a St. Bernard! So, after the painful memories go away (and they usually do), you have another great travel story to add to your dinner party conversation arsenal. As a group travel leader, however, you are not allowed to charge extra for these experiences.

Group #2 / Travel Agencies, Tour Operators and DMC's - This is easy! As a group travel leader, you are a buyer of travel services. Travel Agencies, Tour Operators and DMC's are the supply side of the business and would all love for you to buy from them. You are looking for a friend to handle your travel needs and each and every one of them wants to be your friend!

Again, the key to keeping this business fun is to work _only_ with people you truly like. Talk with these different tour suppliers and their representatives, and zero in on the ones who are not only offering a good deal or the lowest price, but also have a sincere "I want your business and I am willing to earn it" attitude. The problem is, a majority of these people fit this description! So, take your time in selecting who you will use, meet with them if possible, and get recommendations from other group travel leaders.

The longer you have your travel club, the more buying power you represent and the more tour suppliers you will have banging at your door. Here is my suggestion for selecting your travel partners:

1. **Travel agency** - Find one, good local agency that fits all of the descriptions outlined in Chapter Seven and associate yourself with them. As long as the agency does a good job for you, stay with them.

2. **Tour Operators** - In the beginning, talk with _at least_ two or three and get a feel for their operation, what they have to offer, and how they are willing to work with you. Try a couple of different ones on different tours and see who performs the best and offers the best service. Because of the variety of your tours, you may want to have a _few_ preferred operators to work with. Keep your options open. But, if you find one that excels in price and service, and they also have that potential "friend" quality, then you're on to something good!

3. **DMC** – What I said about the Tour Operator above, is exactly the same for the DMC's. Use the following guidelines for all three of the tour suppliers:

    Develop a good business relationship with all of them.

Build it on friendship, trust and mutual respect. As long as they do a good job for you, stay with them. It is still good business to get competitive quotes occasionally to make sure no one is taking you for granted. The closer the relationship you have with these people, the less likely this will happen.

I know you will end up only working with people you like. How do I know this? First, I have run my travel business successfully on this principle for many years. Since I am no "Wonder Boy," I am sure you can build the same kind of travel business that is based on friendships, trust and mutual respect as well as me. Secondly, because it is the nature of the business. Let me explain:

Group #1 - The reason you will like your tour participants and travel club members is simple. It's a natural process and this is how it works. If you don't particularly care for someone, their attitude, their demeanor, or whatever, you will not be outgoing and receptive to them (usually the feelings are mutual). Your personalities just don't mix. Since you both have this "feeling" about each other, one of you will eventually (if not right off the bat) go away. Obviously, since this is your travel club, you are not going anywhere, so Voila!…they leave! Now, who does this leave as the remaining travel club members? *The people you like!* Over a period of years, you will build a travel business full of wonderful people. Many will start out as casual club members and tour participants, but will end up as close, dear friends. You may have to put up with a marginal member for a tour or two, but eventually, they will leave and that's a fact!

Group #2 - The reason you will like your tour and travel providers is that they want your business and they are going to like you no matter what! Whether they do or not is another story. Most of these people are sincere business people and will take good care of you whether they are on your Christmas card list or not. *Your challenge* is to find among all of these very capable people *a few* with whom you want to work closely with and build a longterm relationship. Not an easy task! The end result will be, however, that you will find these special people and they will end up being true friends. That's how it works.

So you see, you can be in a business where you like who you work with *and* who you do business with. As a group travel leader, you can literally "have your cake and eat it too!" Not many people have that opportunity in their careers.

A word about attitude

As you endeavor in your great search for the perfect tour and travel suppliers, you will probably encounter, upon occasion (not often), a person with a blasé attitude toward handling your business because you are new to the business. Ninety nine percent of the time, the suppliers that find out you are just starting in the business will go out of their way to help you. These are the smart ones. They know that if they can work with you now, then as you grow and profit, so will they. These are the people you want to give your business to, the ones that want your business and will help you become successful. If you should happen to get one of the one percent minority, make the conversation short.

Now, after a few successful years in the business, some group travel leaders develop an attitude aimed at the tour suppliers. It is the "I Am Group Travel Leader...Hear Me Roar!" attitude. Once this attitude sprouts its ugly head, there are usually very bad consequences that follow not far behind, as the group travel leader soon finds out. I know this attitude could not possibly take hold of you, but I thought you should be aware of its possible emergence.

To summarize; Have fun and work with people you like *and* who like you. Life is way, way, too short to go through it being miserable.

The title of Chapter Twelve is "Thoughts, Observations, and Miscellaneous Information." It contains a lot of good information presented in a random way. I think you will find it interesting!

The world is a book and those
who do not travel read only one page.

St. Augustine

CHAPTER 12

Thoughts, Observations, and Miscellaneous Information

Something for Everybody

The following are random thoughts, observations, and information that will be of use to you in many areas of your travel business. In this mix, I hope you find several pieces of information that you can incorporate into your business plan, sales and marketing plan, work ethic, etc. There is no sequence to this information, so just dive in!

How to use being new to the group travel business to your best advantage!

Contrary to common belief, being new in a particular business arena is not all bad. With regards to being a new group travel leader, it's true that you do not have the sales and marketing skills or in-depth knowledge of the group travel business that many of the established group leaders have. But that's OK, because as with any business, it takes time. In the meantime, while you are learning the finer points of the business, why not take advantage of being new to the travel industry while you can! Being new will work to your best advantage with the tour and travel suppliers. Most of them, when they find out *(or you happen to mention)* that you are just getting into the group travel business, will go out of their way to help you. They will send you extra materials; they will make an effort to come and meet you personally; they will give you valuable time saving advice, and they will pass on other travel contacts that could also be helpful to you. They do this for a couple of reasons:

1. Most of them love the travel business and are truly excited about your getting into the travel business.

2. They also know that if they help you now, you will probably be a loyal client of theirs for years to come. This is both nice of them and a good business move on their part.

By being nice to you, they have scored a couple of major "Brownie points" as well. When you let them know that you are new to the business, you also make a couple of points with them:

1. They appreciate your being honest and up-front about being new in the travel business (this helps them understand how to work with you better).

2. They appreciate the opportunity to help you get established in the business.

Of course this is all pretty self-serving on both of your parts, but it works, and it works to the advantage of you both! So, do not be shy when speaking with your travel suppliers about setting up your first tours. Tell them you are new and a lost lamb in the world of travel. At that point, they will take you by your hand and lead you on!

Potential High School and College groups

There is a wealth of group travel business to be found in high schools and colleges. The potential travel market is extremely good for anyone who knows the ins and outs of the various school systems. If you are a teacher, a professor, or even a professional college student (come on now, it's time to get a job), your talents and knowledge of how to work within these academic areas of opportunity are invaluable. The following are just a few of the group travel categories you can tap into:

Foreign language groups: Every language class is a strong prospect for a group trip because all foreign language students would love to visit the country whose language they have chosen to speak. Don't you know that in their imaginations, their "dream destination" is alive and well and beckoning them to visit! On top of it, the desire to make that dream trip come true at this stage in their life is very strong.

Also, now it is not just the French or Spanish class going on the trips. The languages being studied today are many and varied, everything from Cantonese to Farsi. So, the opportunity for world travel has opened up considerably when it comes to language groups.

Music Groups: A huge market exists both domestically and internationally for high school bands, college bands, and choir tours. I have a friend who has specialized in this area that has done extremely well. The student group travel market is very large and lucrative and there are many successful travel companies that are dedicated solely to this area of the travel business. Many times, a student, teacher, or parent of a student has a better chance to develop a group than an outside travel company.

More potential group possibilities:

- Social and Fraternal organizations
- Athletic teams
- History / Geography classes
- Art classes

Also, think about a cruise for some of these groups. It could be an easy sell!

Chapter 12   **207**

Travel destinations 5 year cycle

There are many beautiful and exciting places to go in this world to visit, and most of the time you can find a deal to travel to them. There are always deals to be found if you know where to look for them. Popular destinations run hot and cold, and when they're hot, you can't get a deal. When the spotlight is off of them, you *can* get a great buy. Does that make it a bad destination? Not at all, it's all part of a five year cycle.

What starts to make a destination hot? The simple answer is whichever destination is offering the best deals. So, who offers the best deals? The destinations whose business has fallen off over the past few years do. They have to get that business back, they need to be a hot destination...*they need to be #1 again!* Will they be able to revive their popularity? The answer is "yes" because most tourists will follow the dollar (or drachma, or mark, or escudo, etc.) to wherever the best deals are.

All the destination needs is to lower its prices, put together some super packages, and the people will come running back. So this is what the destination's movers and shakers will do: when tourism falls off (for whatever reason) over a period of time, something has to be done to revive it. The tourism bureau representing that city goes intoaction, in cooperation with the major airlines servicing the city, hotels, car rental agencies, restaurants, etc., putting together a power packed promotion to get the tourists to return. All of a sudden, there are *fantastic* roundtrip airfares to this great destination; there are hotel and resort packages at unheard of prices with bargains galore! The tourist who loved them before will return, because of the great deals, and will fall in love with them all over again.

As time goes on, and the crowds keep growing, the great deals get fewer and fewer. Before long, there aren't any *real deals* anymore. What's happened here? *The city has become a hot, hot destination!* When this happens, they peak as one of the "in" destinations and they usually start a slow decline towards *destination tourism hell!* All over the world, there are hot destinations that are growing colder and colder by the day. *These are the destinations you want to watch for deals in the future.* How do you know which ones to look for? Look at the destinations that have been extremely popular over the past five years. They are the destinations next in line to turn cold. Over the past five years, the price of their destination has done nothing but increase, increase to the point that they will drive their loyal tourist to the next new hot destination. Their rates now must start a downturn.

These hot/cold popular tourist destinations are on a five year cycle. They are hot for a few years, and then start to decline (in tourism business) for a couple more years, and then they turn cold. Now, the process begins all over again; tourism bureau, great deals…come and see the new us! Because of the super deals being offered <u>once again</u> (the last deals were 5 years ago), the crowds start flocking back.

Got the picture? Every five years – hot/cold. Why is this important to you? Because you can study the destination cycle and predict where the next hot destinations are going to be! You are now a travel Prophet! As the saying goes "Timing is everything!" Take advantage of this information and track some destinations that you eventually want to visit personally or with your group. If you plan accordingly, you can literally be in the "right place at the right time!"

Waiting lists are good!

Most of the time when you are booking tours, the number of participants you tell the tour supplier is an estimated projection. After you have a few tours under your belt, you will have a good "feel" for the kind of numbers you can actually produce.

Remember this when blocking space for your next group:

1. As I mentioned in Chapter Eight, always block your space

Chapter 12

based on a conservative number of expected tour participants. If you think you can realistically get 35 to 40 pax, then use 30 pax as the minimum number for your tour supplier to base their quote on. If you fall a little short, you may still be OK. If you have more, everybody's happy!

Try this experiment when promoting your next tour:

2. Promote one of your tours on a "limited space reservation, first come, first served basis." Tell your club members that you only have a limited number of seats for this next tour and if they really want to go, sign up now, because *it will sell out!* Let's say for this particular tour, you have a 40 pax block of space with a tour operator.

   You will let everyone know that you only have space for 30 pax. You are sure you will get at least 30 pax for the tour, and you do...because space was limited and these 30 people acted fast because they did not want to be left out! In fact, you have another 10 pax who want to sign up. Even though you already have the space blocked and can book them on the tour immediately, put them on a waiting list! Why? Because the next time you have a "limited space reservation, first come, first served basis," they will be one of the first to sign up.

   Another reason is that people loved to "be cleared" off of a waiting list. During the "clearing process," they will call you daily to find out where they stand. It's a joyous day for them when you call to say, "Good news, we were able to get more space and you're on the tour!" You are a wonderful group travel leader, you got them on the tour! Understand, this should not be a painful process (unless it's one of those members you would like to get rid of), so you will want to "clear" them fairly fast.

Specialized Tours...a gold mine!

I mentioned in Chapter Ten that I thought cruising was the absolute best, most opportune, most profitable, and exciting area of travel you could possibly be in today. Well, I still do (you thought I changed my mind)! BUT, the next best, would definitely be *specialty tours* (some of the specialty tours use a cruise, of course). The opportunity you have to develop specialty tours is unlimited. This is truly a case where you are *limited only by your imagination!*

A great example of taking advantage of the specialized tour market is *Shopping Safaris.com.* The founder, Mark Gaughan, has started a travel club that offers his groups an opportunity to hit the mall or hit the links, catch a trout or catch an off Broadway play. The central theme of his tours is always shopping but each program is always combined with a sightseeing tour that will leave the participant with fond memories of their day or weekend. Many of Mark's tours are escorted by professional educators with degrees in a particular field that he incorporates into his shopping excursions. Brilliant!

This area of travel does not need a lot of explanation, or guidance from me, because a specialty tour will be a *labor of love* on the part of the group travel leader. The effort to package a specialty tour will be minimal because the tour will be developed around someone who is already an expert in a particular field, the group travel leader.

Another classic example of a popular specialty tour is a Flower and Garden Tour. Anyone who is associated with a local or national flower and garden club has an opportunity to organize their own tour (with the possibility of a sanction from the local club if you give the president one of the free tour conductor tickets). Think about this: if you have a hobby that you absolutely love, a tour could probably be developed around it. What's the number one driving force behind most successful, independent, group travel leaders? The desire to travel...the desire to see the world! The following list of potential specialty tour categories is minimal at best. These are just some of the ones that I know about:

- Flower & Garden
- Museum
- Estate & Mansion
- Food & Wine
- Historical
- Religious
- Alumni / Reunion
- Castle & Palaces
- Ethnic
- Railroad
- Antique

Again, these are just a few of the more obvious categories. If you have a hobby you love, build a tour around it, and go!

Direct mail promotions – "A" List and "B" List

The most effective way to market your travel club and tours is by a direct mail campaign. To do your direct mail campaign, you need mailing lists, *good mailing lists*. You can create your own mailing lists or you can purchase them from companies that specialize in that service. You will want to have two categories of mailing lists: an **"A" list** and a **"B" list**. The **"A" list** will be the best and most productive of the two. You will create your very important **"A" list** from people close to you who are:

- family members
- close personal friends
- neighbors
- business acquaintances

- golf partners
- bridge and dance partners
- bowling and bingo friends
- fraternal and social club member acquaintances

Your **"B" list** will be made up of casual and distant acquaintances, along with various targeted mailing lists you will acquire from research or purchase from a mailing list supplier. The mailing list company that I have used for many years is InfoUSA. They have extensive mailing lists for both business (11 million), and private households (113 million). These lists are reasonably priced and can be purchased according to your specifications, such as:

- Average household income
- Average age
- Specific occupation
- Zip code /area code

Look in the Yellow Page section of your telephone book under *Mailing Lists* for a complete listing of these companies, or contact InfoUSA for a sample of what they have to offer. You can reach them at:

- (800) 304-3282 Household lists

- (800) 336-8349 Business lists

Mailing to your "A" list - Getting your first travel club members: To get the nucleus of your travel club established, use the **"A" list** of potential club members and tour participants for your initial mailing.

Because the **"A" list** is made up of family, friends, and business and social acquaintances, you should already have correct addresses and telephone contact information for a majority of these people. *The #1 list of names you should use to initially announce your travel club opening is from your Christmas card or holiday season list (all of these people are on your "A" list).* These are the people closest to you and the ones who have the most potential to help start spreading the word of your new venture.

Your first promotional piece to the **"A" list** prospects should be an invitation to join your travel club along with information on the first two or three tours that you are planning. This can be in the form of a personal letter, a newsletter (easy to produce on a computer), a flyer, or any other method that you think will get attention. Follow-up the mailing with a telephone call to see if they received it and to answer any questions they may have. Questions are good because they give you an opportunity to elaborate on the travel club, the tours, your goals, etc.

Work your **"A" list** to the maximum before starting on the **"B" list** mailing. Also remember, you are running a *first class* operation, so your tour brochures, club information, newsletters, etc., should be sent by first class mail to everyone on your **"A" list**. Regarding your initial mailing, be sure to read the next item, *"5 will get you 10."* This marketing tip can help you double your **"A" list**!

Direct mail marketing tip – 5 will get you 10

Here is a marketing tip that is so simple, but so very effective, you need to use it in your next direct mail promotion. When you print your next tour's main promotional piece, *double the quantity* you usually have printed. Instead of printing 200 brochures or leaflets, print 400, or go from 500 to 1,000. The price when doubling your printing run is very inexpensive, because the main expense you are paying for is getting the press set up to make the initial printing run. After this is done, the rest of the cost is just for paper, ink and cleanup. This is what you will do with the extra copies:

- When you do the initial mailing to your "A" list, instead of just putting one brochure in the envelope, *put two.*

- When someone calls to request a brochure, put two in the envelope and send it off to them.

Why send two? For this reason:

- Most of your tour participants will be booking and paying the tour price that is based on double occupancy. If it is a couple on your "A" list that has received your brochures, what's the first thing they will do with the extra brochure? They will give it to their best friends! Not only will they give it to their best friends, but they will try and convince them to come along on the tour also…now you have outside sales people working for you!

So, if you get five requests, send out ten brochures, and hopefully those five will get you ten!

Here is a good example of how this worked for one group travel leader. Sue and Bob Brown are the group travel leaders for the No Mads, from Fairfield Glade, Tennessee. I had put together a deal for group travel leaders to Greece and the Greek Isles. Sue and Bob had never been to Greece, or on a Mediter-ranean cruise, and they really wanted to go. I packaged a tour for them, and included one free trip (air and land) for every fifteen participants they could get.

It was in the fall of the year, and because Fairfield Glade is a lake resort community, many of the residents had already left to go to their winter homes. Sue was concerned about the size of group she would be able to get together because so many of their club members were scattered around the country. Sue's goal was to get at least fifteen participants. To make a long story short, Sue put two brochures in each of the envelopes, mailed them first class to her **"A" list,** *and got forty eight people in three weeks!* This system works…use it!

Promotional Postcards

Postcards are an economical way to get your travel club and tours some great exposure. Here are a few reasons postcards are so effective:

- They are inexpensive to buy (sometimes they are even free or at a very low cost from tourism bureaus)

- They are inexpensive to mail

- They catch the eye of the person opening the mail

- They are colorful (or should be)

- They get immediately scanned for interest because they don't have to be opened to find out the information

If you just want to make an announcement or send a simple, direct message, the U.S. Post Office has a great program for you to use. You can purchase inexpensive, plain postcards from your local post office for one cent per postcard plus postage. The postcards are already pre-stamped with the correct postage, so all you have to do is print your message on them, put on an address label, and they are ready to go! As of January 1, 2001, the post office charges you one cent for the post card and .20 cents for the postage. There is no limit on how many or how few you can purchase.

If you have the budget and want to get more innovative, custom postcards are a great way to send a special, eye-catching message. There are several companies that specialize in printing postcards and mass-produce them in many sizes and shapes at very reasonable prices. *Any major printing company can print custom post-cards, but to get the very best deal, use a company that specializes in printing only postcards.* The following are your best postcard sources if you want to try a postcard promotion:

- **Plain Postcards**: For plain, very inexpensive postcards, go to your local post office (If you want a large quantity of postcards, give them a day or two to get them together for you).

- **Customized Postcards**: If you want to use a custom postcard, look in the yellow pages of your telephone book under Postcards to see if you have any local printing companies *specializing* in postcards. If you cannot find a local source, then consider contacting Modern Postcard. Modern Postcard is the best company I've found for quality, service and price. Call for a sample packet for your files.

> Modern Postcard
> 1675 Faraday Avenue
> Carlsbad, CA 92008
>
> Tel: (800) 959-8365
> Fax: (760) 431-1939

"If you don't ask for it, you won't get it!"

This statement is so true! There are several ways you can possibly make extra money on your tours. You do this by getting a percentage of the tour providers' "extra" services that they make money on, which is mainly travel insurance and optional tours. The key to getting a percentage of this extra money is that you have to ask for it, because most of the time, your travel provider won't bring it up. Remember, you are bringing this group to them…

this is found money of which you should have a percentage.

- **Commissions on insurance**: Until you get yourself certified as a travel insurance agent (which should be immediately), negotiate a percentage of the travel insurance that the tour provider sells to your group. The commission they receive can vary between 15% to 30% or more. Most tour and travel suppliers that work with group travel leaders understand that you will want a commission split. Just "Ask and ye shall (may) receive!"

- **Commissions on optional tours**: Optional tours are offered for a fee but are not included in your tour package. During the tour program, on days that are at the tour participants' leisure, your travel provider will offer optional tours. The tours they sell to your group are commissionable to them and, as with the insurance, you deserve a percentage of the commission. The commission split for optional tours also varies but is usually between 5% to 10%. Again, just "Ask and ye shall receive!"

- **Promotional allowance and give-a-ways**: When you bring a group to a travel agency or U.S. tour operator, many of them have a per person promotional allowance that they will credit to your final payment. This credit is to help you promote a particular tour that you have selected and can be used however you want e.g., for printing, advertising, entertainment (tour meetings), etc. Like everything else, how much you are allowed is dependent on usually two points:

  1. How big the group is

  2. How expensive the tour is

  Besides the promotional credit, some tour operators also offer promotional items such as travel bags, tee shirts, caps and visors, etc. that you can give away to attendees of your tour meetings. This is a great way to build excitement for your upcoming tour. The recipients of the gift will be a walking advertisement for you since they start using or wearing these items months before the tour. Remember, it's up to you to ask your travel provider for this support.

Note: *The promotional credit is just that, a credit, a certain amount per person that you will deduct from your final payment invoice. Understand that this is not immediate cash in hand.*

- **More frees**: When you negotiate your free trips, make sure you get a clear understanding of how the free trips will be provided. Based on one free for every 15 full paying pax, follow this guideline:

  - Always negotiate a free tour based on both air, land and/or cruise.

  - If you were anticipating a minimum group of 30 pax, but actually end up with 41 pax (not including the two tour conductor tickets), you will have earned *almost* 3 free trips. *Make sure you negotiate a prorated cost for that third free.* In other words, you almost had enough pax for a third free.

    Since you were only 4 pax short of getting the third free trip, they should give you a substantial cost reduction for that third TC. Have the travel provider explain the formula they will use for this situation up-front, when you are in the negotiating stage. As with most contracts, once you've signed on the dotted line...the "honeymoon's over!"

Chapter 12   **219**

Note: The "honeymoon's over" scenario does not pertain just to travel agencies and tour operators, but is pretty much an across the board policy for most travel vendors (hotels, air lines, cruise lines, motorcoach companies, etc.). So, discuss <u>every point of interest</u> regarding your tour prior to signing any contracts!

Insurance

Travel insurance to cover both you, as a group travel leader and owner of a travel club, and your club members/tour participants, is very important. To protect yourself from any litigation brought on by a tour disruption or accident (airline strikes, tour vendor goes out of business, a tour participant is injured during the trip, etc.), you must cover yourself by having proper insurance. Follow this guideline for your insurance coverage:

1. **Purchase E & O insurance** - For your travel club, you will need Errors and Omissions (E & O) insurance, officially known as: Travel Agents/Tour Operators Professional Liability Insurance. Fortunately, this insurance is reasonable in cost, even for a new group travel leader. One of the main E & O insurance providers to the travel industry is The Berkley Group. You can get the insurance you need from The Berkley Group directly, or you can purchase it through one of the group travel leader organizations that you are going to join, such as CLIA or OSSN. After you join several of these organizations (which are going to help you excel as a group travel leader), check out their membership packets for the multitude of benefits (not just insurance) that you are going to receive as a member.

For your files, The Berkley Group can be contacted at:

P.O. Box 9366
Garden City, NY 11530

Tel: (800) 645-2424
Fax: (516) 294-1821

2. **Become a registered agent for a travel insurance company** - *This is a must*, because not only does it help cover you liability-wise, it is also a great source of income. Becoming a licensed agent is not difficult and, if you need assistance, the travel insurance agency will help guide you through the process. The two main things you need to do are 1) contact one of the companies listed below (if you don't know of a company yourself) for a Participation Agreement and 2) check with your state licensing agency for the requirements you will need to qualify (every state has different requirements) to become a state licensed agent. The following are two very good travel insurance agencies that I have worked with over the years that you can contact for information and an application to get set-up as one of their agents.

GlobalCare Insurance Services, Inc.
220 Broadway, Suite 201
Lynnfield, MA 01940

Tel: (800) 821-2488
Fax: (781) 592-7720
E-mail: tvlinstiac.net
Website: www.globalcare-cocco.com

Travel Guard International
1145 Clark Street
Stevens Point, WI 54481-2980

Tel: (715) 345-0505
Fax: (715) 345-0525
Website: www.travel-guard.com

3. **Sell cruise & tour protection insurance to your tour participants** - There are two ways for you to sell the cruise & tour protection insurance once you are a registered agent for one of the travel insurance companies and licensed by your state to sell travel insurance.

    1) Give each of your tour participants a pamphlet and let them decide if they want to take out the insurance or not.

    2) Include the insurance in your tour package.

    Many group travel leaders nowadays are just including the insurance in their tour packages. By including it, you cover your tour participants with comforting travel coverage in case of emergencies or travel occurrences such as:

    - Trip cancellation
    - Trip interruption
    - Travel delay
    - Baggage Loss
    - Baggage delay
    - Emergency medical expenses
    - Car rental damages
    - Travel accident

    This insurance, along with the E & O insurance you have for your travel club and the insurance of your tour operator, should cover any and all liabilities that may come your way.

    As the radio commentator Paul Harvey would say, *"Now here's the rest of the story!"* - The rest of the story for you is: *You also make a good commission by selling travel insurance!* So, by including the insurance in your tour package, you will protect yourself and your travel club from any major liability action, protect your tour participants from any out-of-pocket expenses should there be an emergency, and make money at the same time. Such a deal!

> **Note**: *For those of you developing a senior travel clientele, most of the travel insurance companies have a pre-existing medical condition exclusion waiver. When in effect, this allows anyone with a pre-existing medical condition to take the trip and not have to worry that they are not covered by medical insurance in case of an emergency. Be sure to ask for details about this great policy.*

Internet website

If you are getting into the group travel business in a serious way and for the long haul, you should consider using the Internet as a one of your main sales tools. By establishing a website for your travel club, the market potential you can reach is phenomenal. On top of it, a website is relatively inexpensive to set-up and manage. If working with computers is in your area of expertise, I strongly recommend that you pursue this course. *It will help considerably to advance your travel club.*

To help you with ideas and to better understand how websites function, get on the Internet and look over the various travel company websites (travel agencies, group travel leaders, tour operators, cruise agencies, etc.). Many travel industry people are already utilizing the Internet to their great benefit, which again, is something I am sure will benefit you also.

A fine example of a well produced group travel leader website is **www.sunandbreezes.com**. Dick and Carmen Ingersol decided to get into the group travel business after reading my book. Once motivated, they "jumped" in with both feet and started Sun and Breezes Travel Club. Dick did a great job putting their Sun and Breezes website together. For a shot of inspiration, check out this website!

Note: Also, there is another website, www.infohub.com, on the Internet that you should look over. As a group travel leader you will find it helpful (idea-wise) and interesting.

Passports & Visas

Passports - If you do not have a passport yet, now is the time to get one. First of all, you will need a passport to travel around the world, and secondly, you should have a passport because it proves you are an American citizen. *You have to be an American citizen to get a U.S. passport.* A passport is the ultimate form of identification (from any country).

You can get passport applications from most local post office branches. The current fee for a U.S. passport is $60.00 for adults and is good for ten years. You should allow six to eight weeks for delivery when using normal service. If you urgently need a passport, you can have the process expedited by paying a $30.00 rush fee. Once your application is completed, you can return it to the post office and they will process it for you. You will also need to have a current photo to go with the application. Look in the yellow pages under Passport Services to find a list of businesses that take passport photos. There are also passport and visa service businesses that will do the whole passport process for you (application, photos, rush, etc.) if you want a one-stop service. As normal, you will pay a little more for this personal service.

Visas - When traveling internationally, upon occasion, you may need a visa to enter a particular country. The requirements for obtaining a visa vary widely from country to country. Some visas can be obtained by telephone (e.g., Australia) while for others you will need to send your passport to that particular country's embassy in the U.S. (e.g., Vietnam). Regarding your tours, the travel supplier you select will handle getting the visas for your groups.

Travel club get-togethers

During the first travel club meetings, you will want to

concentrate on promoting and selling the tours you have planned. The initial tour information get-togethers can be revved-up by having someone from the travel company (whoever's handling the tour for you) attend the meeting. These travel professionals (a travel agent or tour rep) can help generate momentum for your tours just by their presence. Since they are very knowledgeable about the tours you have planned, they can answer most of the questions that the group will have, which takes some of the pressure off of you and gives you more freedom to spend time with the attendees. This is also a good time to use some of the give-a-ways that the tour operator has provided.

As the group grows in numbers (and it will), consider having some special gatherings to keep the interest going, such as a:

- **Passport party** - If you are promoting an international tour, many of the tour participants will not have a passport, so this is a good opportunity to get everyone together to fill out the applications, make sure all of the necessary information is correct, answer questions, etc. Besides keeping the excitement of the upcoming tour on a roll, having a passport party also accomplishes another thing for you; When you leave to go on the tour, you will know that your group participants passports are in order!

- **Final travel document party** - Approximately two to three weeks prior to the tour's departure, you will receive the travel documents for your group from your tour operator. The travel document packet will usually include:

  - Airline tickets /cruise line tickets

  - Day-by-day itinerary

  - Travel contact information (address, telephone and fax numbers of hotels and/or cruise ship, local tour operator, etc.)

- Information sheets on the included sightseeing tours, restaurants, special dinners, etc.

- Baggage tags

After you have received the travel documents, you will need to go through each packet to make sure each one has everything necessary, and to double-check the spelling of all names. Once the packets are in order, you may want to personalize the packets by adding your own information sheets (or duplicating some of the tour operators information on your travel club's stationery). After the packets are checked and double-checked, it's time to pass them out.

Instead of just dropping them in the mail, have a travel document party and personally pass them out to your tour members. This will give you an opportunity to answer any questions they may have (and there will always be questions) about what's inside the document packet and a chance to double-check once again that everything is included and all information is correct. It is also a good time to have a final question and answer session regarding the tour departure schedule, how the tour program will work, etc.

If any tour participants miss the travel document party, mail their documents by priority mail and then follow-up with a telephone call or meeting, to go over what they missed at the party.

- **After the tour party / Photos, Pfood & Pfun** - After you return from your *fantastic* tour, it is always a good gesture (and great marketing move) to have a post-tour party. This should actually be more of a party than a meeting, where everyone can be together once again to share stories of the tour and show-off their best photographs. This is a great way to thank these people for their support while building a stronger camaraderie among your members. Of course, there is nothing wrong with talking about how great the next trip is going to be!

Travel Documents

Whoever you use to handle your tour will send you the documentation for your group in a nice, attractive packet. These packets come in various sizes and shapes, and also in a variety of different materials. They can be of a heavy textured paper, plastic, synthetic leather, or canvas. The documents are usually packaged ready for you to hand out to your group. Some tour companies will even try to personalize the packets for you to a certain extent by over-printing your travel club's name on the travel folder and information inside. If you have a tour operator that does this, that's great and you're set to go! If your travel club's name is not on the tour operator's documentation, you may want to repackage it with your own travel packet. The main items to replace are the travel document folder and the suppliers luggage tags.

Having your own travel document folders and luggage tags can help you in several ways:

- They give your travel club recognition.

- They personalize your tour package.

- They help your travel suppliers' baggage handlers to instantly recognize your groups luggage at airports, train stations and piers.

- They help bellmen to deliver and pick up bags more effectively upon arrival and departures at hotels.

While re-packaging is not necessary by any means, it will help build your travel club's name and image. Also, if you start booking your tours direct, without the assistance of a professional tour supplier, you will need to put together your own travel documentation packets for your tour group participants. Following is the name of one of the major travel document suppliers. Call them and request a sample packet to see if this is something you may want to do.

> PFC Products, Inc.
> 46641 Erb Drive
> Macomb, MI 48042-5312
>
> Tel: (800) 344-1343
> Fax: (810) 949-0813

Traveling international – It's less expensive than you think!

In my many dealings with group travel leaders around the U.S., one of the *major mistakes* I see made is to discount the possibility of taking their groups on an international tour. The #1 and #2 reasons of most group travel leaders who do not travel internationally, are usually:

#1. It's too expensive!

#2. My group members aren't interested in going to foreign countries.

Let me address these two objections:

Objection #1 - "It's too expensive." Most of the group travel leaders who make this statement have not seriously investigated an international trip for their group. Anybody who truly wants to travel internationally can certainly do so *and* at a reasonable cost on top of it. Go back to the beginning of this chapter and re-read *Travel Destinations 5 Year Cycle*. That should put anyone who wants to travel the world at a bargain price, on the right track.

Objection #2 - "My group members aren't interested in going to foreign countries." I believe that a majority of people, if they had a choice, would love to travel internationally, as long as they are presented with a quality tour at a reasonable cost. Anyone slightly interested in history *has to realize* the significant difference between 200 years of history and 2,000 years of history! Let me see...Rome, Georgia or Rome, Italy...which one would I choose? Now, nothing against Rome, Georgia, but personally, I'm off to eat some pasta fagiole at a little outdoor tratoria (café) on the Via Veneto!

The main point is: If a group travel leader wants their groups to travel internationally, a multitude of options are there for consideration. All it takes is a little investigation, a few phone calls, a few faxes, and a wonderful international tour can be created for the group! Don't get me wrong, I'm not against seeing the U.S.A. (as I mentioned earlier in the book), but a good group travel leader should present all of the travel options, both domestic and international, to the group members. Motorcoach tours are a great way to see *the world*, not just the United States. They can just as easily be to Brussels, Belgium as Branson, Missouri. Speaking of motorcoach tours...

Day trips and overnight Motorcoach tours

Day trips and short overnight motorcoach trips of a week or less are a huge business in the U.S.A. Every group travel leader needs to consider incorporating some of these short excursions into their over-all travel program for a couple of reasons:

1. These trips are a great momentum builder for your travel club. Since the time away from home is short and the price is reasonable, more people will be able to take advantage of these short trips. Not everyone will be able to take the longer tours, international tours or cruise vacations, but many will be able to take advantage of the short trips.

2. The more frequently you get your members together, the faster and tighter your travel club will grow.

Personally, I have had only minimum experience in this area of the travel business. This is why, in Chapter Eleven, I mentioned what I consider to be a good book on organizing motorcoach tours. In case you missed that part in Chapter Eleven, the book is *Managing Group Tours* by Anita L. Fielder. The book costs $14.95 (plus shipping) and is available through Group Tour Magazine. To order a copy call 1-800-767-3489.

There is a great motorcoach organization called the International Motor Coach Group, Inc. (IMG). The IMG has a very informative booklet (over 70 pages) listing the motorcoach companies that belong to this organization, as well as advice about how to select and work with motorcoach companies, tourism boards, associate travel partners, etc. Many of these companies are not listed in the reference section of my book. For a free copy of the IMG Travel Directory, contact:

International Motor Coach Group, Inc.
5520 Hempstead Way, Suite B
Springfield, VA   22151

Tel: (888) 447-3466
Fax: (703) 642-5201
E-mail: imgi@bellatlantic.net
Website: www.imgcoach.com

Your own personal Cruise Newsletter

For those of you taking my advice and jumping into the cruise business with both feet, there is a great cruise newsletter that can be personalized for your travel club. This is a very classy piece of newsprint that will get your travel club instant attention. The tabloid size, full color newsletter is called Cruise Observer. It is a high quality marketing tool that has the potential to accelerate your cruise business and enhance your travel club's image at the same time! For a free sample of Cruise Observer, contact:

Cruise Observer
28 Kenilworth Road
Asheville, NC 28803

Tel: (828) 275-0086
Fax: (770) 234-5937
E-mail: info@cruiseobserver.com
Website: www.cruiseobserver.com

Commissions & mark-up

There are two ways you will make money by organizing group travel:

1. You can be paid a commission.

2. You can work with a net price (no commission), and you will mark-up the net price with the amount of profit you want to make.

When you book a tour that is commissionable, it's a simple transaction between you and your travel provider. The commission is yours and you can put in the bank! However, when you are working with a travel provider on a net rate, the amount of money you want to make (your mark-up) is your decision.

Sometimes, after you have negotiated a great deal for a particular tour and are working with net rates, there is a temptation to mark-up the tour a bit on the heavy side. Keep in mind, as group travel leaders, we have nothing tangible to sell. What keeps people coming back to us is not just a product they want (people can buy a similar tour from any of our competitors), but rather our ability to give better service than the next group travel leader and keep our tours *operating at a competitive price*. As I have stated throughout the book, the travel business is a great business with wonderful benefits for both the group travel leader and their tour participants. People travel with you because they like you and you offer great tour packages at competitive prices. Since you are always going to be a likeable person (I'm sure of this), the real key to keep this successful formula rolling along is to keep offering great tours at competitive prices. So, when it comes to marking-up your net rates, to say it simply...don't be greedy. You don't need to be the cheapest deal in town, but you do need to keep your tours in the "good deal" range.

One way to gauge how to price your tours is to compare them with similar tours offered in the Sunday travel section of your local newspaper. If your tour can match or under-cut the "super deal" tour in the paper, you are in line with your pricing. If yours are considerably higher, you need to re-work your pricing, if possible. If you are at a minimum profit and can't lower your prices, then get a few more quotes to see if another operator can lower the cost. Also, you do not necessarily need to be the "cheapest deal in town" to have a good following. Once your reputation grows as an outstanding group travel leader, many people just want to travel with you and the price of the tour becomes secondary to them.

So here is the bottom-line on this subject: *Always price your tours with a reasonable amount of profit.* What is a reasonable profit? That will vary from group travel leader to group travel leader and what they need to operate their travel club. If one group leader is operating as a home based business and another has their travel club operation based in a suite of offices in a corporate park, the differences in needed profit could be considerable. If you are working out of your home, a fifteen percent mark-up should be sufficient to run your operation and add some money to your coffers. If you are renting office space, leasing equipment, etc., you will probably need to work on a fifteen to twenty percent mark-up.

Also, you must consider the free trips that you will be taking as part of your compensation. Admittedly, you can't eat those first class seats, but after all, you are traveling around the world in style "for a song." That's why you are in the travel business, to travel free and not have to spend your hard-earned cash. By keeping your mark-up reasonable, your tour participants will increase, thus allowing you to travel more frequently, visit more exciting places, and meet more interesting people than you could ever imagine.

A traveler's peace is found in a home away from home.

Sara Hale

CHAPTER 13

Committing Group Travel Leader Suicide

How to commit it and how to prevent it

This chapter has been written mainly for people just entering the group travel business. For those of you who have been in the business for a while, I can summarize this for you in one sentence and you will probably get the full meaning of what new people need to understand. You can skip this chapter if you understand the full impact of the sentence: *"Don't be a freeloader!"* To those of you who are new to the business, the following is a little humorous and a little sarcastic, but very serious in its message. Please read this chapter with this thought in mind.

New group travel leaders beware! After a few years in the group travel business, there is an infectious disease that can creep into the minds and bodies of seemingly normal group travel leaders. No one knows how or why this happens, but it does, and it seems to affect just certain types of individuals. Fortunately, it is not contagious, nor is it fatal to one's health.

This unfortunate disease can be prevented by understanding some basic principles in the care and maintenance of a group travel leader. I am, of course, speaking of the dreaded *BS Syndrome*. The *BS Syndrome* is defined as:

A malady of the mouth where bold statements and promises are made by a group travel leader who has no intention or ability to fulfill them.

What makes the travel business such a wonderful business is the spirit of cooperation among the different travel and hospitality providers in the travel industry. Everyone has a mutual respect and admiration for each other's chosen profession and they all work together to promote their common cause – travel and tourism. Because of this mutual respect, most travel providers are very generous with their particular travel industry product to the people who bring them business. The airlines, cruise lines, hotels, DMC's, tour operators, car rental agencies, etc., all offer their various services and hospitality in some fashion to their partners in travel. What they offer may be free, or it may be at a discount. Whatever they do is in the *honest* spirit of "I'll help you and you help me."

Consequently, travel agents, meeting planners, group travel leaders, and corporate executives receive wonderful travel benefits throughout the year from these good people. In turn, all the group travel people need to do is send them business when they can. Services and hospitality are usually provided in three ways:

1. There is a standing open invitation from providers to travel industry personnel inviting them to experience their services (airlines, cruise lines, etc.), and products (hotels, resorts, etc). This is a travel industry courtesy.

2. There is a personal invitation by a provider to a group travel planner to experience their services or products. This is called a Familiarization Tour or Educational Tour (See Chapter 14).

3. There is a request by a group travel planner *to be provided* these services or products for free, or at a deep discount, for the purpose of qualifying the services or products for a future group movement or conference meeting (See Chapter 14).

I mention this because the *BS Syndrome* seems to be most prevalent in the group travel planners of point #3. Once contracted, the *BS Syndrome* creates a flaw in some of these group travel leaders (mainly in their character). Because they are flawed, these group travel leaders, technically known in scientific circles as a T3Cat (Type 3 Category) are very susceptible to the final stages of *BS Syndrome*, which causes their once happy world as a group travel leader to come to a grinding halt. These group travel leaders are then categorized as a FGRT (Failed Group Travel Leader). This is truly a sad situation. A majority of group travel leaders are good, happy, healthy, business people, and it's terrible to see a good one start to deteriorate, much less watch their demise. Why does this happen? Research shows us it all started in the early 1970's.

The Great BS Syndrome Plague of the 1970's

It was the best of times, *and it was the best of times...* talk about the "good ol' days!" Throughout the 1970's and early part of the 1980's, anyone who could produce groups was put on a very high pedestal by the tour and travel suppliers. Travel agents, conference and meeting planners, executives of major corporations, and group travel planners...all were courted by the vendors hoping to get a piece of the group action.

If you fell into the group producer category, the world (literally) was yours. We came, we saw, we ate, and we drank...*and it was all free!* We traveled the world as guests of our generous travel partners. In turn, for their generosity and hospitality, all we had to do is bring a group or two back to some of the beautiful and exotic destinations we visited, and many of us did. So, if you actually had a group travel business, this was no problem. If you presented yourself as a group travel specialist, and didn't actually produce any business, that was a problem, but not in the beginning.

In the early days, even though you were a non-group person, you were still invited to join in. Why? Because the group travel partners *actually believed what you told them* (I'm not making this up), namely that you had several groups you would be happy to send their way.

This is how the *BS Syndrome* was first discovered. It seems after a decade of group travel specialists (without any groups) traveling the world at our travel partners' expense, the presence of many of these "flawed" group travel planners was discovered. One day, somebody noticed that the group travel leader/ travel supplier relationship was a little one sided (actually it was a travel supplier that first noticed this). The "cat was out of the bag!" Like so many of the modern day diseases after their initial discovery, all of a sudden everyone has it! This was exactly the case of the *BS Syndrome*. So began what was to be come known as "the Dark Days" (cir. 1985–1995). Although the Plague has subsided considerably, you still hear occasionally about individual FGTL cases. A cure for the *BS Syndrome* has been discovered, and now, this dreaded disease can be totally prevented. The sad part is, there are still some group travel leaders who will not take precautions to prevent the infection. If you feel you are about to be infected with the *BS Syndrome,* take the cure and "nip it in the bud!"

The cure: When you travel, bring a group with you occasionally.

How to commit group travel leader suicide

Take advantage of your travel industry partners generosity and hospitality:

- By accepting their Fam Trip or Educational Tour invitations to experience their services on the pretense that you are a qualified group travel leader with substantial group business. And by giving your hosts the impression that you will reciprocate their generous hospitality by sending them busloads of customers, *and then don't* (most likely can't).

- By requesting a Site Inspection of a particular destination, resort, or cruise line, on the pretense that you are doing this on behalf of a client who is very interested in bringing a large incentive group or conference to their particular product, *and then don't.*

To put it in a nut shell: *Don't pretend to be a "Big Time" group travel planner when you're not, and promise to deliver groups when you can't.* This is Group Travel Leader Suicide.

How to prevent committing group travel leader suicide

As a group travel leader, do not pretend that you represent more business than you actually do. Be patient, take your time and build a solid business based on exceptional service and quality tours. In a few years, you actually *will have* a lot of business to place with your travel partners, and will have thus, avoided the *BS Syndrome* infection and, ultimately, Group Travel Leader Suicide.

Group Travel Leader Suicide – The consequence

Can you say "Persona non grata?" If you can't, you had better learn, because you will be hearing it a lot!

If you abuse the system (take advantage of a travel supplier's hospitality by promising them a group you don't have), your name and reputation will certainly precede you wherever you want to do business. If you think the world is getting smaller, wait until you see

Chapter 13   **239**

how small the travel industry world is…everybody knows everybody! Think long and hard about misrepresenting yourself to your tour and travel partners.

CHAPTER 14

Living the Good Life

If things were any better, I'd need a twin!

Ahhh…the good life, I remember it well. *Of course I still remember...I'm still living it!* We hear a lot about "living the good life," but what exactly defines "the good life" anyway? It will obviously mean many different things to different people. To me, "living the good life" means having the freedom to travel the world… *in style!* Much of this chapter is about my travel experiences, and the life style I lead. I guarantee you this is not an ego trip on my part and believe me, whatever I have done, you can do too. All it takes is time, a desire to travel, and a commitment to make it happen.

I realized at a fairly early age that I had a passion for travel. I wanted to see the world, but I wanted to see it *my way*, not Uncle Sam's way (whose offer to me, while appreciated, was not exactly what I had in mind). So how to travel and cruise my way around the world in first class fashion was my challenge.

There were two possible options to for me to consider:

Option #1: **A career in sales and marketing** – This was certainly a viable option. At the time, I had several offers to go to work (WORK!) for some major corporations. I could have taken one of the jobs, put in my fifty to sixty (plus) hours a week (for thirty years), eventually climb up the corporate ladder until I had an office with a window, and finally arrive at the crowning moment of every corporate executive's dream. *No*, not being made a vice president...*but finally getting six weeks of vacation a year!* Then reality set in...six weeks? Six weeks? What I want is six months! So I proceeded to option #2.

Option #2: **Get into the travel business** - I did.

I figured it this way:

- Why work for a big salary when you are going to spend a big part of it on travel anyway?

- Why pay for travel when you can travel free (or close to free)?

- Why limit yourself to only a few weeks of vacation a year when you can have the whole year?

- Why travel economy class when you can travel in business class or first class?

- *Why go as a tourist when you can go as an invited guest?*

Made sense to me! Basically I traded making a good corporate salary for an opportunity to travel the world, and it was a great decision. After a short while in the travel business, I found the secret to getting my boss to let me go anywhere in the world I wanted to go, whenever I wanted to go. The secret is this: *Get a group of people to go with you wherever you go.* Asking for time off from my boss to take a trip to some exciting destination went like this:

Me: "Say Boss, I want to go to Hong Kong and Singapore

next month for a couple of weeks…and I have forty people who want to go with me." Boss: "Bring me back one of those little paper umbrellas that they put in the drinks over there and don't forget to write!"

I've over-simplified it a little bit, but basically that's how it would work. Also remember, since this was part of my job, I wasn't using any of my vacation time, I wasn't spending any of my money, *I was* getting paid to take the trip, and my boss was happy to let me go! Now that's a job!

This is how I started to make my way around the world. I would pick a place *I had always wanted to go*, put a tour package together, and then got a group of people to join me! Sound familiar? It's Chapter Six all over again!

Back to talking about "the good life." For people like me, and since you bought this book, people like you, the meaning of "the good life" is traveling to exciting destinations, being wined and dined by people you know and like, being courted for our ability to bring business to our hosts, and being touted by our hosts for actually doing it. I suppose the simple definition for "the good life" would be: *Good times, good food, and good friends.*

Familiarization Tours, Educational Tours & Site Inspections

In the travel industry, there are three options you can take to get around the world for free (or at a nominal cost). They are:

1. Organize your own tours and then escort them (your travel club).

2. Participate in a familiarization tour (fam trip) or educational tour.

3. Arrange a site inspection

Chapter 14   **243**

These three travel options listed above are your entre into living "the good life." Let's examine each option:

1. **Organize your own tours**: Since this is the subject of the book from Chapter One, I assume you have a grasp of what you need to get started and established in the group travel business. If you do not totally understand this, go back and re-read it again because the information is there!

2. **Familiarization tour or educational tour**: First of all, a familiarization tour and an educational tour are exactly the same thing. The reason for the two different terms is that familiarization tours got sort of a bad reputation in the 1980's (because of the *BS Syndrome* plague, as explained in Chapter Thirteen). So, several of the airlines and many of the travel industry professionals started calling them "educational" tours because it really defined the purpose. The bottom line is that they are one and the same and the common term used in the industry is "fam trip."

   You will use the fam trip for gaining knowledge, experience, and making connections.

   Here again, is the definition of a fam trip:

   A trip organized for group travel leaders (travel club representative, travel agent, corporate executive, meeting planner, etc.) by a travel provider or providers (airlines, cruise lines, hotels, tourism bureaus, etc.) for the purpose of marketing their services or products.

   During my first fam trip I was treated very specially...*and I liked it.* From then on, I wanted to be treated like that a lot, so I took a fam trip every time the opportunity arose! Because of the many fam trips I took in the early days of my travel career, my knowledge of the world and the travel business grew by leaps and bounds. This will happen to you also; each trip you take will have you wanting to go back for more. The more you travel, the faster you will gain the essential knowledge that it takes to make you a success in the travel business.

In the travel industry today, there is a much better under-standing of how and what each travel entity expects from each other on a fam trip. Now, there is a lot less "blue sky" and more serious business being taken care of. Part of the reason for this "get serious" attitude is that very few fam trips are totally free today. Most of the fam trips nowadays will cost you something, although not much. The price that the organizers charge is usually a very deep discount from a normal rate and it is a tremendous deal for the travel planner.

To the organizer, the fam trip is a marketing tool and is not meant to be a money maker. Even though they charge a nominal fee, the amount you pay will barely cover their expenses of wining and dining you. They are betting that if they give you the "razzle dazzle," you will come back to them in the near future with a group. If the fam trip is to a destination in which you are interested (hopefully it's to one of your "dream destinations!"), you probably *will* return.

The good news is that because you are (more or less) "paying your way," the fam organizers understand that you may be using this trip for educational purposes and not just looking for a destination for your next group. With this understanding, the pressure to "do business now" is off of both of you, and everyone can relax and have a good time! If you liked the destination and had a great time yourself, it's your duty to bring a group back to see this!

3. **Site Inspections**: Site inspections are similar to fam trips but are more serious in nature. Serious means that you are traveling to a certain destination for a specific purpose: to check out the

hotels, restaurants, and sightseeing options for your group with intentions of eventually returning. Once again, a site inspection is:

A request by a group travel planner to be provided services or products for free, or at a deep discount, for the purpose of qualifying the services or products for a future group movement or conference meeting.

Note: Do not start arranging site inspections until you can guarantee a minimum number of participants to take to this destination. If you say you are going to have a group of forty, you had better show up with a group of forty (and hopefully more). If you don't live up to your commitment, your reputation can suffer, because surprisingly, the travel industry is a small world.

By taking cruises and fam trips, you are getting a taste of "the good life." When you start doing site inspections, *you have arrived!* Let me give you an example of one of the site inspections I did this year:

I had not been to Portugal, which is a fantastic country, for many years and I wanted to go back. Because of my solid group business, I knew that I could guarantee a minimum group of eighty pax. I laid out my travel plan of where I wanted to go and what I wanted to see and do (Chapter Six). I called my DMC in Portugal and told him I had a group of eighty pax minimum and I wanted to set up a site inspection. I faxed him the details of the itinerary I had laid out for the site inspection, subject to his suggestions. He went to work getting me hotel accommodations and setting up the sightseeing itinerary. I went to work on my airline tickets. I contacted the sales and marketing department of one of my favorite airlines and told them I was setting-up a site inspection to Portugal for a group of eighty and needed a ticket to get over there. The deal they gave me was 75% off of the economy airfare with an upgrade to business class.

Besides this, when the group goes, I will get another ticket, also upgradable to business class, for free (a TC).

My DMC came back to me with a dynamite itinerary that included three nights in Lisbon and three nights in the Algarve (the Portuguese Riviera) in deluxe hotels. It included sightseeing of castles, palaces, quaint fishing villages, wineries, and Moorish fortresses. I got my ticket, flew to Lisbon (great business class service on this airline), was met at the airport by my DMC and a driver, and spent a week with my DMC being chauffeured all over Portugal in a dark blue Mercedes limousine. Not bad duty!

Obviously, I came back very excited from the site inspection and "chomping at the bit" to get a group over there. As of now, I have one group for 2000 and two groups for 2001!

Portugal was only one of the six site inspections I did in 1999. Besides Portugal, I did site inspections to Australia, Thailand, Vancouver, British Columbia, Quebec, Canada, and Reno, Nevada. Wait, there's more! Besides doing the six site inspections, my wife and I had groups to Holland and Belgium, England, Norfolk, VA, San Francisco, CA, and two Caribbean cruises (I must go on at least two cruises a year or I'll die). Not a bad year I'd say!

Here is the way to proceed on the road to "the good life": Until you get a constant average following of 40 pax or more, take advantage of the fam trips that will be available to you (this also includes cruises). Depending on how aggressive you are, it may take you a couple of years to build to this average. But once you can honestly say that every time you leave town, you have at least a group of forty, then you will be acknowledged as a credible group travel leader and will have earned the respect and trust of your travel partners.

Once you are ready to do a site inspection, this is how you

should proceed and negotiate:

1. Pick a tour operator or DMC.

2. As per your travel plan (Chapter Six), let them know the potential group size and other detailed information regarding your site inspection, including approximate date the group would travel (this is usually one to two years away).

3. The tour operator or DMC will come back to you with a minimum cost for the site inspection trip.

4. You will pay this cost to the tour operator or DMC prior to your arrival, with this stipulation: *The money you pay for the site inspection will be deducted from the final group billing when the group materializes with at least the projected minimum number of participants.*

When it's all said and done, you will have taken two trips to one of your "dream destinations." The cost to you: 25% of a roundtrip economy airfare! That is the major PLUS to site inspections: You get to go to these destinations twice! Once by yourself or with a spouse or friend, and again when you go back with the group!

When you reach the point of doing site inspections, you're reputation is growing, your traveling in style, you're working with some great people, and you're having fun escorting your groups. Good things are starting to happen!

If you follow the advice given in this book, set reasonable goals for yourself, and stay focused on what you really want out of the travel business, good things will continue to happen to you. As they say, "time goes by fast when you're having fun" and this is a fun business. Before you know it, you will truly be on your way to "living the good life!"

I wish I could sit down with each and every one of you and talk to you personally about all of the great opportunities the travel industry has to offer. Unfortunately that is impossible, but I do hope our paths will cross somewhere along the way and we will have a chance to meet.

Being in the travel business will never make you rich beyond your wildest dreams, but it can *enrich your life in many ways* beyond your wildest dreams.

I wish each and every one of you great success in your group travel leader endeavor. I hope that you travel to *all of your "dream destinations"* and that your many successes exceed your highest expectations!

Oh yes, there's one more thing...*never* drink Champagne that's been bottled with a plastic cork. *Here's to "the Good Life!"*

May your heart be light
and your journey carefree.

REFERENCE SECTION INDEX

REFERENCE SECTION INDEX 251

REFERENCE SECTION OVERVIEW 252

GROUP LEADER ORGANIZATIONS 253

GROUP LEADER PUBLICATIONS 259

AIRLINES 265

CAR RENTAL AGENCIES 276

CRUISE LINE COMPANIES 279

DESTINATION MANAGEMENT COMPANIES (DMC) 286

HOTEL CHAINS & REPRESENTATIVES 293

MOTORCOACH COMPANIES 302

RAILROAD COMPANIES 318

TOUR OPERATORS 321

TOURISM OFFICES – INTERNATIONAL 352

TOURISM OFFICES – UNITED STATES 366

TRAVEL ASSOCIATIONS & ORGANIZATIONS 376

TRAVEL GLOSSARY 382

TRAVEL & TOUR RELATED WEBSITES 391

INDEX 393

BOOK ORDER INFORMATION 400

REFERENCE SECTION OVERVIEW

The listings in this section will give you direct access to many of the established, progressive, group travel leader organizations in which you should consider becoming a member.

The fastest way to get registered with these professional organizations is by telephoning or faxing for membership information. Some will even register you over the telephone, which will get you into the group travel leader system immediately. For your convenience, at the top of each page in a bold outlined box, is the organization's name, telephone and fax numbers. Call or fax immediately for information on the ones you want to join.

Regarding the Travel Reference Section, the utmost care has been taken to provide you with as accurate information as possible. The travel industry is ever changing and because of this, there will invariably be some changes. If this occurs, I suggest that you call your local telephone directory service for a new number. Most of these travel providers are alive and well, *somewhere*. America today is on the move, literally, and this probably includes many of the references listed in this book. This book contains information only up to the printing date and therefore is subject to change.

Please feel free to contact me with corrections should you find any. Thank you!

ETC Publishing, Inc.
2254 Emerald Drive
Castle Rock, CO 80104-2703

Tel: 720-733-2003
Fax: 720-733-2046
E-mail: etcpublish@qwest.net

BankTravel

Tel: (330) 332-3841

Fax: (330) 337-1118

BankTravel is the nation's premier membership organization for the Directors of financial institutions senior and travel programs and clubs. Membership is open to all Bank Senior Program Directors nationwide.

BankTravel operates an annual conference that focuses on education, travel, trends, and networking. The BankTravel conference is held in January/February of each year and attracts over 750 Bank Club Directors and travel industry members to this three day conference.

Bank travel members represent the most upscale sector of the mature group travel market with travelers who are deposited clients of the member bank.

Bank Club Directors or Travel industry members should call (330) 332-3841 or e-mail us at glamernet@aol.com.

BankTravel
Box 129
Salem, Ohio 44460
Website: www.banktravel.com

Group Leaders of America (GLAMER)

Tel: (800) 628-0993

Fax: (330) 337-1118

Group Leaders of America (GLAMER) is the nations largest organization for planners of group travel. Our 20,000 members take 4.2 million people on overnight tours every year and organize day trips for 6 million travelers.

Membership in GLAMER is free to qualified group travel leaders, tour operators, travel agents, and national companies in the USA and Canada.

GLAMER operates travel shows in 80 U.S. and Canadian cities annually where the travel industry and group travel planners network and exchange travel and business ideas. GLAMER travel shows include educational seminars, a travel marketplace, and a luncheon. Major sponsors include Ramada Hotels, Southwest Airlines, National Tour Association (NTA), and Cracker Barrel Restaurants.

If you are a group travel planner, please join us free of charge by calling 800-628-0993 or visit on our web site at www.glamer.com.

Travel industry members interested in exhibiting, sponsorships, or mailing lists may contact Rose Conrad at 800-628-0993 or by e-mail at glamernet@aol.com.

GLAMER
Box 129
Salem, Ohio 44460
Website: www.glamer.com

Heritage Clubs International, Inc.

Tel: (515) 423-1600

Fax: (515) 423-0284

The Heritage Club is America's oldest and most successful club program for seniors. The Heritage Club has taught banks coast to coast how to start new senior marketing programs and how to improve their existing ones.

You need proven marketing tools to run a successful seniors marketing program. The Heritage Club program gives you these tools during a two-day training seminar and in the exclusive Heritage Club Manual.

As part of the Heritage Club's National Peer Group, you'll be networking with the best and brightest in the seniors marketing business today. You'll be offered the opportunity to participate in annual peer group meetings with other member banks. And, through the travel network exchange, you'll be provided access to value-added signature tours designed exclusively for bank club seniors.

The baby boomer market will soon become the largest seniors market in history. *Prepare now to take advantage of it with the Heritage Club Program!*

> Heritage Clubs International, Inc.
> P.O. Box 1708
> Mason City, Iowa 50402-1708
> Website: www.heritageclubs.com

International Group Tour Association (IGTA)

Tel: (800) 767-3489

Fax: (616) 393-0085

The International Group Tour Association (IGTA) is a membership-based organization dedicated to growing the group tour industry. We pride our membership with the most qualified and active group travel leaders within the industry. IGTA provides regional trade shows throughout the year. Our program offers educational seminars, familization (FAM) trips, a regional travel marketplace, and a luncheon with superb door prizes. If you are a group travel leader, please join us free of charge by calling (800) 767-3489 or visit our website at www.grouptour.com.

We look forward to seeing you at one of the following marketplace trade shows:

- Eastern Regional
- Midwest Regional
- Western Regional

If you are interested in exhibiting at any of our regional travel shows please conact us at (800) 767-3489.

International Group Tour Association (IGTA)
2465 112th Avenue
Holland, MI 49424
Website: www.group tour.com

National Association of Senior Travel Planners (NASTP)

Tel: (800) 543-9736

Fax: (781) 749-4099

Since 1984, the NASTP has been a leader in the advancement and proliferation of East Coast senior travel planners. The NASTP takes great pride in the quality of services and benefits they offer their members. To name a few:

- **Senior Travel Days Trade Shows** – Held several times annually at various East Coast locations.

- **Tips on Trips Newsletter** – A bi-monthly publication filled with information and group travel specials.

- **Senior Group Travel Network** – A matchmaking and net working service providing group travel leaders with reliable information regarding day trips, overnight trips, destinations, attraction information and more.

- **Exclusive Travel Discounts and Fam Trips** – This great service notifies you of available discounts on airlines, cruises, bus trips, hotel/motel accommodations for your group, and available FAM trips for yourself.

If you are a senior travel planner, please consider joining NASTP and it's membership of successful senior travel planners.

NASTP / P.O. Box 212
Hingham, MA 02043

Outside Sales Support Network (OSSN)

Tel: (561) 743-1900

Fax: (561) 575-4371

OSSN is the International Association for outside sales travel agents, independent contractors, (including group travel leaders) and their "agency partners." A *few of the many benefits* of OSSN are:

- Local chapter meetings
- 180 hour home study course (may be purchased separately)
- Free accounting & travel management software
- List of agencies that want your business
- Fam training programs on land and sea
- Members only Web Site – over 500 pages!
- Library of books, videos, cassettes and software
- Merchant credit card service

Whether you are an established outside sales agent, group travel leader, or just getting into the travel business, you need to join OSSN. OSSN supports all your business needs as a home-based seller of travel. **Join today!**

Mention you heard about OSSN through *How to Organize Group Travel for Fun and Profit* and save $10.00 on your membership fee!

Outside Sales Support Network
1340 U.S. Highway One, Suite 102
Jupiter, Florida 33469
Website: http://www.ossn.com

BankTravel Management Magazine

Tel: (888) 253-0455

Fax: (606) 253-0499

BankTravel Management Magazine is the nations most respected publication dedicated to the development and growth of Bank Travel Clubs.

BankTravel Management is the official publication of BankTravel and is distributed to 4,000 Bank Senior Program Directors bi-monthly.

This full color publication focuses on education and travel information for directors of bank travel programs.

To receive *BankTravel Management*, please call (330) 332-384 and identify your bank and it's club name.

BankTravel Management Magazine
401 West Main Street, Suite 222
Lexington, KY 40507

Group Tour Magazines

Tel: (800) 767-3489

Fax: (616) 393-0085

Group Tour Magazine is the "Group Travel Industry's Planning and Information Resource." Much of our tremendous success with group travel planners over the years can be attributed to the five regional magazines we publish. The regional *Group Tour Magazines* are distributed nationally to over 10,000 qualified group travel planners quarterly. The five regions are:

- New England, Quebec & Atlantic Canada
- Mid-Atlantic
- Southeastern
- Great Lakes
- Western USA & Canada

Unlike any other group travel publication, our single-region format makes *Group Tour Magazine* the unquestionable favorite publication among professional group travel planners!

For more information, please call us on our toll free number, or contact us at:

Group Tour Magazine
2465 112th Avenue
Holland, MI 49424
Website: www.group tour.com

SYTA's Student & Youth Traveler

Tel: (800) 767-3489

Fax: (616) 393-0085

SYTA's Student & Youth Travel Association of North America (SYTA) is the newest edition to the Shoreline Creations, Ltd. family. The official publication, SYTA's *Student & Youth Traveler*, is the only one of its kind. Its mission is to be a resource magazine for student travel planners. The magazine will serve as an educational piece about student friendly destinations, the importance of using SYTA member tour providers and the student and youth market as a whole.

SYTA's Student & Youth Traveler is distributed to 35,000 educational institutions throughout the United States and Canada.

For futher information please contact us at (800) 767-3489 or visit our website at www.grouptour.com.

> SYTA's Student & Youth Travler
> 2465 112th Avenue
> Holland, MI 49424
> Website: www.group tour.com

The Group Travel Leader

Tel: (800) 628-0993

Fax: (606) 253-0499

The Group Travel Leader is the nations premier newspaper for the leaders of traveling senior groups.

Distributed monthly to 30,000 group travel leaders, tour operators, bus companies, and travel industry members, this full color publication is the official newspaper of Group Leaders of America (GLAMER.)

The Group Travel Leader features articles on travel destinations as well as articles of interest to planners of group travel.

Advertising is geared to the traveling group market and features nationwide coverage.

Supplements inserted into the newspaper target specific travel destinations and give you an in depth view of the area.

To receive a free subscription to *The Group Travel Leader* you must be a member of GLAMER. You may join by calling 800-628-0093 and identify yourself as a group travel planner who wishes to join. Travel industry suppliers who wish to advertise call 888-253-0455.

> The Group Travel Leader
> 401 West Main, Suite 222
> Lexington, KY 40507
> Website: www.glamer.com

Leisure Group Travel Magazine

Tel: (630) 964-1431

Fax: (630) 852-0414

Looking to start a travel club, or breath new life into your existing one? Then you should subscribe to Leisure Group Travel Magazine!

Distributed six times per year, our four color publication contains relevant destination information, pertinent editorial and dedicated columns to assist you in making your club the best it can be.

Each edition features a domestic city focus, state feature, cruise section and international travel destination. We also have regular news brief columns to keep you in touch with industry happenings plus each issue contains a reference guide on topics such as convention & visitors bureaus, theaters, casinos and historic attractions.

Leisure Group Travel Magazine has a circulation of 14,000 subscribers and is distributed complimentary to qualified group travel planners.

Leisure Group Travel Magazine
4901 Forest Avenue
Downers Grove, IL 60515
Website: www.leisuregrouptravel.com

Travel Tips

Tel: (630) 964-1431

Fax: (630) 852-0414

Travel Tips is recognized as the number one resource for travel information by our readers. Now in our 13th year, **Travel Tips** publishes six times a year and serves the interests of 11,000 group travel planners and tour organizers for the Western mature market.

Our editorial features review destinations and travel options of specific interest to groups of mature travelers. Our departments include helpful planning hints from experts, festivals and events, theatre, gaming, special offers for seniors and groups, tour operator packages and much more. We also tell you what's new with the airlines and cruise line industry and about upcoming group travel planner trade shows and meetings.

If you are planning day trips or global itineraries, you will find **Travel Tips** your best resource.

Contact us for subscription information. **Travel Tips** is distributed free to qualified travel planers.

> Travel Tips
> 4901 Forest Avenue
> Downers Grove, IL 60515
> Website: www.traveltipsmagazine.com

Aer Lingus (Ireland)
538 Broadhollow Road
Melville, NY 11747
Tel: 800-474-7424
Fax: 516-752-2043
Internet: http://www.aerlingus.ie

Aeroflot (Russia)
335 Palermo Avenue
Miami, FL 33134
Tel: 305-446-9448
Fax: 305-444-4857
Internet: http://www.aeroflot.org

Aerolineas Argentinas
6100 Blue Lagoon Drive, Suite 210
Miami,FL 33126
Tel: 800-333-0276
Fax: 305-266-1204
Internet: http://www.aeroargentinas.com

Aeromexico Airlines
13405 Northwest Fwy.
Houston, TX 77040
Tel: 800-237-6639
Groups: 800-800-9999
Fax: 713-460-3334
Internet: http://www.aeromexico.com

Air Canada
P.O. Box 14000
SAINT LAURENT, QC H4Y IH4
Tel: 800-776-3000
Fax: 800-463-5251
Internet: http://www.aircanada.com

Air China
45 E. 49th Street
New York, NY 10017

Air China - continued
Tel: 800-982-8802
Fax: 212-935-7951
Email: airchinany@aol.com

Air France
142 W. 57th Street, Floor 18
New York, NY 10019
Tel: 800-237-2747
Fax: 212-830-4431
Internet: http://www.airfrance.com

Air-India
570 Lexington Avenue, Floor 15
New York, NY 10022
Tel: 800-223-7776
Fax: 212-407-1412
Internet: http://www.airindia.com

Air Jamaica Ltd./Air Jamaica Express
9525 Queens Blvd., Suite 7
Flushing, NY 11374
Tel: 800-523-5585
Fax: 718-830-0622
Internet: http://www.airjamaica.com

Air New Zealand
1960 E. Grand Avenue, Suite 900
El Segundo, CA 90245
Tel: 800-262-1234
Fax: 310-648-7017
Internet: http://www.airnz.com

Alaska Airlines
19300 Pacific Hwy. S.
P. O. Box 68900
Seattle, WA 98168-0900
Tel: 800-252-7522
Fax: 206-433-3379
Internet: http://www.alaska-air.com

Alitalia (Italy)
666 5th Avenue
New York, NY 10103
Tel: 800-223-5730
Fax: 212-903-3331
Internet: http://www.alitalia.it

All Nippon Airways (Japan)
1251 6th Avenue, 8th Floor
New York, NY 10020
Tel: 800-235-9262
Fax: 212-840-3704
Internet: http://www.ana.com.gp

Aloha Airlines Inc.
371 Aokea Pl.
Honolulu, HI 96819
Tel: 800-367-5250
Fax: 808-836-0303
Internet: http://www.alohaair.com

America West Airlines
4000 E. Sky Harbor Blvd.
Sky Harbor International Airport
Phoenix, AZ 85034
Tel: 800-235-9292
Groups: 800-634-2312
Fax: 602-693-5546

American Airlines
4333 Amon Carter Blvd.
DFW Airport Mail Drop 5397
Fort Worth, TX 76155
Tel: 800-433-7300
Fax: 817-967-2841
Internet: http://www.aa.com

Ansett Australia Airlines
1960 E. Grand Avenue, Suite 900
El Segundo, CA 90245

Ansett Australia Airlines - continued

Tel: 888-426-7388
Fax: 310-648-7017
Internet: http://www.ansett.com

Austrian Airlines

1720 Whitestone Expy.
Whitestone, NY 11357
Tel: 800-843-0002
Fax: 718-670-8619
Internet: http://www.austrianair.com

Avianca Airlines

720 5th Avenue, Floor 5
New York, NY 10019
Tel: 800-284-2622
Fax: 212-399-0811

British Airways

7520 Astoria Blvd.
Flushing, NY 11370
Tel: 800-247-9297
Fax: 718-397-4364
Internet: http://www.british-airways.com

BWIA International (British West Indies Airways)

330 Biscayne Blvd.
Miami, FL 33132
Tel: 800-538-2942
Fax: 868-669-1520
Email: bwipr@wow.net

Canadian Airlines International Inc.

700 2nd Street SW, Suite 2800
Calgary, AB Canada T2P 2W2
Tel: 403-294-2000
Groups: 800-533-0117
Fax: 403-294-2066
Internet: http://www.cdnair.ca

Cathay Pacific Airways (Hong Kong/Asia/Orient)
300 Continental Blvd., Suite 500
El Segundo, CA 90245
Tel: 800-848-5008
Fax: 310-615-0042
Internet: http://www.cathay-usa.com

Cayman Airways
6100 Blue Lagoon Drive, Suite 130
Miami, FL 33126
Tel: 800-422-9626
Fax: 305-267-2925
Internet: http://www.caymanairways.com

China Airlines
6053 W. Century Blvd., Suite 800
Los Angeles, CA 90045
Tel: 800-227-5118
Fax: 310-641-0972
Internet: http://www.china-airlines.com

Continental Airlines Inc.
1600 Smith Street
Houston, TX 77002
Tel: 800-525-0280
Fax: 713-834-2660
Internet: http://www.flycontinental.com

CSA-Czech Airlines
1350 Avenue Of The Americas, 6th Floor
New York, NY 10019
Tel: 800-223-2365
Fax: 212-765-6588

Delta Air Lines
P. O. Box 20706
Atlanta, GA 30320
Tel: 800-221-1212
Fax: 404-767-8499
Internet: http://www.delta-air.com

Egyptair
720 5th Avenue
New York, NY 10019
Tel: 800-334-6787

El Al Israel Airlines
120 W. 45th Street, Floor 18
New York, NY 10036
Tel: 800-223-6700
Fax: 212-852-0641
Internet: http://www.elal.com

Finnair
228 East 45th Street
New York, NY 10017
Tel: 800-950-5000
Fax: 212-499-9040
Internet: http://www.finnair.fi

Frontier Airlines
12015 East 46th Avenue, Suite 200
Denver, CO 80239
Tel: 800-432-1359
Fax: 303-371-7007
Internet: http://www.frontierairlines.com

Grupo TACA International Airlines
5885 NW 18th Ave., Bldg. 71614
Miami, FL 33142
Mailing Address: P.O. Box 591410
Miami, FL 33159-1410
Tel: 800-251-1351
Fax: 503-339-9627
Internet: http://www.grupotaca.com

Hawaiian Airlines
3375 Koapaka Street, Suite G350
Honolulu, HI 96819
Mailing Address: P.O. Box 30008
Honolulu, HI 96820-0008

Hawaiian Airlines - continued

Tel: 800-367-5320
Fax: 808-835-3690
Internet: http://www.hawaiianair.com

Iberia Airlines of Spain

6100 Blue Lagoon Drive, Suite 200
Miami, FL 33126
Tel: 800-772-4642
Fax: 305-267-9401
Internet: http://www.iberia.com

Icelandair

5950 Symphony Woods Road, Suite 410
Columbia, MD 21044
Tel: 800-223-5500
Fax: 410-715-3547
Internet: http://www.icelandair.com

Japan Airlines

655 5th Avenue
New York, NY 10022
Tel: 800-525-3663
Internet: http://www.japanair.com

Korean Air

6101 W. Imperial Highway
Los Angeles, CA 90045
Tel: 800-438-5000
Fax: 310-417-3051
Internet: http://www.koreanair.com

Lan-Chile Airlines

9700 S. Dixie Highway
Penthouse
Miami, FL 33156
Tel: 800-735-5526
Fax: 305-670-9553
Internet: http://www.lanchile.com

Lot-Polish Airlines
500 5th Avenue, Suite 408
New York, NY 10110
Tel: 800-223-0593
Fax: 212-302-0191
Internet: http://www.lot.com

Lufthansa German Airlines
1640 Hempstead Turnpike
East Meadow, NY 11554
Tel: 800-645-3880
Fax: 516-296-9412
Internet: http://www.lufthansa-usa.com

Malaysia Airlines
100 N. Sepulvea Blvd., Suite 400
El Segundo, CA 90245
Tel: 800-552-9264
Fax: 310-535-9088
Internet: http://www.malaysia-airlines.com

Martinair (Caribbean)
5550 Glades Road, Suite 600
Boca Raton, FL 33431
Tel: 800-627-8462
Fax: 561-391-2188
Internet: http://www.martinairusa.com

Mexicana Airlines
9841 Airport Blvd.
Los Angeles, CA 90045
Tel: 800-691-8824
TA: 800-531-7923
Internet: http://www.mexicana.com

Northwest Airlines
5101 Northwest Drive
Saint Paul, MN 55111
Tel: 800-225-2525
Fax: 612-726-3306
Internet: http://www.nwa.com

Northwest/KLM Royal Dutch Airlines
565 Taxter Road
Elmsford, NY 10523
Tel: 800-374-7747
Fax: 914-784-2102
Internet: http://www.klm.com

Olympic Airways (Greece)
645 5th Avenue
New York, NY 1002
Tel: 800-223-1226
Fax: 212-735-0215

Philippine Airlines
447 Sutter Street
San Francisco, CA 94108
Tel: 800-435-9725
Fax: 415-433-6733

Qantas Airways
841 Apollo Street, Suite 400
El Segundo, CA 90245
Tel: 800-227-4500
Fax: 310-726-1401
Internet: http://www.qantas.com

Royal Jordanian
6 East 43rd Street
New York, NY 10017
Tel: 800-777-6732
Fax: 212-949-0485
Internet: http://www.royaljordanian.com

Sabena Belgian World Airlines
1155 Northern Blvd.
Manhasset, NY 11030
Tel: 800-950-1000
TA: 800-950-1000
Fax: 516-562-9323
Internet: http://www.sabena-usa.com

Scandinavian Airlines
9 Polito Avenue
Lyndhurst, NJ 07071
Tel: 800-221-2350
Fax: 201-896-3725
Internet: http://www.flysas.com

Singapore Airlines
5670 Wilshire Blvd., Suite 1800
Los Angeles, CA 90036
Tel: 800-742-3333
Fax: 213-934-4482
Internet: http://www.singaporeair.com

South African Airways
515 E. Las Olas Blvd.
Fort Lauderdale, FL 33301
Tel: 954-769-5000
Fax: 954-769-5079
Email: saausa@baxter.net

Southwest Airlines
P. O. Box 36611
Dallas, TX 75235
Tel: 800-433-5368
Fax: 210-615-2518
Internet: http://www.southwest.com

Swiss International Air Lines
41 Pinelawn Road
Melville, NY 11747
Tel: 800-221-4750
Fax: 631-844-4559
Internet: http://www.swissair.com

Tap Air Portugal
399 Market Street
Newark, NJ 07105
Tel: 800-221-7370
Fax: 973-344-8966
Internet: http://www.tap-airportugal.pt

REFERENCE SECTION

Thai Airways International
222 N. Sepulveda Blvd., Suite 1950
El Segundo, CA 90245
Tel: 800-426-5204
Fax: 310-322-8657
Internet: http://www.thaiair.com

Trans World Airlines
515 N. 6th Street
One City Center
St. Louis, MO 63101
Tel: 800-221-2000
Fax: 314-589-3129
Email: twaweb@twa.com

Turkish Airlines
437 Madison Avenue
New York, NY 10022
Tel: 800-874-TURK
Fax: 212-339-9683
Internet: http://www.thy.com

United Airlines
P. O. Box 66100
Chicago, IL 60666
Tel: 800-241-6522
Internet: http://www.ual.com

US Airways
2345 Crystal Drive
Arlington, VA 22202
Tel: 800-428-4322
Fax: 703-418-5139
Internet: http://www.usairways.com

Virgin Atlantic Airways Ltd.
747 Belden Avenue
Norwalk, CT 06850
Tel: 800-847-4461 (group line)
Fax: 203-750--6490
Internet: http://www.fly.virgin.com

Alamo Rent A Car
P. O. Box 22776
Fort Lauderdale, FL 33335
Tel: 800-327-9633, 954-522-0000
Fax: 954-769-6437

Allstate Rent A Car
5175 Rent Car Road
Las Vegas, NV 89119
Tel: 800-634-6186, 702-736-6147
Fax: 702-736-4555

Avis Rent-A-Car Systems Inc.
900 Old Country Road
Garden City, NY 11530
Tel: 800-331-1212, 516-222-3000
Fax: 516-222-4796
Internet: http://www.avis.com

Budget Rent A Car Corp.
4225 Naperville Road
Lisle, IL 60532
Tel: 800-527-0700, 630-955-7419
Fax: 630-955-7799
Internet: http://www.budgetrentacar.com

Budget Rent A Car Hawaii
550 Paiea Street, Suite 236
Honolulu, HI 96819
Tel: 808-838-2221, 808-537-3600
Fax: 808-838-2381

Budget Rent A Car of Canada Ltd.
185 The West Mall, Suite 900
Etobicoke, ON Canada M9C 5L
Tel: 800-268-8900, 416-622-3366
Fax: 416-622-5555
Internet: http://www.budgetrentacar.com

Dollar Rent A Car
5330 E. 31st Street
Tulsa, OK 74135
Tel: 800-800-4000, 918-669-3000
Fax: 918-669-3007
Internet: http://www.dollar.com

Dollar Rent A Car of Florida
2002 N. Lois Avenue
Tampa, FL 33607
Tel: 800-800-4000, 813-877-5507
Fax: 813-673-3470
Internet: http://www.dollarcar.com

Dollar Rent A Car of Hawaii
1600 Kapiolani Blvd., Suite 825
Honolulu, HI 96814
Tel: 800-367-7006, 808-944-1544

Enterprise Rent A Car Co.
600 Corporate Park Drive
St. Louis, MO 63105
Tel: 800-325-8007, 314-781-8232
Fax: 314-781-4613

The Hertz Corporation
225 Brae Blvd.
Park Ridge, NJ 07656
Tel: 800-654-3131, 201-307-2000
Internet: http://www.hertz.com

The Kemwel Group
106 Calvert Street
Harrison, NY 10528
Tel: 800-678-0678, 914-835-5555
Fax: 914-835-5449
Internet: http://www.kemwel.com

National Car Rental System Inc.
7700 France Avenue S.
Minneapolis, MN 55435
Tel: 800-227-7368, 612-830-2121
Fax: 612-830-2558
Internet: http://www.nationalcar.com

Payless Car Rental System Inc.
2350 34th Street N.
St. Petersburg, FL 33713
Tel: 800-729-5377, 818-321-6352
Fax: 813-323-3729
Internet: http://www.paylesscar.com

Renault Euro Drive
650 1st Avenue
New York, NY 10016
Tel: 800-221-1052
Fax: 212-725-5379

Thrifty Car Rental
P. O. Box 35250
Tulsa, OK 74153-0250
Tel: 800-367-2277, 918-665-3930
Fax: 918-669-2253
Internet: http://www.thrifty.com

Alaska Sightseeing/Cruise West
2401 4th Avenue, Suite 700
Seattle, WA 98121
Tel: 800-426-7702, 206-441-8687
Fax: 206-441-4757
Internet: http://www.cruisewest.com

Amazon Tours & Cruises
8700 W. Flagler Street, Suite 190
Portsmouth, RI 02871
Tel: 800-423-2791, 305-227-2266
Fax: 305-227-1880
Internet: http://www.amazontours.com

American Cruise Lines
One Marine Park
Haddam, CT 06438
Tel: 800-814-6880, 860-345-3311
Fax: 860-345-4265
Internet: http://www.americancruiselines.com

American Hawaii Cruises
Robin Street Wharf
1380 Port of New Orleans Place
New Orleans, LA 70130-1890
Tel: 800-765-7000, 504-586-0631
Fax: 504-585-0630
Internet: http://www.cruisehawaii.com

Carnival Cruise Lines
3655 NW 87th Avenue
Miami, FL 33178
Tel: 800-327-9501, 305-599-2600
Fax: 305-471-4700
Internet: http://www.carnival.com

Celebrity Cruises Inc.
1050 Caribbean Way
Miami, FL 33132

Celebrity Cruises Inc. - continued
Tel: 800-437-4111, 305-530-6000
Fax: 305-384-7354
Internet: http://www.celebrity-cruises.com

Commodore Cruise Line
4000 Hollywood Blvd., Suite 385 South Tower
Hollywood, FL 33021
Tel: 800-237-5361, 954-967-2100
Fax: 954-967-2147
Internet: http://www.commodorecruise.com

Costa Cruise Lines
World Trade Center Building
80 SW 8th Street
Miami, FL 33130-3097
Tel: 800-462-6782, 305-358-7325
Fax: 305-375-0676
Internet: http://www.costacruises.com

Crystal Cruises Inc.
2049 Century Park East, Suite 1400
Los Angeles, CA 90067
Tel: 800-446-6620, 310-785-9300
Fax: 310-785-3891
Internet: http://www.crystalcruises.com

Cunard Line Ltd.
6100 Blue Lagoon Drive, Suite 400
Miami, FL 33126
Tel: 800-223-0764, 305-463-3000
Fax: 305-463-3010
Internet: http://www.cunardline.com

Danube Cruises
80 Richmond Street West, Suite 1502
Toronto, ON Canada M5H 2A4
Tel: 800-268-4155, 416-362-5000
Fax: 416-362-8024

Delta Queen Steamboat Co.
1380 Port Of New Orleans Pl.
New Orleans, LA 70130
Tel: 800-543-1949, 504-486-0631
Fax: 504-585-0630
Internet: http://www.deltaqueen.com

Disney Cruise Vacations
210 Celebration Place, Suite 400
Celebration, FL 34747 - 4600
Tel: 800-511-1333, 407-566-3500
Fax: 407-566-3510
Internet: http://www.disneycruise.com

EuroCruises Inc.
33 Little West 12th Street, Suite 106
New York, NY 10014-1314
Tel: 800-688-3876, 212-691-2099
Fax: 212-366-4747
Internet: http://www.eurocruises.com

French Country Waterways
P. O. Box 2195
Duxbury, MA 02331
Tel: 800-222-1236, 781-934-2454
Fax: 781-934-9048

Holland America Line
300 Elliott Avenue West
Seattle, WA 98119
Tel: 800-426-0327, 206-281-3535
Fax: 206-281-7110/283-2687
Internet: http://www.hollandamerica.com

KD River Cruises of Europe
2500 Westchester Avenue, Suite 113
Purchase, NY 10577
Tel: 800-346-6525, 914-696-3600
Fax: 914-696-0833
Internet: http://www.rivercruise.com

Mediterranean Shipping Cruises
420 Fifth Avenue, 8th Floor
New York, NY 10018 - 2702
Tel: 212-764-4800
Fax: 212-764-8592
Internet: http://www.msccruisesusa.com

Norwegian Coastal Voyage, Inc.
405 Park Avenue
New York, NY 10022
Tel: 212-319-1300
Fax: 212-319-1390
Internet: http://www.coastalvoyage.com

Norwegian Cruise Line
7665 Corporate Center Drive
Miami, FL 33126 – 1201
Tel: 800-327-7030, 305-436-4000
Fax: 305-436-4120
Internet: http://www.ncl.com

Orient Lines, Inc.
1510 SE 17th Street, Suite 400
Fort Lauderdale, FL 33316
Tel: 800-582-0175, 954-527-6660
Fax: 954-527-6657
Internet: http://www.orientlines.com

Peter Deilmann Cruises
1800 Diagonal Road, Suite 170
Alexandria, VA 22314
Tel: 800-348-8287, 703-549-1741
Fax: 703-549-7924
Internet: http://www.deilmann-cruises.com

Princess Cruises
10100 Santa Monica Blvd., Suite 1800
Los Angeles, CA 90067
Tel: 800-421-0522, 310-553-1770
Fax: 310-277-6175
Internet: http://www.princesscruises.com

Radisson Seven Seas Cruises
600 Corporate Drive, Suite 410
Fort Lauderdale, FL 33334
Tel: 800-477-7500, 954-776-6123
Fax: 954-772-3763
Internet: http://www.rssc.com

Regal Cruises
300 Regal Cruises Way
Palmetto, FL 34221
Tel: 941-721-7300
Fax: 941-723-0900
Internet: http://www.regalcruises.com

Renaissance Cruises Inc.
P.O. Box 350307
Fort Lauderdale, FL 33335-0307
Tel: 800-525-5350, 954-463-0982
Fax: 954-463-8125
Internet: http://www.renaissancecruises.com

Royal Caribbean Cruise Line
1050 Caribbean Way
Miami, FL 33132
Tel: 800-327-6700, 305-539-6000
Royal Caribbean Cruise Line - continued
Fax: 305-374-7354
Internet: http://www.royalcaribbean.com

Royal Hawaiian Cruises
P. O. Box 29816
Honolulu, HI 96820
Tel: 800-852-4183, 808-924-1515
Fax: 808-924-0485
Email: rhcms@aloha.net

Royal Olympic Cruises
805 3rd Avenue
New York, NY 10022

Royal Olympic Cruises - continued

Tel: 800-872-6400, 212-688-7555
Fax: 212-688-2304
Internet: http://www.royalolympiccruises.com

Sea Escape Cruises Limited

3020 NW 33rd Avenue
Fort Lauderdale, FL 33311
Tel: 800-327-7400, 954-453-3333
Fax: 954-453-6555
Internet: http://www.seaescapecruise.com

Seabourn Cruise Line

6100 Blue Lagoon Drive
Miami, FL 33126
Tel: 415-391-7444
Fax: 415-391-8518
Internet: http://www.seabourn.com

Silversea Cruises

110 E. Broward Blvd.
Fort Lauderdale, FL 33301
Tel: 800-722-9955. 954-522-4477
Fax: 954-522-4499
Internet: http://www.silverseacruises.com

Tall Ship Adventures, Inc.

1389 S. Havana Street
Aurora, CO 80012
Tel: 800-662-0090, 303-755-7983
Fax: 303-755-9007
Internet: http://www.tallshipadventures.com

Windjammer Barefoot Cruises Ltd.

P.O. Box 190120
Miami, FL 33119-0120
Tel: 800-327-2601, 305-672-6453
Fax: 305-674-1219
Internet: http://www.windjammer.com

Windstar Cruises Ltd.
300 Elliott Avenue West
Seattle, WA 98119
Tel: 800-258-7245, 206-281-3535
Fax: 206-281-0627
Internet: http://www.windstarcruises.com

World Explorer Cruises
555 Montgomery Street, Suite 1400
San Francisco, CA 94111
Tel: 800-854-3835, 415-393-1565
Fax: 415-391-1145
Internet: http://www.wecruise.com

Zeus Cruises
209 W. 40th Street, Floor 3
New York, NY 10018
Tel: 800-447-5667, 212-221-0006
Fax: 212-764-7912
Internet: http://www.zeustours.com

AUSTRIA / BELGIUM

**ADM - Blaguss Austria Destination Management –
Euromic Austria**
Schleifmühlgasse 1/14
1040 Vienna, Austria
Tel: +43-1- 585 39 39-0
Fax: +43-1- 585 39 39 39
E-mail: austria@euromic.com

Brussels International Travel Service – Euromic Belgium
Rue Arthur Diderich 30
1060 Brussels, Belgium
Tel: +32-2-543 10 10
Fax: +32-2-538 12 94
E-mail: belgium@euromic.com

CYPRUS

Drakos Travel Ltd – Euromic Cyprus
Drakos Beach House
20 Georgiou A'Street,
P.O. Box 258 Limassol, Cyprus
Tel: +357-5-32 48 00
Fax: +357-5-32 49 21
E-mail: cyprus@euromic.com

DENMARK

First United A/S – Euromic Denmark
H.C. Andersens Boulevard 38
1553 Copenhagen V, Denmark
Tel: +45-33 11 75 75
Fax: +45-33 11 79 79
E-mail: denmark@euromic.com

EGYPT

Emeco Travel – Euromic Egypt
 2, Talaat Harb Street
P.O. Box 1294

EGYPT

Emeco Travel – Euromic Egypt...continued
Cairo 11 111, Egypt
Tel: +20-2-574 93 60
Fax: +20-2-574 42 12
E-mail: egypt@euromic.com

FINLAND

Next Travel Ltd – Euromic Finland
Tunturikatu 15B
00100 Helsinki, Finland
Tel: +358-9-43 42 590
Fax: +358-9-43 42 5920
E-mail: finland@euromic.com

FRANCE

Holt Travel Welcome Service – Euromic France
12, rue du Helder
75 009 Paris, France
Tel: +33-1-45 23 08 14
Fax: +33-1-42 47 19 89
E-mail: france@euromic.com

VIP Riviera Service – Euromic France/Riviera
205, Promenade des Anglais
06203 Nice, France
Tel: +33-4-93 44 22 33
Fax: +33-4-93 37 49 93
E-mail: riviera@euormic.com

GREAT BRITAIN

Sterling Travel Associates – Euromic Great Britain
41 Queen Street, Maidenhead
Berkshire, SL6 1ND, Great Britain
Tel: +44-628 783682
Fax: +44-628 773415
E-mail: uk@euromic.com

GREECE

Cruise Club Holidays
85 Vouliagmenis Ave.
Athens 166 75, Greece
Tel: 011-30-1-960-4250
Fax: 011-30-1-964-4943
E-mail: sales@cruiseclub.gr

Horizon Travel – Euromic Greece
50 Praxitelous Street
176 74 Kallithea, Athens, Greece
Tel: +30-1 94 70 700
Fax: +30-1 94 29 600
E-mail: greece@euromic.com

HUNGARY

Blaguss-Volanbusz / ADM Hungary – Euromic Hungary
Erzsébet tér, Autobuszpalyaudvar
1051 Budapest, Hungary
Tel:+36-1-317 77 77
Fax: +36-1-266 14 90
E-mail: hungary@euromic.com

ICELAND

Atlantik – Euromic Iceland
Grandagardi 14
101 Reykjavik, Iceland
Tel: +354-511-2010
Fax: +354-511-2015
E-mail: iceland@euromic.com

ISRAEL

Amiel Destination Management – Euromic Israël
5 Yoni Netanyahu Street
60 376 Or Yehuda, Israël
Tel: +972-3-538 84 44
Fax: +972-3-533 60 69
E-mail: israel@euromic.com

ITALY

Fourth Dimension Tours – Euromic Italy
Via Quintino Sella 20
00 187 Rome, Italy
Tel: +39-06-474 10 46
Fax: +39-06-474 10 40
E-mail: italy@euromic.com

JORDAN

International Traders – Euromic Jordan
P.O. Box 408
Amman 11 118, Jordan
Tel: +962-6-560 70 14
Fax: +962-6-566 99 05
E-mail: jordan@euromic.com

MALTA

Traveltrade Incentives – Euromic Malta
Paolo Court, G. Cali Street
Ta' Xbiex MSD 14, Malta
Tel: +356-33 35 10/1
Fax: +356-31 44 05
E-mail: malta@euromic.com

NETHERLANDS

I.T.B. Amsterdam
Olympisch Stadion 14
1076 DE Amsterdam. Netherlands
Tel: 011-31-20-3051358
Fax: 011-31-20-6758651
E-mail: jaap@itbams.nl

Delta Travel Service B.V. – Euromic Netherlands
Hobbemastraat 16
1071 ZB Amsterdam, Netherlands
Tel: +31-20-575 57 55
Fax: +31-20-675 05 99
E-mail: netherlands@euromic.com

POLAND

Mazurkas Travel - DMC Poland – Euromic Poland
Ul. Dluga 8/14
00 238 Warsaw, Poland
Tel: +48-22 831 60 92
Fax: +48-22 831 59 50
E-mail: poland@euromic.com

PORTUGAL

Especialtur
Av. Santos Dumont, 63 – 8. B
1050-202 Lisboa, Portugal
Tel: 011-351-1-793- 7420
Fax: 011-351-1-793-7419
E-mail: portugal@especialtur.mailpac.pt

Intervisa Travel Service – Euromic Portugal
Av. Republica 85 - 1°-Dto
1050 Lisbon, Portugal
Tel: +351-217 990 460
Fax: +351-217 955 151
E-mail: portugal@euromic.com

Intervisa Travel Service – Euromic Madeira (Portugal)
Av. Arriaga, 30-3
9000 Funchal, Madeira, Portugal
Tel: +351-291 225 641
Fax: +351-291 225 020
E-mail: madeira@euromic.com

Intervisa Travel Service – Euromic Algarve (Portugal)
Praca D. Filipa de Lencastre, 8-1
4000 Porto, Portugal
Tel: +351-222 079 212 / 222 079 213
Fax: +351-222 059 552
E-mail: oporto@euromic.com

SPAIN

Lib/Go
69 Spring Street
Ramsey, NJ 07446
Tel: (800) 899-9800
Fax: (201) 934-3821
E-mail: crespoe@libgotravel.com

Latitud 4 Destination Management – Euromic Spain
Plaza Urquinaona 6-15 Planta
Torre Urquinaona
08 010 Barcelona, Spain
Tel: +34-93 304 32 14
Fax: +34-93 304 32 44
E-mail: spain@euromic.com

SWEDEN

Grand European North – Euromic Sweden
P.O. Box 1383
111 93 Stockholm, Sweden
Tel: +46-8-58 76 13 00
Fax: +46-8-58 76 13 13
E-mail: sweden@euromic.com

SWITZERLAND

SM Travel SA – Euromic Switzerland - Geneva
1-3 Rue de Chantepoulet
1201 Geneva, Switzerland
Tel: +41-22 731 65 20
Fax: +41-22 738 72 46
E-mail: switzerland@euromic.com

SM Travel SA – Euromic Switzerland - Zurich
Ringstrasse 14
8057 Zurich, Switzerland
Tel: +1-311 35 00
Fax: +1-312-31 29
E-mail: zurich@euromic.com

SWITZERLAND - continued

Montreux Tourist Organization & Regional DMC
P.O. Box 1557
Burnsville, MN 55337
Tel: 800-590-4686
Fax: 952-892-1639

TURKEY

VIP Tourism DMC – Euromic Turkey
Cumhuriyet Caddesi 271
80 230 Harbiye-Istanbul, Turkey
Tel: +90-212 241 65 14
Fax: +90-212 230 66 76
E-mail: turkey@euromic.com

Adam's Mark Hotels & Resorts
11330 Olive Blvd.
St. Louis, MO   63141
Tel: 800-444-2326, 314-567-9000
Fax: 314-567-0602
Internet: http://www.travelweb.com

Alexander Associates
2607 Nostrand Avenue
Brooklyn, NY   11210
Tel: 800-221-6509, 718-253-9400
Fax: 718-258-5623

American/Wolfe International
1890 Palmer Avenue, Suite 202
Larchmont, NY   10538
Tel: 800-223-6595, 914-833-3303
Fax: 914-833-3308

ANA Hotels International
725 S. Figueroa Street, Suite 970
Los Angeles, CA   90017
Tel: 213-955-7677
Fax: 213-955-7678
Internet: http://www.ananet.or.jp

Aristos International
319 S. 11th Street
McAllen, TX   78501
Tel: 800-527-4786, 956-631-2000
Fax: 956-631-8416
Internet: http:/www.aristoshotels.com

Aston Hotels & Resorts
2155 Kalahaua Avenue, Suite 500
Honolulu, HI 96815
Tel: 800-922-7866, 808-931-140
Fax: 808-922-8785
Internet: http://www.aston-hotels.com

Best Western International
P.O. Box 10203
Phoenix, AZ   85064-0203
Tel: 800-528-1234, 601-957-4200
Fax: 602-957-5643
Internet: http://www.bestwestern.com

Canadian Pacific Hotels
1 University Avenue,Suite 1400
Toronto, ON Canada M5J 2P1
Tel: 800-441-1414, 416-367-7111
Fax: 416-863-6097

Castle Resorts & Hotels
1150 South King Street
Honolulu, HI 96814
Tel: 800-367-5004, 808-591-2235
Fax: 800-477-2329, 808-596-0158
Internet: http://www.castle-group.com

Choice Hotels International
10750 Columbia Pike
Silver Spring, MD   20901
Tel: 800-424-6423, 301-592-5125
Fax: 301-592-6227
Internet: http://www.choicehotels.com

Conrad International
9336 Civic Center Drive
Beverly Hills, CA   90210
Tel: 800-445-8667, 310-278-4321
Fax: 310-859-2513
Internet: http://www.hilton.com

Destination Resorts Hawaii
3750 Wailea Alanui Drive
Kihei, HI   96753
Tel: 800-367-5246, 808-879-1595
Fax: 808-874-3554

Destination Resorts Hawaii - continued
Internet: http://www.destinationresortshi.com

Doubletree Hotels Corporation
755 Crossover Lane
Memphis, TN   38117
Tel: 800-222-8733, 901-374-5000
Internet: http://www.doubletreehotels.com

Four Seasons Hotels & Resorts
1165 Leslie Street
Toronto, ON   Canada M3C 2K8
Tel: 800-545-4000, 416-449-1750
Fax: 212-697-1445

Golden Tulip Worldwide
360 Lexington Avenue, Suite 200
New York, NY   10017
Tel: 800-344-1212, 212-220-6588
Fax: 212- 220-6589

Hilton Hotels Corporation
P.O. Box 5567
Beverly Hills, CA   90209-5567
Tel: 800-445-8667, 310-278-4321
Fax: 310-859-2313
Internet: http://www.hilton.com

Hyatt Hotels Corporation
200 W. Madison Street
Chicago, IL   60606
Tel: 800-233-1234, 312-750-1234
Fax: 312-750-8579
Internet: http://www.hyatt.com

Inter-Continental Hotels & Resorts
1120 Avenue of the Americas, Floor 19
New York, NY   10036
Tel: 800-327-0200, 212-852-6400

Inter-Continental Hotels & Resorts - continued

Fax: 212-852-6470
Internet: http://www.interconti.com

ITR-International Travel & Resort, Inc.

300 East 40th Street
New York, NY   10016
Tel: 800-223-9815, 212-476-9444
Fax: 212-476-9467

Jarvinen Worldwide Hotels

3142 Wilshire Blvd, Suite 204
Los Angeles, CA   90010
Tel: 800-876-5278, 213-380-2633
Fax: 213-380-5765

Jolly Hotels

22 East 38th Street, Floor 3
New York, NY   10016
Tel: 800-221-2626, 212-213-1468
Fax: 212-212-2369

Kempinski Hotels International

420 Lexington Avenue, Room 626
New York, NY   10170
Tel: 800-426-3135, 212-697-8600
Fax: 212-697-5153
Internet: http://www.hilton.com

Krystal Hotels of Mexico

2500 Wilcrest Drive, Suite 300
Houston, TX   77042
Tel: 800-231-9860, 713-952-7791
Fax: 713-952-9941

LHW- The Leading Hotels of the World Ltd.

747 Third Avenue
New York, NY   10017

LHW- The Leading Hotels of the World Ltd. - continued
Tel: 800-223-6800, 212-838-3110
Fax: 212-758-7368
Internet: http://www.interactive.lin.com/lead

Loews Hotel
667 Madison Avenue
New York, NY   10021
Tel: 800-235-6397, 212-545-2000
Fax: 212-521-2714
Internet: http://www.loewshotels.com

Mandarin Oriental Hotel Group
509 Madison Avenue, Suite 1902
New York, NY   10022
Tel: 800-526-6566, 212-207-8880
Fax: 212-207-8886
Internet: http://www.mandarin-oriental.com

Marriott Corporation
One Marriott Drive
Washington, DC   20058
Tel: 800-228-9290, 301-380-9000
Fax: 301-380-5728
Internet: http://www.marriott.com

Meredien Hotels
888 Seventh Avenue
New York, NY   10106
Tel: 212-956-3501
Fax: 212-765-1524

Miyako Hotels
312 East 1st Street, Suite 510
Los Angeles, CA   90012
Tel: 213-488-0011
Fax: 213-621-7627

New Otani Hotels
520 Madison Avenue, Floor 24
New York, NY   10022
Tel: 800-421-8795, 212-308-7491
Fax: 212-980-1932
Internet: http://www.newotani.co.jp

Nikko Hotels International
160 Central Park South
New York, NY   10019
Tel: 800-645-5687, 212-765-4789
Fax: 212-757-2091
Internet: http://www.nikko.com

Omni Hotels
420 Decker Drive, Suite 200
Irving, TX   75062
Tel: 800-843-6664, 972-730-6664
Fax: 972-871-5667
Internet: http://www.omnihotels.com

Orient Hotel Reservations
37 Bowery, Confucius Plaza
New York, NY   10002
Tel: 800-628-1168, 212-925-3388
Fax: 212-925-6483
Internet: http://www.asiavacation.com

Outrigger Hotels & Resorts
2375 Kuhio Avenue
Honolulu, HI   96815
Tel: 800-688-7443, 808-921-6600
Fax: 808-921-6655
Internet: http://www.outrigger.com

Pan Pacific Hotels & Resorts
177 Post Street, Suite 800
San Francisco, CA   94108
Tel: 800-533-6465, 415-732-7747

Pan Pacific Hotels & Resorts - continued
Fax: 415-732-5800
Internet: http://www.panpac.com

Park Plaza International Hotels & Resorts
6263 N. Scottsdale Road, Suite 200
Scottsdale, AZ   85250
Tel: 800-670-7275, 602-951-3335
Fax: 602-951-3050
Internet: http://www.parkhtls.com

Peabody Hotel Group
5118 Park Avenue, Suite 245
Memphis, TN   38117
Tel: 800-732-2639, 901-762-5444
Fax: 901-762-546

Pointe Hilton Resorts
7600 North 16th Street, Suit 130
Phoenix, AZ 85020
Tel: 800-876-4683, 602-997-6000
Fax: 602-870-2783
Internet: http://www.hilton.com

Preferred Hotels & Resorts Worldwide
311 South Wacker Drive, Suite 1900
Chicago, IL   60606
Tel: 800-323-7500, 312-913-0400
Fax: 312-913-0444
Internet: http://www.preferredhtls.com

Promus Hotel Corporation
755 Crossover Lane
Memphis, TN   38120
Tel: 901-374-5000
Fax: 90-374-5620

Radisson Hospitality Worldwide
P.O. Box 59159

Radisson Hospitality Worldwide - continued

Minneapolis, MN   55459-8200
Tel: 800-333-3333, 612-540-5526
Fax: 612-449-3400
Internet: http://www.radisson.com

The Ritz-Carlton Hotel Co.

3414 Peachtree Road NE, Suite 300
Atlanta, GA   30326
Tel: 800-241-3333, 404-237-5500
Fax: 404-261-0119
Internet: http://www.ritzcarlton.com

Shangri La Hotels & Resorts

5777 W. Century Blvd, Suite 1105
Los Angeles, CA   90045
Tel: 800-942-5050, 310-665-2000
Fax: 310-665-2020
Internet: http://www.shangri-la.com

Sonesta International Hotels Corp.

200 Clarendon Street
Boston, MA   02116
Tel: 800-766-3782, 617-421-5400
Fax: 617-421-5402
Internet: http://www.sonesta.com

SRS Worldhotels

152 W. 57th Street, Floor 33
New York, NY   10019
Tel: 800-223-5652, 212-956-0200
Internet: http://www.srs-worldhotels.com

Starwood Hotels & Resorts Worldwide Inc.

777 Westchester Avenue
White Plains, NY   10604
Tel: 800-343-9136, 914-640-8100
Fax: 914-696-1138
Internet: http://www.starwoodlodging.com

Supranational Hotels
774 Main Street, 4th Floor
Moncton, NB   Canada   E1C 9Y3
Tel: 800-843-3311, 506-877-3060
Fax: 506-877-3160

Thistle Hotels
152 West 57th Street, Floor 33
New York, NY   10019
Tel: 800-847-4358, 212-957-1168
Fax: 212-957-1171

Utell International
810 North 94th Street
Omaha, NE   68114
Tel: 800-448-8355, 402-398-3200
Fax: 402-398-5484
Internet: http://www.hotelbook.com

Utell Resorts
360 Lexington Avenue, Fmt 2
New York, NY   10017
Tel: 800-223-6510, 212-220-6590
Fax: 212-220-8994
Internet: http://www.rezolutions.com

A Yankee Line Inc.
370 W. 1st Street
Boston, MA 02127
Tel: 800-942-8890, 617-268-8890
Fax: 617-268-6960

Abbott Tours
1704 Granby Street NE
Roanoke, VA 24012
Tel: 800-433-1111, 540-343-1133
Fax: 540-345-2052

Alaska Sightseeing/Cruise West
2401 4th Avenue, Suite 700
Seattle, WA 98121
Tel: 800-426-7702, 206-441-8687
Fax: 206-441-4757

American Charters Ltd.
1251 W. Craighead Road
Charlotte, SC 28206
Tel: 800-330-3286, 704-864-3286
Fax: 704-865-5382

American Coach Lines
P. O. Box 646
Norcross, GA 30091
Tel: 770-449-1806
Fax: 770-246-9397
Internet: http://www.amebus.com

American Sightseeing Tours Inc.
11077 NW 36th Avenue
Miami, FL 33167
Tel: 800-275-8687, 305-677-7700
Fax: 305-681-8134
Internet: http://www.sightseeing.com

Anderson Coach & Tour
1 Anderson Plaza
Greenville, PA 16125
Tel: 800-345-3435, 724-588-8310
Fax: 724-588-0257
Internet: http://www.andersoncoach.com

Arrow Line/Coach USA
P. O. Box 280807
East Hartford, CT 06128
Tel: 800-243-9560
Fax: 860-289-1535
Internet: http://www.arrowline.com

Auto Europe LLC
39 Commercial St.
Portland, ME 04101
Tel: 800-223-5555, 207-842-2000
Fax: 207-842-2222
Internet: http://www.autoeurope.com

Back Bay Coach Inc.
31 Fargo Street
P. O. Box 217
Boston, MA 02117-0217
Tel: 617-728-8686
Fax: 617-728-8699

Blue Bird Coach Lines
501 E. 19th Street
Erie, PA 16503
Tel: 800-352-0979, 814-459-5500
Fax: 814-454-7071

Blue Bird Coach Lines
1 Bluebird Sq.
Olean, NY 14760
Tel: 800-441-1111, 716-372-5500
Fax: 716-372-3200

Blue Bird Coach Lines (Rochester, NY Division)
420 Summit Point Drive
Henrietta, NY 14467
Tel: 800-278-9915, 716-334-2222
Fax: 716-334-2686

California Charter Inc.
3333 E. 69th Street
Long Beach, CA 90805
Tel: 800-642-3287, 562-634-7969
Fax: 562-634-5818

California Parlor Car Tours
1101 Van Ness Avenue
San Francisco, CA 94109
Tel: 800-227-4250, 415-474-7500
Fax: 415-673-1539
Email: reservations@calpartours.com

California Wine Tours
22455 Broadway
Sonoma, CA 95476
Tel: 800-294-6386, 707-253-1300
Fax: 707-938-4249
Internet: http://www.californiawinetours.com

Capitol Bus Lines/Capital Tours
2926 Leaphart Road
West Columbia, SC 29169
Tel: 800-968-8037, 803-767-4310
Fax: 803-767-4325
Internet: http://www.capitol-tours.com

Cardinal Coach Lines Ltd.
732-41 Avenue NE
Calgary, AB Canada T2E 3P9
Tel: 800-661-6161, 405-531-3945
Fax: 403-230-9304
Email: cardinal@cardinal-cal.com

Central West Motor Stages Inc.
P.O. Box 177649
Irving, TX 75017-7649
Tel: 800-533-1939, 972-399-1059
Fax: 972-986-7262
Internet: http://www.bus-charter.com/centralcontac.html

Chat Tours/Traveline
214 Bedford Road
Toronto, ON Canada M5R 2K9
Tel: 800-268-1180, 416-967-4333
Fax: 416-967-6147
Email: travline@netcom.ca

CIE Tours International
P. O. Box 501
Cedar Knolls, NJ 07927-0501
Tel: 800-338-3964, 973-292-3899
Fax: 973-292-0463
Internet: http:///www.cietours.com

Cityrama
45 East 34th Street, Suite 500
New York, NY 10016
Tel: 800-214-1148, 212-683-8120
Fax: 800-320-0417, 212-683-1299

Coach USA
950 McCarty Street
Houston, TX 77029
Tel: 800-344-4441, 713-671-0991
Fax: 713-671-2079
Internet: http://www.coachusa.com

Coach USA
4950 L B McLeod Road
Orlando, FL 32811
Tel: 407-999-0199
Fax: 407-999-0196

Coach USA/ Gray Line of Los Angeles
660 W. Avenue L
Lancaster, CA   93534
Tel: 800-618-7259, 805-948-8421
Fax: 805-949-9891

Coach USA Phoenix
4001 S. 34th Street
Phoenix, AZ   85040
Tel: 800-777-3484, 602-437-3484
Fax: 602-437-3515
Internet: http://www.coachusa.com

Dillon's Bus Service Inc.
P.O. Box 409
Millersville, MD 21108-0409
Tel: 800-827-3490, 410-647-2321
Fax: 410-647-8827
Internet: http://www.dillonbus.com

East Coast Transportation
14125 Beach Blvd.
Jacksonville Beach, FL 32250
Tel: 800-829-7433, 904-992-2022
Fax: 904-223-9698
Internet: http://www.ectravel.com

Eyre Bus Service & Tour & Travel Ltd.
P. O. Box 239
Glenelg, MD 21737-0239
Tel: 800-321-3973, 410-442-1330
Fax: 410-531-5517
Internet: http://www.eyre.com

Good Life Transportation Inc.
8200 Fletcher Avenue
Lincoln, NE 68507
Tel: 800-233-0404
Fax: 402-467-5714

Gray Line of Albuquerque
800 Rio Grande Blvd. NW, Suite 22
Albuquerque, NM 87104
Tel: 800-256-8991, 505-242-3880
Fax: 505-243-0692
Internet: http://www.rt66.com

Gray Line of Anaheim
2001 S. Manchester Avenue
Anaheim, CA 92802
Tel: 800-828-6699
Fax: 714-978-2921
Internet: http://www.pacificcoastgrayline.com

Gray Line of Atlantic City
P. O. Box 1619
Atlantic City, NJ 08404-1619
Tel: 800-524-1351, 609-646-7549
Fax: 609-347-0246

Gray Line of Black Hills
P. O. Box 1106
Rapid City, SD 57709-106
Tel: 800-456-4461
Fax: 605-341-5152
Internet: http://www.blackhillsgrayline.com

Gray Line of Charleston
P.O. Box 219
Charleston, SC   29402
Tel: 800-423-0444, 843-722-4444
Fax: 843-722-0173

Gray Line of Chicago
27 E. Monroe Street, Suite 515
Chicago, IL 60603
Tel: 800-621-4153, 843-722-4444
Fax: 312-251-3108

Gray Line of Denver
P. O. Box 17646
Denver, CO 80217
Tel: 800-348-6877, 303-289-2841
Fax: 303-286-7052

Gray Line of Indianapolis
9075 N. Meridian Street
Indianapolis, IN 46260
Tel: 800-447-4526
Fax: 317-573-0410

Gray Line of Jackson Hole
1680 W. Martin Lane
Jackson, WY 83001
Tel: 800-443-6133, 304-733-4325
Fax: 307-733-2689
Email: alltrans@sisna.com

Gray Line of Las Vegas
4020 E. Lone Mountain Road
North Las Vegas, NV 89031
Tel: 800-634-6579
Fax: 702-632-2135

Gray Line of Minneapolis/St. Paul
21160 Holyoke Avenue
Lakeville, MN 55044
Tel: 800-530-9686, 612-469-5020
Fax: 612-469-1020

Gray Line of Mobile
P. O. Box 1711
Mobile, AL 36633
Tel: 800-338-5597, 334-432-2229
Fax: 334-432-5296
Internet: http://www.graylineofmobile.com

Gray Line of Montreal
1140 Wellington Street
Montreal, QC Canada H3C 1V8
Tel: 514-934-1222, 514-937-0288
Fax: 514-398-9946
Internet: http://www.graylinemontreal.com

Gray Line of New Orleans
2 Canal Street, Suite 1300
New Orleans, LA 70130
Tel: 800-535-7786, 504-569-1401
Fax: 504-587-1401

Gray Line of New York
1740 Broadway
New York, NY 10019
Tel: 800-669-0051, 212-397-2620
Fax: 212-247-6956

Gray Line of Niagara Falls
3466 Niagara Falls Blvd.
North Tonawanda, NY 14120
Tel: 800-695-1603
Fax: 716-692-4398

Gray Line or Orlando/Coach USA
9712 Recycle Center Rd.
Orlando, FL   32824
Tel: 800-781-8999, 407-826-9999
Fax: 407-826-5880

Gray Line of Ottawa/Ottawa Tours
1335 Carling Avenue, Suite 101
Ottawa, ON Canada K1Z 8N8
Tel: 800-297-6422
Fax: 613-725-9240

Gray Line of Philadelphia
3101 Orthodox Street

Gray Line of Philadelphia - continued
Philadelphia, PA 19137
Tel: 800-577-7745
Fax: 215-744-1196
Internet: http://www.grayline.com

Gray Line of Pittsburgh
110 Lenzner Court
Sewickley, PA 15143
Tel: 800-342-2349, 412-741-2720
Fax: 412-741-7754
Internet: http://www.motorcoach.com/lenzner

Gray Line of Portland/Evergreen
P. O. Box 17306
Portland, OR 97217-0306
Tel: 800-422-7042, 503-285-9545
Fax: 503-285-5202

Gray Line of Quebec
P. O. Box 246
Quebec City, QC Canada G1R 4P8
Tel: 418-653-9722,
Fax: 418-653-9834

Gray Line of St. Louis
312 W. Morris Street
Caseyville, IL 62232
Tel: 800-542-4287, 314-241-1224
Fax: 314-638-3737

Gray Line of Salt Lake City
553 W. 100 S.
Salt Lake City, UT 84101
Tel: 800-309-2352
Fax: 801-521-7086
Internet: http://www.coachusa.com

Gray Line of San Antonio
217 Alamo Plaza
San Antonio, TX 78205
Tel: 800-472-9546, 210-226-1706
Fax: 210-226-2515

Gray Line of San Diego
1775 Hancock Street, Suite 130
San Diego, CA 92110
Tel: 800-331-5077, 619-491-0011
Fax: 619-491-0884
Internet: http://www.graylinesandiego.com

Gray Line of San Francisco
350 8th Street
San Francisco, CA 94103
Tel: 800-826-0202
Fax: 415-554-0349
Internet: http://www.graylinesanfrancisco.com

Gray Line of Savannah
215 W. Boundary Street
Savannah, GA 31401
Tel: 800-426-2318, 912-236-9604
Fax: 912-233-3959

Gray Line of Seattle
4500 W. Marginal Way SW
Seattle, WA 98106
Tel: 800-544-0739206-624-5077
Fax: 206-626-5209
Internet: http://www.graylineofseattle.com

Gray Line of Tucson
425 W. Paseo Redondo
Tucson, AZ 85701
Tel: 800-276-1528, 520-622-8811
Fax: 520-622-8838

Gray Line of Vancouver
255 E. 1st Avenue
Vancouver, BC Canada V5T 1A7
Tel: 800-667-0882
Fax: 604-879-1105
Internet: http://www.glyvr.vom

Gray Line of Victoria Ltd.
700 Douglas Street
Victoria, BC Canada V8W 2B3
Tel: 800-663-8390
Fax: 250-388-9461
Internet: http://www.victoriatours.com

Gray Line of Yellowstone
P. O. Box 1168
Red Lodge, MT 59068-1168
Tel: 800-733-2304, 406-638-8271
Fax: 406-446-2828

Greene Coach Charters & Tours
126 Bohannon Avenue
Greeneville, TN 37745
Tel: 800-338-5469, 423-638-8271
Fax: 423-638-5541
Internet: http://www.greenecoach.com

Greyhound Lines Inc. Tour & Travel Div.
P. O. Box 660606
Dallas, TX 75266-0606
Tel: 800-327-8019, 972-789-7067
Fax: 972-789-7029
Internet: http://www.greyhound.com

Hammond Transportation Ltd.
P. O. Box 569
Bracebridge, ON Canada P1L 1T8
Tel: 705-645-5431
Fax: 705-645-3629

Hotard Vacations
2838 Touro Street
New Orleans, LA 70122
Tel: 800-553-4895, 504-944-0253
Fax: 504-944-8650
Internet: http://www.hotard.com

Hubers Bus Service Inc.
103 Weels Avenue
Glen Burnie, MD 21061
Tel: 410-766-1108
Fax: 410-760-9576

James River Bus Lines & Story Land Tours
603 N. Allen Avenue
Richmond, VA 23220
Tel: 804-342-7300
Fax: 804-342-7373
Internet: http://www.jrbl.com

Jefferson Lines
2100 E. 26th Street
Minneapolis, MN 55404
Tel: 800-767-5333, 612-359-3401
Fax: 612-332-5532
Email: charters@jeffersonlines.com

Keeshin Charter Service Inc.
615 W. 41st Street
Chicago, IL 60609
Tel: 800-843-3247, 312-254-6400
Fax: 773-247-7682
Internet: http://www.keeshin.com

Kerrville Bus and Tour Company/Coach USA
800 Spring Street, Suite 100
Shreveport, LA 71101
Tel: 800-442-8705, 318-227-2882
Fax: 318-227-2486

Kerrville Bus Greyline Coach USA
710 Davis Street
Grand Prairie, TX 75050
Tel: 800-256-4723, 972-263-0294
Fax: 972-262-2761
Internet: http://www.kerrville-bus.com

Lakefront Lines
13315 Brookpark Road
Brookpark, OH 44142
Tel: 800-683-6338, 216-267-8810
Fax: 216-362-3797

Lakeland Bus Lines Inc.
425 E. Blackwell Street
Dover, NJ 07801
Tel: 973-366-0600
Fax: 973-366-3145
Internet: http://www.lakelandbus.com

Landmark Charter Coach Service Inc.
4405 W. Washington Center Road
Fort Wayne, IN 46818
Tel: 219-489-1059
Fax: 219-489-7818

Mears Transportation Group
324 W. Gore Street
Orlando, FL 32806
Tel: 407-839-1570
Fax: 407-422-6923
Internet: http://www.mears-net.com

Miller Transportation Inc.
7917 Old 3rd Street Road
Louisville, KY 40214
Tel: 800-544-2383, 502-368-5644
Fax: 502-368-7253
Internet: http://www.millertransportation.com

Mountaineer Coach Inc.
260 Industrial Park Road
Beaver, WV 25813
Tel: 304-255-5925
Fax: 304-255-1336

Mr. Canada's Transportation Network Inc.
160 Hargrave Street, Penthouse #1
Winnipeg, MB Canada R3C 3H3
Tel: 204-957-1513
Fax: 204-943-0476

Orange Belt Stages
P. O. Box 949
Visalia, CA 93279-0949
Tel: 800-266-7433, 209-733-4408
Fax: 209-733-0538
Internet: http://www.orangebelt.com

Ozark Pastimes Inc.
2200 E. Sunshine Street, Suite 100
Springfield, MO 65804
Tel: 417-883-0119

Pacific Coach Lines Ltd.
1150 Station Street, Suite 210
Vancouver, BC Canada V6A 4C7
Tel: 800-661-1725, 604-662-7575
Fax: 604-681-1515
Internet: http://www.pacificcoach.com

Peoria Charter Coach Company
2600 NE Adams Street
Peoria, IL 61603
Tel: 800-448-0572, 309-688-9523
Fax: 309-688-9520
Internet: http://www.peoriacharter.com

Raz Transportation and Tours
11655 SW Pacific Highway
Portland, OR 97223
Tel: 888-684-3322, 503-684-3322
Fax: 503-968-3223

Rockland Coaches Inc.
126 N. Washington Avenue
Bergenfield, NJ 07621
Tel: 201-384-2400
Fax: 201-384-2765

Rohrer Bus Service
P. O. Box 100
Duncannon, PA 17020-0100
Tel: 717-957-3811
Fax: 717-957-4884

Star Transit
3860 W. Tompkins Avenue
Las Vegas, NV 89103
Tel: 800-338-8111, 702-646-4661
Fax: 702-646-3040

Sun Valley Stages Inc.
P. O. Box 936
Twin Falls, ID 83303
Tel: 800-574-8661, 208-733-3921
Fax: 208-733-3993

Tour Carriage Inc./SignaTours
P. O. Box 1529
Black Canyon City, AZ 85324
Tel: 800-445-0628, 602-716-9700
Fax: 602-716-9799
Email: singatours@aol.com

Trailways Transportation System
1001 Connecticut Avenue NW, Suite 225

Trailways Transportation System - continued
Washington, DC 20036
Tel: 202-737-5820
Fax: 202-638-5211
Internet: http://www.trailways.org

Trentway Wagar
P. O. Box 1017
Peterborough, ON K9J 7A5
Tel: 800-461-7661, 705-748-6411

Fax: 705-748-2452
Internet: http://www.trentway.com

Turner Coaches Inc./Bee Travelers
P. O. Box 2852
Terre Haute, IN 47802-0852
Tel: 800-873-5252, 812-232-5252
Fax: 812-232-6884

Unlimited Inc./Gray Line
P. O. Box 332
Myrtle Beach, SC 29578-0332
Tel: 843-448-9483
Fax: 843-626-1513
Email: ltupromo@sccoast.net

Vermont Transit Co. Inc.
106 Main Street
Burlington, VT 05401-8420
Tel: 800-552-8737, 802-862-9671
Fax: 802-862-7812
Internet: http://www.vermonttransit.com

World Transportation Inc.
9712 Recycle Center Road
Orlando, FL 32824
Tel: 800-781-8999, 407-826-9999
Fax: 407-826-5880

Alaska Railroad
327 W. Ship Creek Avenue
P. O. Box 107500
Anchorage, AK 99510-7500
Tel: 800-544-0552, 907-265-2494
Fax: 907-265-2323
Internet: http://www.akrr.com

Amtrak National Railroad Passenger Corp.
60 Massachusetts Avenue NE
Washington, DC 20002
Tel: 800-872-7245, 202-906-3000
Fax: 202-906-3306
Internet: http://www.amtrak.com

BC Rail Passenger Service
P.O. Box 8770
North Vancouver, BC Canada V6B 4X6
Tel: 800-663-8238, 604-984-5500
Fax: 604-984-5505
Email: bc.com@bcrtass.com

DER Travel Services (Europe)
9501 W. Devon Avenue
Rosemont, IL 60018
Tel: 800-782-2424, 847-692-4141
Fax: 800-282-7474
Internet: http://www.dertravel.com

Durango & Silverton Narrow Gauge Railroad & Museum
479 Main Avenue
Durango, CO 81301
Tel: 970-247-2733
Fax: 970-259-3570
Internet: http://www.durangotrain.com

Eastern & Oriental Express
1520 Kensington Road
Hinsdale, IL 60523

Eastern & Oriental Express - continued
Tel: 800-323-7308, 630-954-2944
Fax: 630-954-3324

Grand Canyon Railway
235 N. Grand Canyon Blvd.
Williams, AZ 86046
Tel: 800-843-8724, 520-773-1976
Fax: 520-773-1610
Internet: http://www.thetrain.com

Great Rail & River Journeys of Britian & Europe
1520 Kensington Road
Oak Brook, IL 60523
Tel: 800-323-7308, 630-954-2944
Fax: 630-954-3324
Internet: http://www.abercrombie.com

Great Smoky Mountains Railway
P. O. Box 397
Dillsboro, NC 28725-0397
Tel: 800-872-4681, 704-586-8811
Fax: 704-586-8806
Internet: http://www.gsmr.com

Japan Railways Group
1 Rockefeller Plaza, Room 1622
New York, NY 10020
Tel: 212-332-8686
Fax: 212-332-8690

Orient-Express Trains & Cruises
1520 Kensington Road, Suite 212
Oak Brook, IL 60523
Tel: 800-524-2420, 630-954-2944
Fax: 630-954-3324

Rocky Mountaineer Railtours
1150 Station Street, 1st Floor

Rocky Mountaineer Railtours - continued
Vancouver, BC Canada V6A 2X7
Tel: 800-665-7245, 604-606-7200
Fax: 604-606-7201
Internet: http://www.rkymtnrail.com

The Royal Scotsman
1520 Kensington Road, Suite 212
Oak Brook, IL 60523
Tel: 800-323-7308, 630-954-2944
Fax: 630-954-3324
Internet: http://www.abercrombiekent.com

Verde Canyon Railroad
300 N. Broadway
Clarkdale, AZ 86324
Tel: 800-293-7245, 520-639-0010
Fax: 520-639-1653

White Pass and Yukon Route
P. O. Box 435
Skagway, AK 99840
Tel: 800-343-7373, 907-983-2217
Internet: http://www.whitepassrailroad.com

Abercrombie & Kent International
1520 Kensington Road, Suite 212
Oak Brook, IL 60523
Tel: 800-323-7308, 630-954-2944
Fax: 630-954-3324
Internet: http://www.abercrombiekent.com

Abreu Tours Inc.
25 W. 45th Street, Suite 1309
New York, NY 10036
Tel: 800-223-1580, 212-869-1840
Fax: 212-354-1840
Internet: http://www.abreu-tours.com

Absolute Asia
180 Varick Street, Floor 16
New York, NY 10014
Tel: 800-736-8187, 212-627-1950
Fax: 212-627-4090
Internet: http://www.absoluteasia.com

Absolute Australia
180 Varick Street
New York, NY 10014
Tel: 888-285-6094
Fax: 212-627-4090
Internet: http://www.absoluteaustralia.com

Across Continent Travel & Safaris
9100 S. Sepulveda Blvd., Suite 122
Los Angeles, CA 90045
Tel: 800-933-9756, 310-645-1659
Fax: 310-645-3426
Internet: http://www.actsafaris.com

Action Whitewater Adventures
P. O. Box 1634
Provo, UT 84603
Tel: 800-453-1482, 801-375-4111

Action Whitewater Adventures - continued
Fax: 801-375-4175
Internet: http://www.riverguide.com

Adventure Center
1311 63rd Street, Suite 200
Emeryville, CA 94608
Tel: 800-227-8747, 510-654-1879
Fax: 510-654-4200
Internet: http://www.adventure-center.com

Adventure Tours U.S.A.
10726 Plano Road
Dallas, TX 75238
Tel: 800-999-9046, 214-210-6100
Fax: 214-210-6193
Internet: http://www.atusa.com

AESU Travel
3922 Hickory Avenue
Baltimore, MD 21211
Tel: 800-638-7640, 510-366-6999
Fax: 410-366-5494
Internet: http://www.aesu.com

African Portfolio
225 E. 79th Street
New York, NY 10021
Tel: 800-700-3677, 212-737-0144
Fax: 212-737-6930
Internet: http://www.africanportfolio.com

Africa Tours Inc.
875 Avenue Of The Americas, Suite 2108
New York, NY 10001
Tel: 800-235-3692, 212-563-3686
Fax: 212-563-4459
Internet: http://www.africasafaris.com

Alaska Passages Inc.
P. O. Box 213
Petersburg, AK 99833
Tel: 907-772-3967
Fax: 907-772-3967
Internet: http://www.alaska.net/~akpassag

Alaska Sightseeing/Cruise West
2401 4th Avenue, Suite 700
Seattle, WA 98121
Tel: 800-426-7702, 206-441-8687
Fax: 206-441-4757
Internet: http://www.cruisewest.com

All Aboard America
230 S. Country Club Drive
Mesa, AZ 85210
Tel: 800-848-4728, 602-962-6502
Fax: 602-962-5727
Internet: http://www.pcslink.com/~alaboard

Allied Tours Inc.
165 W. 46th Street, Floor 10
New York, NY 10036
Tel: 212-869-5100
Fax: 212-302-6129
Internet: http://www.alliedtours.com

Ambassador Tours Inc.
717 Market Street
San Francisco, CA 94103
Tel: 800-989-9000, 415-357-9876
Fax: 415-357-9877
Internet: http://www.ambassadortours.com

American Christian Tours Inc.
201 E. South Street
Rice Lake, WI 54868
Tel: 800-367-4484, 715-234-6500

American Christian Tours Inc. - continued
Fax: 715-234-1898
Internet: http://www.acts-tours.com

American Tours & Travel Inc.
4490 35th Street
Orlando, FL 32811
Tel: 800-243-4365, 407-351-2500
Fax: 407-352-2962
Internet: http://www.bandfest.com

American Travel Abroad Inc.
4801 W. Peterson Avenue, Suite 618
Chicago, IL 60646
Tel: 800-342-5315, 773-725-9500
Fax: 773-725-8089
Internet: http://www.amta.com

American Travel Abroad Inc.
250 W. 57th Street, Suite 1120
New York, NY 10107
Tel: 800-228-0877, 212-586-5230
Fax: 212-581-7925
Internet: http://www.amta.com

AmericanTours International Inc.
6053 W. Century Blvd.
Los Angeles, CA 90045
Tel: 310-641-9953
Fax: 310-216-5807
Internet: http://www.americantours.com

Apple Vacations East
7 Campus Blvd.
Newton Square, PA 19073
Tel: 800-727-3400, 610-359-6700
Fax: 610-359-6519
Internet: http://www.applevacations.com

Apple Vacations West
101 NW Point Blvd.
Elk Grove Village, IL 60007
Tel: 800-365-2775, 847-640-1150
Fax: 847-640-1950
Internet: http://www.applevacations.com

Around Town Tours Inc.
2075 Bayberry Road, Suite 102
Bensalem, PA 19020
Tel: 800-468-0906, 215-245-6600
Fax: 215-245-8051
Internet: http://www.aroundtown.com

Asian Journeys Inc.
4720 Interlachen Lane
Austin, TX 78747
Tel: 800-426-0777
Fax: 512-291-0576
Internet: http://www.asianjourneys.com

ATA Vacations
7337 W. Washington Street
Indianapolis, IN 46231
Tel: 800-225-9919, 317-23-4561
Fax: 317-243-4168
Internet: http://www.ata.com

Auto Europe LLC
39 Commercial Street
Portland, ME 04101
Tel: 800-223-5555, 207-842-2000
Fax: 207-842-2222
Internet: http://www.autoeurope.com

AutoVenture
425 Pike Street, Suite 502
Seattle, WA 98101
Tel: 800-426-7502, 206-624-6033

AutoVenture - continued
Fax: 206-340-8891
Internet: http://www.autoventure.com

Avanti Destinations
851 SW 6th Avenue, Suite 1010
Portland, OR 97204
Tel: 800-422-5053, 503-295-1100
Fax: 503-295-2723
Internet: http://www.avantidestinations.com

Bahamas Travel Network
1043 SE 7th Street
Fort Lauderdale, FL 33301
Tel: 800-513-5535, 954-467-1133
Fax: 954-467-7544
Internet: http://www.bahamastravelnet.com

Baja Expeditions
2625 Garnet Avenue
San Diego, CA 92109
Tel: 800-843-6967, 619-581-3311
Fax: 619-581-6542
Internet: http://www.bajaex.com

Baobab Safari Company Inc.
210 Post Street, Suite 911
San Francisco, CA 94108
Tel: 800-835-3692, 415-391-5788
Fax: 415-391-3752
Internet: http://www.baobabsafaris.com

Barbachano Tours/Cozumel Central Reservations
480 W. 83rd Street
Miami Lakes, FL 33014
Tel: 800-327-2254, 305-362-6200
Fax: 305-362-6100
Internet: http://www.barbachano.com

Branson Country Tours
1140 W. 76 Hwy.
Branson, MO 65616
Tel: 800-841-2376, 417-336-2220
Fax: 417-336-2224
Internet: http://www.bransoncountrytours.com

Brendan Tours
15137 Califa Street
Van Nuys, CA 91411
Tel: 800-421-8446, 818-785-9696
Fax: 818-902-9876

Brennan Tours
1402 3rd Avenue
Joseph Vance Bldg., Suite 717
Seattle, WA 98101,
Tel: 800-237-7249, 206-622-9155
Fax: 206-622-9160
Internet: http://www.brennantours.com

British Air Tours
5728 Major Blvd., Suite 750
Orlando, FL 32819
Tel: 800-359-8722, 407-345-0114
Fax: 407-351-9403
Internet: http://www.british-airways.com

California Wine Tours
22455 Broadway
Sonoma, CA 95476
Tel: 800-294-6386, 707-253-1300
Fax: 707-938-4249
Internet: http://www.californiawinetours.com

Camino Tours Inc.
7044 18th Avenue NE
Seattle, WA 98115

Camino Tours Inc. - continued
Tel: 800-938-9311, 206-523-1764
Fax: 206-523-8256
Internet: http://www.webtravel.com/caminotour

Canadian Travel Abroad LTD.
80 Richmond Street West, Suite 804
Toronto, ON Canada M0H 2A4
Tel: 800-387-1876, 416-364-2738
Fax: 416-364-6951
Internet: http://www.baxter-net/cantrav

CanAm Holidays Inc.
202 Golden Mile Centre
3806 Albert Street
Regina, SK Canada S4S 3R2
Tel: 800-667-3540, 306-586-4644
Fax: 306-585-0060
Internet: http://www.canamholidays.com

Caradonna Caribbean Tours Inc.
435 Douglas Avenue, Suite 2205
Altamonte Springs, FL 32714
Tel: 800-328-2288, 407-774-9000
Fax: 407-682-6000
Internet: http://www.caradonna.com

Caravan Tours Inc.
401 N. Michigan Avenue
Chicago, IL 60611
Tel: 800-227-2826, 32-321-9800
Fax: 312-321-9845
Internet: http://www.caravantours.com

Central Holidays
P. O. Box 1664
Englewood Cliffs, NJ 07632
Tel: 800-935-5000, 201-798-5777
Fax: 201-228-5355

Central Holidays - continued
Internet: http://www.centralholidays.com

Certified Vacations
110 E. Broward Blvd.
Fort Lauderdale, FL 33301
Tel: 800-367-9112, 954-522-1440
Fax: 954-357-4672
Internet: http://www.leisureweb.com

Championship Tennis Tours Inc.
8040 E. Morgan Trail, Suite 12
Scottsdale, AZ 85258
Tel: 800-468-3664, 602-443-9449
Fax: 602-443-8982
Internet: http://www.tennistours.com

China Travel Service
575 Sutter Street
San Francisco, CA 94102
Tel: 800-899-8618, 415-398-6627
Fax: 415-398-6669
Internet: http://www.chinatravelservice.com

CIE Tours International
P. O. Box 501
Cedar Knolls, NJ 07927-0501
Tel: 800-338-3964, 973-292-3899
Fax: 973-292-0463
Internet: http://www.cietours.com

CIT Tours Corp.
80 Tiverton Court, Suite 401
Markham, ON Canada L3R 0G4
Tel: 800-387-0711, 905-415-1060
Fax: 905-415-1063
Internet: http://www.cit-tours.com

CIT Tours Inc. of Canada
1450 City Councillors Street, #750
Montreal, QC Canada H3A 2E6
Tel: 514-845-9101
Fax: 514-845-9137
Internet: http://www.cit-tours.com

City Tours Inc.
26A Oak Street
East Rutherford, NJ 07073
Tel: 800-248-9868, 201-939-4154

Club Europa
802 W. Oregon Street
Urbana, IL 61801
Tel: 800-331-1882, 217-344-5863
Fax: 217-344-4072
Internet: http://www.clubeuropatravel.com

Collette Travel Service Inc.
162 Middle Street
Pawtucket, RI 02860
Tel: 800-832-4656, 401-728-3805
Fax: 401-727-4745
Internet: http://www.collettetravel.com

Contiki Holidays
300 Plaza Alicante, Suite 900
Garden Grove, CA 92840
Tel: 800-266-8454, 714-740-0808
Fax: 714-740-0818
Internet: http://www.contiki.com

Continental Airlines Vacations
110 E. Broward Blvd.
Fort Lauderdale, FL 33301
Tel: 800-634-5555, 954-522-1440
Fax: 954-357-4661
Internet: http://www.coolvacations.com

Costa Rica Connection
975 Osos Street
San Luis Obispo, CA 93401
Tel: 800-345-7422, 805-543-8823
Fax: 805-543-3626
Internet: http://www.crconnect.com

Country Heritage Tours Inc.
P. O. Box 59
Amherst, NH 03031-0059
Tel: 800-346-9820, 603-673-0640
Fax: 603-673-5839
Internet: http://www.quilt.com/cht/countryheritage.html

Country Squire Tours
P. O. Box 937
Centerville, MA 02632
Tel: 800-225-8051
Fax: 508-420-2263
Internet: http://www.newenglandtours.com

Creative Leisure International
P. O. Box 750189
Petaluma, CA 94975
Tel: 707-778-1800
Fax: 707-778-1223
Internet: http://www.creativeleisure.com

Cultural Tours, Europe & Beyond Inc.
7758 Wisconsin Avenue, Suite 67
Bethesda, MD 20814
Tel: 800-826-7995, 202-333-5747
Fax: 301-718-8251
Internet: http://www.fairwindtravel.com

Delta Dream Vacations
110 E. Broward Blvd., Suite 720
Fort Lauderdale, FL 33301
Tel: 800-301-6400, 954-522-1440

Delta Dream Vacations - continued
Fax: 954-357-4680
Internet: http://www.deltavacations.com

Destination Ireland & Great Britain Inc.
13 Sterling Place, Suite 4A
Brooklyn, NY 11217
Tel: 800-832-1848, 718-622-4717
Fax: 718-622-4874

Diplomat Tours
3174 Arden Way
Sacramento, CA 95825
Tel: 800-727-8687, 916-972-1500
Fax: 916-481-4728
Internet: http://www.diplomattours.com

Distinctive Journeys International Ltd.
53 W. Jackson Blvd., Suite 926
Chicago, IL 60604
Tel: 800-922-2060, 312-922-5227
Fax: 312-922-5231
Internet: http://www.distinctivejourneys.com

Donna Franca Tours
470 Commonwealth Avenue
Boston, MA 02215
Tel: 800-225-6290, 617-375-9400
Fax: 617-266-1062
Internet: http://www.donnafranca.com

Educational Field Studies (EFS)
14325 Willard Road, Suite 102
Chantilly, VA 20151
Tel: 800-654-4750, 703-631-7078
Fax: 703-631-6904
Internet: http://www.efsworld.com

Educational Tours Inc.
104 Wilmot Road
Deerfield, IL 60015
Tel: 800-962-0060, 847-374-0088
Fax: 847-374-9515
Internet: http://www.et-educationaltours.com

Escapade Vacations
630 3rd Avenue
New York, NY 10017
Tel: 800-224-7360, 212-370-1477
Fax: 212-370-1477
Internet: http://www.isram.com/escapade

Especially Britain
P. O. Box 121398
Fort Worth, TX 76121-1398
Tel: 800-869-0538, 817-763-5754
Fax: 817-870-1125
Internet: http://www.expresspages.com/e/especiallybritain

Euro-Bike & Walking Tours
P. O. Box 990
De Kalb, IL 60115
Tel: 800-321-6060, 815-758-8851
Fax: 815-758-8851
Internet: http://www.eurobike.com

Euro Lloyd Travel/Tours Inc.
1640 Hempstead Turnpike
East Meadow, NY 11554
Tel: 800-334-2724, 516-794-1253
Fax: 516-228-8258
Internet: http://www.eurolloyd.com

European Waterways-Luxury Hotel Barges
140 E. 56th Street, Apt. 4C
New York, NY 10022
Tel: 800-217-4447, 212-688-9489

European Waterways-Luxury Hotel Barges - continued
Fax: 212-688-3778
Internet: http://www.europeanwaterways.com

Fam-Fax
P. O. Box 3396
Carmel, CA 93921
Tel: 831-626-1212
Fax: 831-616-1252
Internet: http://www.traveldiscounts.com

Fantasy Holidays
400 Jericho Turnpike, Suite 301
Jericho, NY 11753
Tel: 800-645-2555, 516-935-8500
Fax: 516-932-4622
Internet: http://www.fantasyholidays.com

Flemming Tours
P.O. Box 456
Valley Park, MO 63088
Tel: 800-967-9597, 314-861-9010
Fax: 314-825-9540

Forum Travel International
91 Gregory Lane, Suite 21
Pleasant Hill, CA 94523
Tel: 925-671-2900
Fax: 925-671-2993
Internet: http://www.foruminternational.com

4th Dimension Tours
7101 SW 99th Avenue, Suite 105-106
Miami, FL 33173
Tel: 800-343-0020, 305-279-0014
Fax: 305-273-9777
Internet: http://www.4thdimension.com

The French Experience
370 Lexington Avenue
New York, NY 10017
Tel: 800-283-7262, 212-986-1115
Fax: 212-986-3808
Internet: http://www.frenchexperience.com

Friendly Holidays
1983 Marcus Avenue, Suite C130
New Hyde Park, NY 11042
Tel: 800-221-9748, 516-358-1200
Fax: 516-358-1320
Internet: http://www.friendlyholidays.com

Funday Discovery Tours Inc.
233 E. New Haven Avenue, Floor 2
Melbourne, FL 32901
Tel: 407-725-0796
Fax: 407-724-0736
Internet: http://www.fundaytours.com

Funjet Vacations
P. O. Box 1460
Milwaukee, WI 53201-1460
Tel: 800-558-3050
Fax: 414-351-1453
Internet: http://www.funjet.com

GEO Expeditions
P. O. Box 3656
Sonora, CA 95370-3656
Tel: 800-351-5041, 209-532-0152
Fax: 209-532-1979
Internet: http://www.geoexpeditions.com

Geographic Expeditions Inc.
2627 Lombard Street
San Francisco, CA 94123
Tel: 800-777-8183, 415-922-0448

Geographic Expeditions Inc. - continued
Fax: 415-346-5535
Internet: http://www.geoex.com

Globus & Cosmos
5301 S. Federal Circle
Littleton, CO 80123
Tel: 800-221-0090, 303-797-2800
Fax: 303-347-2080
Internet: http://www.globusandcosmos.com

Go Ahead Vacations
One Education Street
Cambridge, MA 02141
Tel: 800-242-4686
Fax: 617-619-1901
Internet: http://www.goaheadvacations.com

Gogo Worldwide Vacations
69 Spring Street
Ramsey, NJ 07446
Tel: 800-229-4999
Fax: 201-934-3888
Internet: http://www.gogowwv.com

Golf Getaways
30423 Canwood Street, Suite 227
Agoura Hills, CA 91301
Tel: 800-423-3657, 818-991-7015
Fax: 818-991-9270
Internet: http://www.golfgetaways.com

GolfPac Inc.
417 Whooping Loop, Suite 1701
Altamonte Springs, FL 32701
Tel: 800-327-0878, 407-260-2288
Fax: 407-260-8989
Internet: http://www.golfpacinc.com

Gray Line of Alaska
300 Eilliott Avenue W.
Seattle, WA 98119
Tel: 800-544-2206, 206-281-3535
Fax: 206-301-5282

GTI Travel Inc.
420 Madison Avenue
New York, NY 10017
Tel: 800-868-7484, 212-759-7780
Fax: 212-759-7736
Internet: http://www.gti2italy.com

G.W.T. Inc.
190 Moore Street, Suite 470
Hackensack, NJ 07601
Tel: 800-868-7498, 617-449-5460
Fax: 201-343-7591

Health Tours International
25 W. 43rd Street, Suite 805
New York, NY 10036
Tel: 800-997-9972, 212-997-8510
Fax: 212-997-8453
Internet: http://www.erols.com/htours

Heritage Festivals/America's Travel Centre
P. O. Box 571187
Salt Lake City, UT 84157-1187
Tel: 800-223-4367, 801-23-3445
Fax: 801-265-2314
Internet: http://www.heritagefestivals.com

Homeric Tours Inc.
55 E. 59th Street
New York, NY 10022
Tel: 800-223-5570, 212-753-1100
Fax: 212-753-0319
Internet: http://www.homerictours.com

Horizon Tours
1634 I Street NW, suite 301
Washington, DC 20006
Tel: 888-780-0720, 202-783-8482
Fax: 202-393-1547
Internet: http://www.horizontours.com

Insight International Tours Inc.
745 Atlantic Avenue
Boston, MA 02111
Tel: 800-582-8380. 617-482-2000
Fax: 800-622-5015
Internet: http://www.insighttours.com

Intrav
7711 Bonhomme Avenue
Saint Louis, MO 63105
Tel: 800-825-2900, 314-727-6198
Fax: 314-727-7500
Internet: http://www.intrav.com

Island Resort Tours, Inc.
300 E. 40th St.
New York, NY   10016
Tel: 800-251-1755, 212-476-9400
Fax: 212-476-9452
Internet: http://www.islandresorttours.com

Isram World of Travel
630 3rd Ave.
New York, NY   10017
Tel: 800-223-7460, 212-922-1002
Fax: 212-093-9350
Internet: http://www.isram.com

ITC/ITC Golf Tours
4134 Atlantic Avenue, suite 205
Long Beach, CA   90807
Tel: 800-257-4981, 562-595-6905

ITC/ITC Golf Tours - continued
Fax: 562-424-6683
Internet: http://www.travelsource.com/golf/itc.html

Jet Vacations
880 Apollo St., Suite 41
El Segundo, CA   90245
Tel: 800-538-0999, 888-538-4755
Fax: 310-640-1700
Internet: http://www.jetvacations.com

Jetset Tours (North America), Inc.
5120 W. Goldleaf Cir, Suite 310
Los Angeles, CA   90056
Tel: 800-638-3273, 213-290-5800
Fax: 213-294-0432
Internet: http://www.jetsettours.com

Keith Prowse & Co. (USA) Ltd.
234 W. 44th St., Suite 1000
New York, NY 10036
Tel: 800-669-8687, 212-398-1430
Fax: 212-302-4251
Internet: http://www.keithprowse.com

Kemwel's Premier Selections
106 Calvert St.
Harrison, NY   10528
Tel: 800-234-4000
Fax: 212-381-8802
Internet: http://www.kemwel.com

Ker & Downey
2825 Wilcrest Dr., Suite 600
Houston, TX   77042
Tel: 800-423-4236, 713-917-0048
Fax: 713-917-0123
Internet: http://www.kerdowney.com

Kesher Kosher Tours
370 Lexington Avenue, Rm 1805
New York, NY 10017
Tel: 800-847-0700, 212-949-9580
Fax: 212-599-6086
Internet: http://www.keshertours.com

Key Tours International
11096-B Lee Highway, Suite 104
Fairfax, VA   22030
Tel: 800-576-1784, 703-591-3550
Fax: 703-591-3553
Internet: http://www.keytours.com

Knightly Tours
4138 California Avenue SW
Seattle, WA   16366
Tel: 800-426-2133, 206-938-8657
Fax: 206-937-8498

Kompas Holiday USA, Inc.
2826 E. Commercial Blvd.
Ft. Lauderdale, FL   33308
Tel: 800-233-6422, 954-771-9200
Fax: 954-771-9841

Kuoni Travel, Inc.
11 East 44th Street
New York, NY   10017
Tel: 212-687-7190
Fax: 212-986-4158

Ladatco Tours
2220 Coral Way
Miami, FL   33145
Tel: 800-327-6162, 305-854-8422
Fax: 305-285-0504
Internet: http://www.ladatco.com

Lynott Tours, Inc.
350 Fifth Avenue, Suite 2619
New York, NY   10118
Tel: 800-221-2474, 212-760-0101
Fax: 212-695-8347
Internet: http://www.lynottours.com

Magnatours, Inc.
410 New York Avenue, Suite 100
Huntington, NY 11743
Tel: 800-856-2462, 516-424-2000
Fax: 800-936-2462, 516-424-6700

Maupintour, Inc.
1421 Research Park Drive, Suite 300
Lawrence, KS   66049
Tel: 800-255-4266, 785-331-1000
Fax: 785-331-1057
Internet: http://www.maupintour.com

Mayflower Tours & Travel
P.O. Box 490
Downers Grove, IL   60515-0490
Tel: 800-323-7605, 630-435-8500
Fax: 630-960-3575
Internet: http://www.mayflowertours.com

Mexitours
405 Smith Street
Farmingdale, NY   11735
Tel: 800-423-1004
Fax: 407-834-3337

MISR Travel
630 Fifth Avenue, Suite 1460
New York, NY   10111
Tel: 800-233-4978, 212-332-2600
Fax: 212-332-2609

Mountain Travel/Sobek
6420 Fairmount Avenue
El Cerrito, CA   94530
Tel: 800-227-2384, 510-527-8100
Fax: 510-525-7710
Internet: http://www.mtsobek.com

Nawas International Travel
777 Post Road
Darien, CT   06820
Tel: 800-221-4984, 203-656-3033
Fax: 203-655-1577

New Horizons Tour & Travel
1931 Horton Road, Suite 13
Jackson, MI   49203
Tel: 800-327-4695, 517-788-6822
Fax: 310-670-7707

Newmans South Pacific Vacations
6033 W. Century Blvd, Suite 1270
Los Angeles, CA   90045
Tel: 800-421-3326, 310-348-8282
Fax: 310-215-9705

Noel-Olson Travelworld
1145 Clark Street
Stevens Point, WI   54481
Tel: 800-826-4026, 715-345-0505
Fax: 715-345-1397

Oberammergau Tours
16701 SW 92nd Avenue
Miami, FL   33157
Tel: 800-228-1590, 305-232-1555
Fax: 305-233-9168

Olympia Tours
20335 Biscayne Blvd, Suite 10

Olympia Tours - continued

Aventura, FL   33180
Tel: 800-367-6718, 305-935-4555
Fax: 305-937-4025
Internet: http://www.olympiatours.com

Orbis Polish Travel Bureau

342 Madison Avenue, Room 1512
New York, NY   10173
Tel: 800-223-6037, 212-867-5011
Fax: 212-682-4715
Internet: http://www.orbis-usa.com

Orient Flexi-Pax Tours

630 Third Avenue
New York, NY   10017
Tel: 800-545-5540, 212-692-9550
Fax: 212-661-1618
Internet: http://www.isram.com/ofpt

Overseas Adventure Tours

625 Mount Auburn St.
Cambridge, MA   02138
Tel: 800-221-0814, 617-876-0533
Fax: 617-876-0455

Pacific Delight Tours, Inc.

132 Madison Avenue
New York, NY   10016
Tel: 800-221-7179, 212-684-7707
Fax: 212-532-3406

Pathfinders Tours

6426 N. Glenwood Avenue
Chicago, IL   60626
Tel: 800-455-7477, 773-743-7426
Fax: 773-743-7466
Internet: http://www.pathfinders.co.uk

Perillo Tours
577 Chestnut Ridge Road
Woodcliff Lake, NJ 07675
Tel: 800-431-1515, 201-307-1234
Fax: 201-307-1808
Internet: http://www.perillotours.com

Pierbusseti World Travel
542 S. Dearborn Street, Suite 550
Chicago, IL 60605
Tel: 800-621-1047, 312-939-2890
Fax: 312-939-8727

Pleasant Holidays
2404 Townsgate Road
Westlake Village, CA 91361
Tel: 800-242-9244, 818-991-3390
Fax: 805-379-4039
Internet: http://www.pleasant.net

Presley Tours, Inc.
16 Presley Park Dr.
Makanda, IL 62958
Tel: 800-621-6100, 618-549-0704
Fax: 618-549-0404

Princess Tours
2815 Second Avenue, Suite 400
Seattle, WA 98121
Tel: 206-443-1979, 206-728-4202
Fax: 206-443-1979

Qantas Vacations
300 Continental Blvd., Suite 610
El Segundo, CA 90245
Tel: 800-641-8772, 310-322-6359
Fax: 310-535-1057
Internet: http://www.jetabout.com

Rail Travel Center
139 Main Street, Suite 606B
Brattleboro, VT   05301
Tel: 800-458-5394, 802-254-7788
Fax: 802-254-7755
Internet: http://www.railtvl.com

Resort Golf Vacations
2441 Bellevue Avenue
Daytona Beach, FL   32114
Tel: 800-351-9575, 904-252-2332
Fax: 904-252-9215
Internet: http://www.resort.golf.com

Roads Less Traveled
2840 Wilderness Place, Suite F
Boulder, CO   80301
Tel: 800-488-483, 303-4130-0938
Fax: 303-413-0926
Internet: http://www.roadslesstraveled.com

Russian Travel Bureau, Inc.
225 East 44th Street
New York, NY   10017
Tel: 800-847-1800, 212-986-1500
Fax: 212-490-1650
Internet: http://www.astanet.com/get/russntrvl

Sanborn's Viva Tours, Inc.
2015 South 10th Street
McAllen, TX   78503
Tel: 800-395-8482, 956-682-9872
Fax: 956-682-0016
Internet: http://www.sanborns.com

Sea Air Holidays Ltd.
733 Summer Street
Stamford, CT   06901
Tel: 800-732-6247, 203-356-9033

Sea Air Holidays Ltd. - continued
Fax: 203-965-7297
Internet: http://www.seaairholiday.com

SITA World Travel Inc.
8125 San Fernando Road
Sun Valley, CA   91352
Tel: 800-421-5643, 818-767-0039
Fax: 818-767-4346
Internet: http://www.sitatours.com

Smolka Tours
82 Riveredge Road
Tinton Falls, NJ   07724
Tel: 800-722-0057, 732-576-8813
Fax: 732-224-9356

Society Expeditions
2001 Western Avenue, Suite 300
Seattle, CA   98121
Tel: 800-548-8669, 206-728-9400
Fax: 206-728-2301
Internet: http ://www.societyexpeditions.com

Spanish Heritage Tours, Inc.
11647 Queens Blvd.
Forest Hills, NY   11375
Tel: 800-221-2580, 718-544-2752
Fax: 718-793-4278
Internet: http://www.shtours.com

Spectacular Sport Specials
5813 Citrus Blvd.
New Orleans, LA   70123
Tel: 800-451-5772, 504-734-9511
Fax: 504-734-7075
Internet: http://www.spectacularsport.com

Sports World Tours
614 SW 11th Avenue, Suite 400
Portland, OR   97205
Tel: 800-634-2555, 503-241-4701
Fax: 503-241-4872
Internet: htt ://www.sportsworldtours.com

Sun Islands Hawaii
2299Kuhio Avenue, Floor 1
Honolulu, HI 96815
Tel: 808-926-3888
Fax: 808-922-6951
Internet: http://www.suntrekshawaii.com

Sunny Land Tours, Inc.
166 Main Street
Hackensack, NJ   07601
Tel: 800-783-7839, 201-487-2150
Fax: 201-487-1546

Sunspots International
1918 NE 181st Avenue
Portland, OR   97230
Tel: 800-334-5623, 503-666-3893
Fax: 503-661-7771
Internet: http://www.sunspotintl.com

Suntrek Tours
77 West 3rd Street
Santa Rosa, CA   95401
Tel: 800-786-8735, 707-523-1800
Fax: 707-523-1911
Internet: http://www.suntrek.com

Tauck Tours
P.O. Box 5027
Westport, CT 06881-5027
Tel: 800-468-2825, 203-226-6911
Fax: 203-221-6866

REFERENCE SECTION   **347**

Tourco, Inc.
29 Bassett Lane
Hyannis, MA   02601
Tel: 800-537-5378, 508-771-5165
Fax: 508-790-1115

Tourlite International, Inc.
551 Fifth Avenue
New York, NY   10176
Tel: 800-272-7600, 212-599-2727
Fax: 212-370-0913
Internet: http://www.tourlite.com

Tours & Travel Dimensions
18 West 45th Street, Suite 612
New York, NY   10036
Tel: 800-437-9085, 212-268-9691
Fax: 212-268-9697

Town & Country Tours
808 East Osborn Road
Phoenix, AZ   85014
Tel: 800-528-0421, 602-234-3622
Fax: 602-248-8026
Internet: http://www.atus.com

Trafalgar Tours, Inc.
29-76 Northern Blvd.
Long Island City, NY 11101
Tel: 800-854-0103
Fax: 800-830-1731
Internet: http://www.trafalgartours.com

Travcoa, Travel Corporation of America
P.O. Box 2630
Newport Beach, CA 92658-2630
Tel: 800-992-2003, 949-476-2800
Fax: 949-476-2538
Internet: http://www.travcoa.com

Travel Bound, Inc.
599 Broadway
New York, NY   10012
Tel: 800-456-2004, 212-334-1350
Fax: 800-208-2080, 212-334-1357

Triaena Tours, Inc.
850 7th Avenue
New York, NY   10019
Tel: 800-223-1273, 212-245-3700
Fax: 212-582-8815
Internet: http://www.trieana.com

Ulysses Tours, Inc.
645 Fifth Avenue, Floor 5
New York, NY   10022
Tel: 800-431-1424, 212-371-7646
Fax: 212-371-1579

Unitours, Inc.
411 W. Putnam Avenue
Greenwich, CT 06830
Tel: 800-777-7432, 203-629-3900
Fax: 203-629-1905
Internet: http://www.unitours.com

Universal Travel System
1434 Sixth Street
Santa Monica, CA 90401
Tel: 800-255-4338, 310-393-0261
Fax: 310-395-9511
Internet: http://www.uts-travel.com

University Educational Travel
19355 Business Center Drive, Suite 2
Northridge, CA   91324
Tel: 800-525-0525, 818-886-0633
Fax: 818-993-5243
Internet: http://www.uet.com

Uniworld
16000 Ventura Blvd, Suite 200
Encino, CA   91436
Tel: 800-733-7820, 818-382-7820
Fax: 818-382-7829

Vacations Hawaii
1314 S. King Street, Suite 1062
Honolulu, HI   96814
Tel: 800-591-4700, 808-591-4777
Fax: 808-591-4790

Vagabond Tours
118 Somerset Street, Floor 2
New Brunswick, NJ   08901
Tel: 800-700-0790, 732-745-2449
Fax: 732-745-2440
Internet: http://www.vagabondtours.com

Value Holidays
10224 N. Port Washington Road
Mequon, WI   53092
Tel: 800-558-6850, 414-241-6373
Fax: 414-241-6379
Internet: http://www.valhol.com

Venture Travel & Tours
2008 Riverside Drive E.
Burlington, VT   05401
Tel: 800-552-8737, 802-862-9671
Fax: 802-862-7812
Internet: http://www.vermonttransit.com

Villas International Ltd.
950 Northgate Drive, Suite 206
San Rafael, CA   94903
Tel: 800-221-2260, 415-499-9490
Fax: 415-499-9491
Internet: http://www.villasintl.com

Walt Disney Travel Co.
1441 S. West Street
Anaheim, CA   92802
Tel: 800-854-3104, 714-520-5050
Fax: 714-520-6099
Internet: http://www.disneyland.com

Wilderness Travel
1102 9th Street
Berkeley, CA   94710
Tel: 800-368-2794, 510-558-2488
Fax: 510-558-2489
Internet: htt ://www.wildernesstravel.com

Wildlife Safari
346 Rheem Blvd, Suite 107
Moraga, CA   94556
Tel: 800-221-8118, 925-376-5595
Fax: 925-376-5059
Internet: htt ://www.wildlife-safari.com

Ya'lla Tours
4711 SW Huber Street, Suite 2
Portland, OR   97219
Tel: 800-644-1595, 503-977-3758
Fax: 503-977-3765
Internet: htt ://www.yallausatours.com

Zeus Tours & Yacht Cruises, Inc.
209 West 40th Street, Floor 3
New York, NY   10018
Tel: 800-447-5667, 212-221-0006
Fax: 212-764-7912
Internet: http://www.zeustours.com

Antigua & Barbuda Dept. of Tourism
610 Fifth Avenue, Room 311
New York, NY   10020-2403
Tel: 212-541-4117
Fax: 212-757-1607
Internet: http://www.antigua/barbuda.org

Argentina Tourist Information Office
5055 Wilshire Blvd., Suite 210
Los Angeles, CA   90036-6100
Tel: 213-930-0681
Fax: 213-934-9076

2655 LeJeune Road, Suite F
Miami, FL   33134
Tel: 305-442-1366
Fax: 305-441-7029
Internet: http://www.sectur.gov.ar

Aruba Tourism Authority
1000 Harbor Blvd.
Weehawken, NJ 07087-6727
Tel: 800-682-7822, 201-330-0800
Fax: 201-330-8757
Internet: http://www.aruba.com

Australia Tourist Commission
2049 Century Park East, Suite 1920
Los Angeles, CA   90067-3121
Tel: 310-449-2800
Fax: 310-277-2258
Internet: http://www.australia.com/ENGLISH.html

Austria National Tourist Office
P.O. Box 1142
New York, NY   10108-1142
Tel: 212-944-6880
Fax: 212-730-4568
Internet: http://www.anto.com

Tourist Information Office of Austria
11601 Wilshire Blvd, Suite 2180
Los Angeles, CA   90025-1770
Tel: 310-477-2038
Fax: 310-477-5141

Tourist Information Office of the Bahamas
2050 N. Stemmons Fwy, Suite 116
Dallas, TX 75258-9997
Tel: 214-742-1886
Fax: 214-741-4118

Bahamas Tourist Center
150 East 52nd Street, Floor 28
New York, NY   10022-6017
Tel: 212-758-2777
Fax: 212-753-6531

19495 Biscayne Blvd., Suite 809
Miami, FL   33180-2321
Tel: 305-932-0051
Fax: 305-682-8758

Barbados Tourism Authority
3440 Wilshire Blvd.
Los Angeles, CA   90010-2101
Tel: 213-380-2198
Fax: 213-384-3763

800 2nd Avenue
New York, NY   10017-4709
Tel: 800-221-9831, 212-986-6516
Fax: 212-573-9850

Belgium Tourist Office
780 Third Avenue, Suite 1501
New York, NY   10017-2024
Tel: 212-758-8130
Fax: 212-355-7685

Bermuda Department of Tourism
44 School Street, Suite 1010
Boston, MA   02108-4201
Tel: 617-742-0405
Fax: 617-723-7786

205 East 42nd Street, 16th Floor
New York, NY   10017-5706
Tel: 212-818-9800

British Virgin Islands Tourist Board
370 Lexington Avenue, Suite 1605
New York, NY   10017-6503
Tel: 800-835-8530, 212-696-0400
Fax: 212-949-8254

Cayman Islands Department of Tourism
420 Lexington Avenue, Suite 2733
New York, NY   10170-0149
Tel: 212-682-5582
Fax: 212-986-5123

Cayman Islands Tourist Information Office
6100 Blue Lagoon Drive, Suite 150
Miami, FL   33126-2085
Tel: 305-226-2300
Fax: 305-267-2932

820 Gessner Road, Suite 170
Houston, TX   77024-4261
Tel: 713-461-1317
Fax: 713-461-7409

3440 Wilshire Blvd., Suite 1202
Los Angeles, CA   90010-2113
Tel: 213-738-1968
Fax: 213-738-1829

Danish Tourism Board
655 Third Avenue, Floor 18
New York, NY   10017-5617
Tel: 212-885-9700
Fax: 212-885-9710
Internet: http://www.visitdenmark.com

Egyptian Tourist Authority
8383 Wilshire Blvd., Suite 215
Beverly Hills, CA   90211-2402
Tel: 213-653-8815
Fax: 213-653-8961

630 Fifth Avenue, Suite 1706
New York, NY   10111-0100
Tel: 212-332-2570
Fax: 212-956-6439

645 N. Michigan Avenue, Suite 829
Chicago, IL   60611-2879
Tel: 312-280-4666
Fax: 312-280-4788

Fiji Visitors Bureau
5777 W. Century Blvd., Suite 220
Los Angeles, CA   90045-5669
Tel: 800-932-3454, 310-568-1616
Fax: 310-670-2318

Finnish Tourist Board
655 Third Avenue
New York, NY   10017-5617
Tel: 212-885-9737
Fax: 212-885-9710
Internet: http://www.thekingsroad.com

French Government Tourist Office
9454 Wilshire Blvd., Suite 715
Beverly Hills, CA   90212-2906

French Government Tourist Office - continued

Tel: 310-271-6665
Fax: 310-276-2835

676 N. Michigan Avenue, Suite 3360
Chicago, IL 60611-2846
Tel: 312-751-7800
Fax: 312-337-6339

444 Madison Avenue, Floor 16
New York, NY 10022-6903
Tel: 212-838-7800
Fax: 212-838-7855
Internet: http://www.francetourism.com

German National Tourist Office

122 East 42nd Street, Floor 52
New York, NY 10168-5298
Tel: 212-661-7200
Fax: 212-661-7174
Internet: http://www.germany-tourism.de

(Great Britain) British Tourist Authority

551 Fifth Avenue, Suite 701
New York, NY 10176-0701
Tel: 212-986-2266
Fax: 212-986-1188
Internet: http://www.visitbritain.com

Greek National Tourist Organization

645 Fifth Avenue, Lobby 5
New York, NY 10022-5910
Tel: 212-421-5777
Fax: 212-826-6940
Internet: http://www.greektourism.com

Hong Kong Tourist Association

401 N. Michigan Avenue, Suite 1640
Chicago, IL 60611-4255

Hong Kong Tourist Association - continued
Tel: 312-329-1828
Fax: 312-329-1858

10940 Wilshire Blvd., Suite 1220
Los Angeles, CA   90024-3940
Tel: 310-208-4582
Fax: 310-208-1869

Hungarian National Tourist Office
150 East 58th Street, Floor 33
New York, NY   10155-0002
Tel: 212-355-0240
Fax: 212-207-4103
Internet: http://www.hungary.com/tourinform

(Iceland) Scandinavian Tourist Boards
P.O. Box 4649
New York, NY   10163-4649
Tel: 212-885-9700
Fax: 212-885-9710
Internet: http://www.artic.is/touristb/practical.html

Irish Tourist Board
345 Park Avenue
New York, NY   10154-0004
Tel: 800-223-6470, 212-418-0800
Fax: 212-371-9052
Internet: http://www.ireland.travel.ie

Tourist Information of Israel
5 South Wabash Avenue, Suite 1402
Chicago, IL   60603-3011
Tel: 312-782-4306
Fax: 312-782-1243

5151 Belt Line Road, Suite 1280
Dallas, TX   75240-6740
Tel: 800-514-1188, 972-991-9097
Fax: 972-392-3521

Tourist Information of Israel - continued

6380 Wilshire Blvd, Suite 1700
Los Angeles, CA   90048-5019
Tel: 323-658-7462
Fax: 323-658-6543

Italian Government Tourist Board

500 North Michigan Avenue, Suite 2240
Chicago, IL   60611-3776
Tel: 312-644-0996
Fax: 312-644-3019

12400 Wilshire Blvd., Suite 550
Los Angeles, CA   90025-1030
Tel: 310-820-1898
Fax: 310-820-6357

630 Fifth Avenue, Suite 1565
New York, NY   10111-0100
Tel: 212-245-3027
Fax: 212-586-9249

Japan National Tourist Organization

401 N. Michigan Avenue, Suite 770
Chicago, IL   60611-4278
Tel: 312-222-0874
Fax: 312-222-0876

515 s. Figuerora Street, Suite 1470
Los Angeles, CA   90071-3331
Tel: 213-623-1952
Fax: 213-623-6301

1 Rockefeller Plaza, Suite 1250
New York, NY   10020-2002
Tel: 212-757-5640
Fax: 212-307-6754

Japan National Tourist Organization - continued

360 Post Street, Suite 305
San Francisco, CA   94108-4903
Tel: 415-986-4764
Fax: 415-986-3989

Jordan Information Bureau

2319 Wyoming Avenue NW
Washington, DC   20008-1600
Tel: 202-265-1606
Fax: 202-667-0777

Kenya Tourist Office

424 Madison Avenue, Suite 1401
New York, NY   10017-1106
Tel: 212-486-1300
Fax: 212-688-0911

Korean National Tourism Corp.

205 N. Michigan Avenue, Suite 2212
Chicago, IL   60601-5923
Tel: 312-819-2560
Fax: 312-819-2563

2 Executive Drive, Suite 750
Fort Lee, NJ   07024-3395
Tel: 201-585-0909
Fax: 201-585-9041

3435 Wilshire Blvd., Suite 1110
Los Angeles, CA   90010-1912
Tel: 213-382-3435

Luxembourg National Tourist Office

17 Beekman Place
New York, NY   10022-8003
Tel: 212-935-8888
Fax: 212-935-5896

Malaysia Tourism Promotion Board
818 West 7th Street, Suite 802
Los Angeles, CA   90017-3431
Tel: 213-689-9702
Fax: 213-689-1530
Internet: http://www.tourism.gob.m4.com

595 Madison Avenue, Suite 1800
New York, NY   10022-1907
Tel: 212-754-1113
Fax: 212-754-1116
Internet: http://www.interknowledge.com/malaysia

Mexico Tourism Board
Tel: 800-446-3942 (800-44-MEXICO)
Fax: 541-312-5620
Internet: http://www.visitmexico.com

Moroccan National Tourist Office
P.O. Box 22663
Lake Buena Vista, FL   32830-2663
Tel: 407-827-5337

20 East 46th Street, Suite 1201
New York, NY   10017-7587
Tel: 212-557-2520
Fax: 212-949-8148

Netherlands Board of Tourism
225 North Michigan Avenue, Suite 1854
Chicago, IL   60601-7667
Tel: 312-819-1500
Fax: 312-819-1740
Internet: http://www.nbt.nl/holland

9841 Airport Blvd.
Los Angeles, CA   90045-5409
Tel: 310-348-9015
Fax: 310-348-9339

INetherlands Board of Tourism - continued

355 Lexington Avenue, Floor 21
New York, NY   10017-6688
Tel: 212-370-7360
Fax: 212-370-9507

New Zealand High Tourism Board

501 Santa Monica Blvd, Suite 300
Santa Monica, CA   90401-2443
Tel: 800-388-5494, 310-395-7480
Fax: 310-395-5453

Northern Ireland Tourist Board

551 Fifth Avenue, Suite 701
New York, NY   10176-9799
Tel: 800-326-0036, 212-922-0101
Fax: 212-922-099

Norwegian Tourist Board

P.O. Box 4649
New York, NY   10261-4649
Tel: 212-885-9700
Fax: 212-885-9710
Internet: http://www.norway.org

Philippine Department of Tourism

3660 Wilshire Blvd., Suite 216
Los Angeles, CA   90010-2708
Tel: 213-487-4525
Fax: 213-386-4063

556 Fifth Avenue
New York, NY   10036-5002
Tel: 212-575-7915
Fax: 212-302-6759

447 Sutter Street, Suite 507
San Francisco, CA   94108-4619
Tel: 415-956-4060
Fax: 415-956-2093

Polish National Tourist Office
275 Madison Avenue, Suite 1711
New York, NY   10016-1101
Tel: 212-338-9412
Fax: 212-338-9283
Internet: http://www.polandtour.org

Portugese National Tourist Office
590 Fifth Avenue, Floor 4
New York, NY   10036-4702
Tel: 212-354-4403
Fax: 212-764-6137
Internet: http://www.portugal.org

Puerto Rico Tourism Co.
901 Ponce de Leon Blvd., Suite 101
Coral Gables, FL   33134-3073
Tel: 800-815-7391, 305-445-9450

3575 Cahuenga Blvd. West, Suite 405
Los Angeles, CA   90068-1343
Tel: 800-874-1230, 213-874-5991

7 Cypress Street
Plymouth, MA 02360-5631
Tel: 800-223-6530, 508-759-1238

(Russia) Inturholding USA, Inc.
610 Fifth Avenue, Suite 603
New York, NY   10020-2403
Tel: 212-757-3884
Fax: 212-459-0031

(Slovakia) Central Europe Holiday
10 East 40th Street, Suite 3601
New York, NY   10016-0301
Tel: 212-213-3865
Fax: 212-213-4461

Tourism Board of the Republic of South Africa
500 Fifth Avenue, Suite 2040
New York, NY   10110-2099
Tel: 800-822-5368, 212-730-2929
Fax: 212-764-1980

Tourist Office of Spain
8383 Wilshire Blvd, Suite 956
Beverly Hills, CA   90211-2408
Tel: 213-658-7188
Fax: 213-658-1061
Internet: http://www.okspain.org

845 North Michigan Avenue, Suite 915E
Chicago, IL   60611-2201
Tel: 312-642-1992
Fax: 312-642-9817

1221 Brickell Avenue, Suite 1850
Miami, FL   33131-3259
Tel: 305-358-1992
Fax: 305-358-8223

666 Fifth Avenue
New York, NY   10103-0001
Tel: 888-657-7246, 212-265-8822
Fax: 212-265-8864

St. Lucia Tourist Board
800 Second Avenue, Suite 400J
New York, NY   10017-4709
Tel: 800-456-3984, 212-867-2950
Fax: 212-867-2795

St. Maarten Tourist Information
675 Third Avenue, Suite 1806
New York, NY   10017-5704
Tel: 212-953-2084
Fax: 212-953-2145

St. Vincent Tourist Office
6505 Covecreek Place
Dallas, TX   75240-5453
Tel: 800-235-3029, 972-239-6451
Fax: 972-239-1002

801 Second Avenue, Floor 21
New York, NY   10017-4768
Tel: 212-687-4981
Fax: 212-949-5946

Switzerland Tourism
222 North Sepulveda Blvd, Suite 1570
El Segundo, CA   90245-4366
Tel: 310-640-8900
Fax: 310-335-0131

608 Fifth Avenue
New York, NY   10020-2303
Tel: 212-757-5944
Fax: 212-262-6116

Tahiti Tourism
444 Madison Avenue, Floor 16
New York, NY   10022-6903
Tel: 212-838-8663
Fax: 212-838-9576

Tourism Authority of Thailand
611 North Larchmont Blvd.
Los Angeles, CA   90004-1322
Tel: 323-461-9814
Fax: 323-461-9834

5 World Trade Center, Suite 3443
New York, NY   10048-0205
Tel: 212-432-0433
Fax: 212-912-0920

Tourism Development Corp. - Trinidad/Tobago

359 Fifth Avenue, Suite 6316
New York, NY   10118-6399
Tel: 800-748-4224, 201-662-3403
Fax: 201-869-7628

Venezuelan Tourism Association

P.O. Box 3010
Sausalito, CA   94966-3010
Tel: 415-331-0100
Fax: 415-332-9197

Virgin Islands Tourist Office (U.S.)

500 North Michigan Avenue, Suite 2039
Chicago, IL   60611-3791
Tel: 312-670-8784
Fax: 312-670-8788

2655 South LeJeune Road, Suite 907
Coral Gables, FL   33134-5813
Tel: 305-442-7200
Fax: 305-445-9044

3460 Wilshire Blvd., Suite 412
Los Angeles, CA   89919-2224
Tel: 213-739-0138
Fax: 213-739-2005

Alabama Bureau of Tourism & Travel
401 Adams Avenue
Montgomery, AL   36104
Tel: 800-252-2262, 334-242-4493
Fax: 334-242-4554
Internet: http://www.touralabama.org

Alaska Division of Tourism
P.O. Box 110801
Juneau, AK 9811-0801
Tel: 907-465-2010, 907-465-2012
Fax: 907-465-2287
Internet: http://www.commerce.state.ak.us

Arizona Office of Tourism
2702 N. 3rd Street, Suite 4015
Phoenix, AZ   85004
Tel: 800-842-8257, 602-230-7733
Fax: 602-240-5475
Internet: http://www.airzonaguide.com

Arkansas Dept. of Parks & Tourism
1 Capitol Mall
Little Rock, AR 72201
Tel: 800-628-8725, 501-682-7777
Fax: 501-682-1364
Internet: http://www.arkansaw.com

California Division of Tourism
801 K Street, Suite 1600
Sacramento, CA   95814
Tel: 800-462-2543, 916-322-2881
Fax: 916-322-3402
Internet: http://www.gocalif.ca.gov

Colorado Travel & Tourism Authority
1127 Pennsylvania Street
Denver, CO 80203
Tel: 800-252-2262, 303-832-6171

Colorado Travel & Tourism Authority - continued
Fax: 303-832-6174
Internet: http://www.colorado.com

Connecticut Dept. of Economic-Tourism Division
505 Hudson Street
Hartford, CT   06106
Tel: 800-282-6863, 860-270-8081
Fax: 860-270-8077
Internet: http://www.state.ct.us/tourism/

Delaware Tourism Office
99 Kings Highway
Dover, DE   19901
Tel: 800-441-8846, 302-739-4271
Fax: 302-739-5749
Internet: http://www.state.de.us

Washington, DC Convention & Visitors Association
1212 New York Avenue NW, Suite 600
Washington, DC   20005
Tel: 800-635-6338, 202-789-7000
Fax: 202-789-7037
Internet: http://www.washington.org

Visit Florida
P.O. Box 1100
Tallahassee, FL   32302-1100
Tel: 850-488-5607
Fax: 850-224-2938
Internet: http:// www.flusa.com

Georgia Dept. of Industry, Trade & Tourism
P.O. Box 1776
Atlanta, GA   30301-1776
Tel: 404-656-3590
Fax: 404-651-9063
Internet: http://www.georgia.org

Hawaii Visitors & Convention Bureau
2270 Kalakaua Avenue, Suite 801
Honolulu, HI   96815
Tel: 808-923-1811
Fax: 808-924-0290
Internet: http://www.gohawaii.com

Idaho Dept. of Commerce Div. Of Tourism Dev.
P.O. Box 83720
Boise, ID   83720
Tel: 800-635-7820, 208-334-2470
Fax: 208-334-2631
Internet: http://www.idoc.state.id.us

Illinois Bureau of Tourism
100 W. Randolph Street, Suite 3-400
Chicago, IL   60601
Tel: 800-226-6632, 312-814-4732
Fax: 312-814-6175
Internet: http://www.enjoyillinois.com

Indiana Dept. of Commerce, Tourism Dev. Division
1 North Capitol Ave, Suite 700
Indianapolis, IN   46204
Tel: 800-759-9191, 317-232-8860
Fax: 317-233-6887
Internet: http:// www.indianatourism.com

Iowa Division of Tourism
200 East Grand Avenue
Des Moines, IA   52241
Tel: 800-345-4692, 515-242-4705
Fax: 515-242-4749
Internet: http://www.state.la.us/tourism

Kansas Travel & Tourism Division
700 SW Harrison Street, Suite 1300
Topeka, KS   66603
Tel: 800-252-6727, 785-296-2009

Kansas Travel & Tourism Division - continued
Fax: 785-296-6988
Internet: http://www.kansascommerce.com

Kentucky Department of Travel
500 Mero Street, 22nd floor
Frankfort, KY   40601
Tel: 800-225-8747, 800-255-7275
Fax: 502-564-5695
Internet: http://www.kentuckytourism.com

Louisiana Office of Tourism
1051 North 3rd Street
Baton Rouge, LA   70802
Tel: 800-227-4386, 504-342-8100
Fax: 504-342-8380
Internet: http://www.louisianatravel.com

Maine Office of Tourism
59 State House Sta, 33 Stone Street
Augusta, ME   04333
Tel: 888-624-6345, 207-287-5711
Fax: 207-287-8070
Internet: http:// www.mainetourism.com

Maryland Office of Tourism
217 E. Redwood Street, F19
Baltimore, MD   21202
Tel: 800-634-7386, 410-767-3400
Fax: 410-333-6643
Internet: http://www.mdisfun.org

Massachusetts Office of Travel & Tourism
10 Park Plaza, Suite 4510
Boston, MA   02116
Tel: 800-447-6277, 617-727-3201
Fax: 617-727-6525
Internet: http://www.mass-vacation.com

Travel Michigan
201 N. Washington Square, 2nd floor
Lansing, MI   48913
Tel: 800-543-2937, 517-373-0670
Fax: 517-373-0059
Internet: http://www.michigan.org

Minnesota Office of Tourism
121 7th Place East, Suite 100
St. Paul, MN   55101
Tel: 800-657-3600, 651-286-5029
Fax: 651-296-7095
Internet: http://www.exploreminnesota.com

Mississippi Div. of Tourism Development
P.O. Box 849
Jackson, MS   39205
Tel: 800-927-6378, 601-359-3297
Fax: 601-359-5757
Internet: http:// www.mississippi.org

Missouri Division of Tourism
P.O. Box 1055
Jefferson City, MO   65102
Tel: 800-877-1234, 573-751-4133
Fax: 573-751-5160
Internet: http://www.missouritourism.org

Montana Travel Promotion Division
1424 9th Avenue
Helena, MT   59620
Tel: 800-847-4868, 406-444-2654
Fax: 406-444-1800
Internet: http://www.travel.mt.gov

Nebraska Division of Travel & Tourism
P.O. Box 98907
Lincoln, NE   68509
Tel: 800-228-4307, 402-471-3794

Nebraska Division of Travel & Tourism - continued
Fax: 402-471-3026
Internet: http://www.visitnebraska.org

Nevada Commission of Tourism
401 N. Carson Street
Carson City, NV   89701
Tel: 800-237-0774, 702-687-4322
Fax: 702-687-6779
Internet: http://www.travelnevada.com

New Jersey Division of Travel & Tourism
P.O. Box 826
Trenton, NJ   08625-0826
Tel: 800-537-7397, 609-292-2470
Fax: 609-633-7418
Internet: http://www.state.nj.us/travel

New Mexico Department of Tourism
491 Old Santa Fe Trail, Room. 751
Santa Fe, NM   87501
Tel: 800-545-2040, 505-827-7400
Fax: 505-827-7402
Internet: http://www.newmexico.org

New York State Division of Tourism
P.O. Box 2603
Albany, NY   12220-0603
Tel: 800-225-5697, 518-474-4116
Fax: 518-486-6416
Internet: http://www.iloveny.state.ny.us

North Carolina Tourism Office
P.O. Box 25249
Raleigh, NC   27601
Tel: 919-733-4171
Fax: 919-733-8582
Internet: http://www.visitnc.com

North Dakota Department of Tourism
604 E. Boulevard Avenue, 2nd Floor
Bismarck, ND   58505-0820
Tel: 800-435-5663, 701-328-2525
Fax: 701-328-4878
Internet: http://www.ndtourism.com

Ohio Division of Travel & Tourism
P.O. Box 1001
Columbus, OH   43085
Tel: 800-282-5393, 614-466-8844
Fax: 614-466-6744
Internet: http://www.ohiotourism.com

Oklahoma Travel & Tourism
15 N. Robinson Avenue, Suite 801
Oklahoma City, OK 73102
Tel: 800-652-6552, 405-521-2406
Fax: 405-236-0205
Internet: http:// www.travelok.com

Oregon Tourism Commission
775 Summer Street NE
Salem, OR   97310
Tel: 800-547-7842, 503-986-0000
Fax: 503-986-0001
Internet: http://www.traveloregon.com

Pennsylvania Travel Council
902 North 2nd Street
Harrisburg, PA   17102
Tel: 800-237-4363, 717-787-5453
Fax: 717-787-0687
Internet: http://www.state.pa.us

Rhode Island Tourism Division
1 West Exchange St.
Providence, RI   02903
Tel: 800-556-2484, 401-222-2601

Rhode Island Tourism Division - continued
Fax: 401-273-8270
Internet: http://www.riedc.com

South Carolina Dept. of Parks, Recreation & Tourism
1205 Pendleton St.
Columbia, SC   29201
Tel: 800-346-3634, 803-734-0122
Fax: 803-734-0133
Internet: http://www.travelsc.com

South Dakota Tourism
711 East Wells Avenue
Pierre, SC   57501
Tel: 800-732-5682, 605-773-3301
Fax: 605-773-3256
Internet: http:// www.travelsd.com

Tennessee Dept. of Tourist Development
320 6th Avenue North, Floor 5
Nashville, TN   37243
Tel: 800-462-8366, 615-741-9065
Fax: 615-741-7225
Internet: http://www.state.tn.us/tourdev/

Texas Dept. of Economic Development, Tourism Div.
P.O. Box 12728
Austin, TX   78711-2728
Tel: 800-888-8839, 512-462-9191
Fax: 512-936-0089
Internet: http://www.traveltex.com

Utah Travel Council
300 North State St.
Salt Lake City, UT 84114
Tel: 800-200-1160, 801-538-1030
Fax: 801-538-1399
Internet: http://www.utah.com

Vermont Department of Marketing & Tourism
6 Baldwin Street, #33
Montpelier, VT   05602
Tel: 800-837-6668, 802-828-3236
Fax: 802-828-3233
Internet: http://www.utah.com

Virginia Tourism Corporation
901 E. Byrd Street
Richmond, VA   23219
Tel: 800-847-4882, 804-786-2051
Fax: 804-786-1919
Internet: http:// www.virginia.org

Washington State Dept. of Economic Dev.-Tourism
210 11th Avenue SE, Suite 10
Olympia, WA   98501
Tel: 800-544-1800, 360-753-5601
Fax: 360-753-4470
Washington State Tourism - continued
Internet: http://www.tourism.wa.gov

West Virginia Division of Tourism & Parks
Capital Complex, Bldg. 17
Charleston, WV   25305
Tel: 800-225-5982, 304-558-2766
Fax: 304-558-2279
Internet: http://www.state.wv.us/tourism/default.htm

Wisconsin Department of Tourism
P.O. Box 7976
Madison, WI   53707-7976
Tel: 800-372-2737, 608-266-7621
Fax: 608-266-3403
Internet: http://www.state.wi.us

Wyoming Business Council Division of Tourism
1-25 at College Drive
Cheyenne, WY   82002

Wyoming Business Council Division of Tourism - cont.

Tel: 800-225-5996, 307-777-7777
Fax: 307-777-6904
Internet: http://www.commerce.state.wy.us/west

Africa Travel Association
347 Fifth Avenue, Room 610
New York, NY   10016
Tel: 212-447-1926
Fax: 212-725-8253
Internet: http://www.africatrvl.aol.com

American Bus Association (ABA)
1100 New York Avenue NW, Suite 1050
Washington, DC 20005-3934
Tel: 800-283-2877, 202-842-1645
Fax: 202-842-0850
Internet: http://www.buses.org

American Hotel & Motel Association (AHMA)
1201 New York Avenue, Suite 600
Washington, DC   20005-3931
Tel: 202-289-3100
Fax: 202-289-3199
Internet: http://www.ahma.com

American Sightseeing International (ASI)
490 Post Street, Suite 1701
San Francisco, CA   94102
Tel: 800-225-4432, 415-986-2082
Fax: 415-986-2703
Internet: http://www.sightseeing.com

American Society of Travel Agents (ASTA)
1101 King Street, Suite 200
Alexandria, VA   22314
Tel: 800-275-2782, 703-739-2782
Fax: 703-684-8319
Internet: http://www.astanet.com

The American Tourism Society
419 Park Avenue S., Room 505
New York, NY   10016
Tel: 212-545-9641

The American Tourism Society - continued
Fax: 212-545-9641
Internet:

Bed & Breakfast: The National Network
P.O. Box 764703
Dallas, TX   75376-4703
Tel: 800-899-4538, 972-298-8586
Fax: 972-298-7118
Internet: http://www.tnn4bnb.com

Caribbean Hotel Association
1000 Ponce de Leon, Floor 5
San Juan, PR   00907
Tel: 787-725-9139
Fax: 787-725-9108
Internet: http://www.chahotels.com

Caribbean Tourism Organization
80 Broad Street, Floor 32
New York, NY   10004
Tel: 212-682-0435
Fax: 212-635-9511
Internet: http://www.caribbeantourism.com

Colorado Dude & Guest Ranch Association
P.O. Box 300
Tabernash, CO   80278-0300
Tel: 970-887-3128
Fax: 970-887-9248
Internet: http://www.coloradoranch.com

Cruise Lines International Association (CLIA)
500 Fifth Avenue, Suite 1407
New York, NY   10110
Tel: 800-372-2542, 212-921-0066
Fax: 212-921-0549
Internet: http://www.cruising.org

The Dude Ranchers Association
P.O. Box 471
Laporte, CO   80535
Tel: 970-223-8440
Fax: 970-223-0201
Internet: http://www.duderanch.org

Elderhostel
75 Federal Street
Boston, MA 02110
Tel: 617-426-7788
Fax: 617-426-8351
Internet: http://www.elderhostel.org/

European Travel Commission
1 Rockefeller Plaza, Room 214
New York, NY   10020
Tel: 212-218-1200
Fax: 212-307-1205

Int'l Association of Convention & Visitors Bureaus (IACVB)
2000 L Street NW, Suite 702
Washington, DC   20036
Tel: 202-296-7888
Fax: 202-296-7889
Internet: http://www.iacvb.org

Int'l Association of Amusement Parks & Attractions
1448 Duke Street
Alexandria, VA   22314
Tel: 703-836-4800
Fax: 703-836-4801

International Gay Travel Association (IGTA)
4331 N. Federal Highway, Suite 304
Ft. Lauderdale, FL   33308
Tel: 800-448-8550, 954-776-2626
Fax: 954-776-3303

National Association of Commissioned Travel Agents
P.O. Box 2398
Valley Center, CA   92082
Tel: 760-751-1197
Fax: 760-751-1309
Internet: http://www.nacta.com

National Association of Cruise Oriented Agencies (NACOA)
7600 Red Road, Suite 128
Miami, FL 33143
Tel: 305-663-5626
Fax: 305-663-5625
Internet: http//www.nacoa.com

National Association of Railroad Passengers
900 2nd Street NE, Suite 308
Washington, DC   20002
Tel: 202-408-8362
Fax: 202-408-8287
Internet: http://www.narprail.org

National Park Service
P.O. Box 37127
Washington, DC   20013-7127
Tel: 202-208-6843
Fax: 202-219-0910
Internet: http://www.nps.gov

National Tour Association (NTA)
546 E. Main Street
Lexington, KY   40508
Tel: 800-682-8886, 606-226-4444
Fax: 606-226-4404

Outside Sales Support Network Association (OSSN)
1340 S. US Highway 1, Suite 102
Jupiter, FL 33477
Tel: 800-771-7327, 561-743-1900

Outside Sales Support Network Assoc. (OSSN) - cont.
Fax: 561-575-4371
Internet: http://www.ossn.com

Pacific Asia Travel Organization
1 Montgomery Street, Suite 1000
San Francisco, CA   94104
Tel: 415-986-4646
Fax: 415-986-3458
Internet: http://www.pata.org

Religious Conference Management Association (RCMA)
1 RCA Dome, Suite 120
Indianapolis, IN   46225
Tel: 317-632-1888
Fax: 317-632-7909

Society for Advancement of Travel for the Handicapped
347 Fifth Avenue, Room 610
New York, NY   10016
Tel: 212-447-7284
Fax: 212-725-8253
Internet: http://www.sath.org

Society of Incentive Travel Executives (SITE)
21 W. 38th Street, Floor 10
New York, NY   10018
Tel: 212-575-0910
Fax: 212-575-1838
Internet: http://www.site-intl.org

Travel & Tourism Research Association (TTRA)
546 East Main Street
Lexington, KY   40508
Tel: 606-226-4344
Fax: 606-226-4355
Internet: http://www.ttra.com

Travel Industry Association of America
1100 New York Avenue NW, Suite 450
Washington, DC   20005
Tel: 202-408-8422
Fax: 202-408-1255
Internet: http://www.tia.org

U.S. Tour Operators Association (USTOA)
342 Madison Avenue, Room 1522
New York, NY   10173
Tel: 212-599-6599
Fax: 212-599-6744
Internet: http://www.ustoa.com

World Tourism Organization
Internet: http://www.world-tourism.org

ADA Room: Hotel rooms that comply with the requirements of the Americans with Disabilities Act. Also known as special needs accommodations.

Advance Deposit: Partial payment in advance for goods and services.

All-suite Hotels: Relatively new class of property containing only suites, or rooms with a separate parlor area and bedroom area.

American Plan (AP): A hotel rate which includes "full board", meaning three meals per day.

Back of the House: Area of a hotel separated from the public areas and usually only used by hotel staff.

Banquet Rooms: Meeting rooms set aside for private functions in a hotel, convention center, or public building.

Bed & Breakfast (B&B): A private house which rents sleeping rooms and includes breakfast in the total cost.

Bed Night: A standard measure of overnight tourist traffic. One bed night equals one person spending one night in a room, while ten people staying 10 nights would be 100 bed nights.

Blocked Space: The amount of sleeping rooms that are reserved (or "blocked") with suppliers by group leaders, travel agents, or wholesalers, in anticipation of resale.

Brochure Shell: Sheets of high quality paper in various sizes bordered with full color pictures to be used for promotional mailings.

Bulk Rate: A very low net rate is paid by certain companies that purchase large quantities of airline seats or hotel rooms. The company, in turn, resells the seats or rooms at a slight increase (or bulk rate) which is still much lower than retail.

Commercial Rate: A discounted rate offered to a company or special customer.

Commission: A fee (usually a percentage amount) paid to a group leader or travel agent for providing customers to a supplier for their products or services.

Concierge: A hotel staff member in charge of porters and personal services for guests. Also handles ground arrangements and general information.

Continental Breakfast: Normally includes rolls, coffee and juice only.

Continental Plan (CP): Hotel rate which includes continental breakfast.

Convention & Visitor's Bureau (CVB): An organization which promotes meetings and incoming travel to a community. Normally run by local authorities.

Corporate Rate: A reduced hotel rate for business travelers which is normally received through special negotiations.

Currency Conversion: The act of determining what the equivalent US dollar amount is to a quoted foreign currency amount.

Deluxe: Intended to mean "of the highest quality", but in the travel industry, this is only a good guideline when part of an official and independent rating system.

Demi-pension and Half-pension: A hotel rate (sometimes referred to as "half-board" in Europe) which includes bed, breakfast and either lunch or dinner.

Deposited Reservation: A reservation for which a hotel has received advance payment for at least one night, making it obliged to hold the room, regardless of the guest's arrival time. Policies vary and should be checked.

DMC: Destination Management Company - A business which customizes a travel package in a specified country or area by handling ground operations, hotel accommodations, etc. Normally works with group leaders and travel agents as the "local" representative and expert on the area.

Documents: When used as in "tour documents", means the paperwork including itinerary, vouchers, and instructions regarding a trip or cruise.

Documentation Requirements: Governmental demands (on foreign citizens to enter their country) which provide proof of the traveler's citizenship and/or permission to entry a country, e.g., passports and visas.

Double Occupancy (DBL): A hotel room for two persons with appropriate bedding to accommodate them.

Double-double: A room with two double or queen beds to accommodate 2-4 people. Also see "twin double"

Double Occupancy Rate: Room rate for a double or twin room when it is occupied by two people.

Downgrade: to change to a lower class of service or accommodation.

DSM: District Sales Manager

E&O Insurance: Errors and omissions coverage purchased from an insurance company which helps to cover mistakes made by the group leader, travel agent, or tour operator.

Efficiency: Accommodation with some cooking facilities in the same room as the sleeping area.

English Breakfast: Full breakfast of cereal, bacon, sausages, eggs, toast, juice, and tea or coffee.

European Plan (EP): Hotel rate that includes only the sleeping room and no meals. Sometimes referred to as "room only".

Executive Floor: Hotel floor reserved for business travelers and usually charged at a higher room rate. Normally includes concierge and some complimentary facilities and services.

Familiarization Trip: A complimentary or reduced rate trip or tour offered to group leaders or travel agents to educate them on a destination. Usually abbreviated to "fam trip".

Family Plan: Discounts for family groups staying at hotels and various resorts.

Flight Manifest: A list of passengers who are confirmed on a specific flight.

Frequent Flyer Program: A plan in which airlines reward repeat passengers with a variety of benefits. Also acts as incentive to persuade passengers to continue using the same airline.

Frequent Guest Program: A plan in which hotels reward regular guests with a range of benefits. Also acts as incentive to persuade customers to continue using the same hotel group.

Front Office: The reception or "front" desk of a hotel.

Full-pension: A hotel rate (sometimes referred to as "full-board" in Europe) which includes bed and three meals a day. In the US, usually referred to as "American Plan".

Guaranteed Reservation: A hotel reservation secured by the guest (usually through a credit card) to pay for the room even if it is not used.

Guarantee Policy: A hotel promises to hold a room for late arrivals, but they will quote a time by which the reservation can be cancelled without charging the credit card on file.

High Season: The busiest season for travel and tourism,

normally involving the maximum rates. Time of year differs from destination to destination.

Hospitality Suite: A hotel suite or large room for entertaining conference or group delegates.

IATAN: International Airlines Travel Agent Network, an organization committed to upholding the professional business standards of the travel industry.

Incentive Tour: A travel package offered to those persons in a company (and normally paid by that company) who have achieved certain sales or performance goals and, hence, have earned a travel reward.

Inclusive Resort: A property which includes sleeping rooms, meals, facilities and activities in the price.

Independent Hotel: One which is not affiliated with a chain or group.

Inside cabin: A room, or cabin, on board a ship with no windows or porthole.

Junior Suite: A large hotel room with a partition separating the sleeping area and the sitting area.

King Room: A hotel room with a king-size bed.

Lanai: A balcony or patio area overlooking water or a garden.

Late Charge: Charges for services, such as restaurant or telephone, which have not appeared on a guest's bill at check-out.

Logo: The emblem or trademark of a company, organization, etc.

Low Season: The least busy season for travel and tourism, normally involving the minimum rates. Time of year differs from destination to destination.

Modified American Plan (MAP): A hotel rate which includes breakfast and one other meal. Usually referred to as "half-board" or "demi-pension".

National Tourist Office (NTO): usually a government-run organization to promote its country and increase inbound tourism through an international network of offices called NTOs.

Net Rate: A wholesale rate to be marked up for retail sale.

No-Show: A passenger or guest who fails to arrive.

NT: abbreviation for "night", usually used as in "per nt" when referring to the hotel rate for each night.

Occupancy Rate: The ratio between the number of rooms a hotel has sold and the number still available.

Option Date: The deadline by which payment of deposit must be made or the room, seat, or tour will no longer be held.

Outside cabin: A room, or cabin, on board a ship with either windows or portholes.

Overbooking: The practice by a supplier/operator/airline of taking more bookings than the capacity allows, in expectation of cancellations.

Override: Extra commission paid by a supplier as a sales incentive.

OW: One-way, usually used in reference to airline transportation or motorcoach transfers

Package: A group of products and services at a hotel or on a tour combined together to create a comprehensive program with one total rate.

Pax: A shortened term for "passenger" but commonly used in all aspects of the industry including airline, hotel and tour.

Peak Season: The busiest season for travel and tourism, normally involving the highest rates.

Positive Space: A confirmed reservation at a hotel or a flight.

PP: Per person

Pre-registration: Details of a guest's room and arrival-departure dates.

Protected: A supplier's or wholesaler's guarantee to pay the agent's commission and a client a full refund on prepaid, confirmed bookings, regardless of cancellations.

Quadruple (QUAD): A hotel room for four persons with appropriate bedding to accommodate them.

Quad Occupancy Rate: A hotel room with sufficient bedding for four people.

Queen Room: A room with a queen-sized bed.

Rack Rate: The usual rate for a hotel room.

Rep: A representative employed by a hotel, airline, tour operator, etc. to offer various services to travelers, operators, group leaders and travel agents.

Res Agent: Short for "reservations agent", is a person who takes a reservation or sells tickets.

Room Night: A room being occupied by one or more guests for one night.

Rooming List: A list provided by the group leader or travel agent to a hotel showing the guest names in a particular group.

RT: Roundtrip, usually used in reference to airline transportation or motorcoach transfers

Run-of-the-House Rate: A flat price at which a hotel agrees to offer any of its rooms to a group, regardless of room quality or location in the hotel.

Seats: The term used by airlines to designate the individual product they have to sell on board their aircraft.

Seat Assignments: The designation of specific seat numbers on board an aircraft for each passenger. Depending on the airline, these can be reserved at a certain number of days prior to the flight.

Shoulder Season: The in-between or medium season between "peak" and "low", normally involving mid-range rates.
Time of year differs from destination to destination.

Single (SGL): A service or facility for use by one person only.

Single Occupancy Rate: A discount for one person occupying a double room.

Single Supplement: An additional charge for one person occupying a hotel room fit for two or more people.

Special-Needs Accommodation: Rooms designed for the comfort of the disabled which include such amenities as wider doors, low sinks, TTD telephones, etc.

Suite: Rooms with at least two rooms including one bedroom and a parlor, and which may also have a kitchen.

Supplement: The price for an extra or better grade of service.

Supplier: Company offering travel products or services for sale through travel agents, group leaders, or directly to the customer.

Tour Conductor or Tour Escort: The group leader who travels with the group as the planner, decision maker and problem solver.

Tour Guide: A professional who has studied the area's history, culture, economics, geography, and politics, and provides this information to the group members as they travel. Normally is "licensed" by the city, state, or country.

Tour Operator: Organization selling and marketing pack-aged tours and/or travel services through group leaders, travel agents, or direct to the public.

Transfer: Transportation from one point to another, e.g.; airport to hotel. Usually designated as being either one-way (OW) or roundtrip (RT).

Triple (TPL): A hotel room for four persons with appropriate bedding to accommodate them.

Twin (TWN): A hotel room with two single beds for two guests.

Twin Double: A hotel room with two double beds for up to four guests. Also see "double double."

Upgrade: To move to a higher standard of accommodation or class of services. Also means to make improvements to a facility.

Value Added Tax (VAT): A levy on goods and services which is imposed by a country's government.

Vouchers: Coupons issued by tour operators which can be presented as payment for accommodations, meals, sightseeing, and various other services.

Wholesaler: A company which purchases large quantities of product or services from suppliers at a greatly discounted rate; they then develop complete packages for re-sale through travel agents or group leaders.

Airline Passenger Rights:
http://www.1travel.com

Cultural Events:
http://www.culturefinder.com

Cultural Behavior:
http://www.getcustoms.com/omnibus.html

Cruise Critic:
http://www.travelosity.com

Currency Conversion:
http://www.xe.net/currency

Currency Exchange List:
http://www.xe.net/cus

Destination Information:
http://www.city.net
http://www.lonelyplanet.com
http://www.travelocity.com

Destination Maps:
http://www.tiger.census.gov
http://www.randmcnally.com
http://www.expediamaps.com

Foreign Language Primer:
http://www.travlang.com/languages

Passports & Documentation Requirements:
http://www.americanpassport.com
http://www.instantpassport.com
http://www.visaadvisors.com/vforentryreq.html

Time zones:
http://www.timezoneconverter.com/cgi-bin/tzc.tzc
http://www.page1.com/time

Travelers Health:
> http://www.cdc.gov/travel

US Government Customs Requirements:
> http://www.customs.ustreas.gov/travel/travel.html

US Government Travel Advisory:
> http://travel.state.gov/travel_warnings.html

World Travel Guide:
> http://www.wtgonline.com

Index

A

"A" list -- 215
accounting --- 59
Accredited Cruise   Counselor (ACC) --------------- 177
Advertising ----------------------------------- 154, 157
Airline ticketing --------------------------------- 73
airline ticketing ------------------------------- 102, 104
associations ------------------------------------- 39
attitude -- 203
Automobile Expense ----------------------------- 63

B

"B" list -- 212
Baggage delay ------------------------------------- 222
Baggage Handling --------------------------------- 139
Baggage Loss ------------------------------------- 222
Baggage tags ------------------------------------- 226
Bank Shot Newsletter ----------------------------- 48
Bank Travel Management Magazine ----------------- 48
BankTravel -- 45
Benefits -- 49
Booking Arrangements Directly ------------------ 110
Booking Directly --------------------------------- 148
Brochures --- 154
BS Syndrome ------------------------------------- 236
bulk fare --- 108
Bureaus of Tourism ------------------------------- 84
business cards ----------------------------------- 72
Business travel expenses ------------------------- 62

C

Car rental damages ------------------------------- 222
Chambers of Commerce --------------------------- 84

CLIA -------- 7, 78, 83, 113, 165, 167, 169, 175, 177
-- 178, 220
commission ------------------------------ 60, 73, 103, 231
Commissions on insurance ---------------------------- 218
Commissions on optional tours ---------------------- 218
complications -- 199
computer --65
consolidator --- 107
Continuing education --------------------------------49
Convention and Visitors Bureaus (CVB) ------------ 193
corporation --59
cruise counselor ----------------------------- 172, 177
Cruise Industry ------------------------------------- 165
cruise line industry --------------------------------- 166
Cruise Line International Association -------------- 77, 165
cruise market --------------------------------------- 166
Cruise Observer ------------------------------------- 231
custom ring feature ----------------------------------71
Customized Postcards ------------------------------- 217

D

deck plans -- 171
destination --93
Destination Management Company ---------------- 85, 102
direct mail -- 212
direct marketing ------------------------------------ 154
DMC ----- 85, 91, 102, 105, 113, 117, 132, 147, 194
-- 200, 201
documentation -------------------------------------- 227
Domestic -- 112
dream destinations --------------------------------- 249

E

E & O insurance ----------------------------------- 220, 222
e-mail --71
Educational Tours ------------------------------ 76, 243, 244
Emergency medical expenses ----------------------- 222
Entertainment -------------------------------------- 158
EP -- 136

Errors and Omissions (E & O) insurance ------- 220, 222
escorting group tours ------------------------------------ 197
Escorting tours --- 195
Expatriates --- 38

F

Familiarization Tours ---------------------------- 76, 243, 244
FAP or AP -- 136
fax machine -- 64
foreign currency -- 109
Free travel -- 89
free trips --- 219, 232
Full Breakfast --- 136
full-time business ----------------------------------- 88, 102

G

GLAMER --- 45, 50, 76
GLAMER, NASTP, OSSN, IGTA ---------------------- 54
GlobalCare Insurance Services, Inc. ------------------- 221
gross profit --- 152
group leader organizations ----------------------------- 36
Group Leaders of America ------------------------------ 45
group participants --------------------------------------- 89
Group Proposal Request -------------------------- 132, 160
Group Proposal Request Worksheet ------------------- 140
Group Size --- 133
Group Tour Magazines --------------------------------- 48
group travel publications ------------------------------- 76

H

Heritage Club International ----------------------- 45, 46
hobby --- 88, 91, 102
home-based business ----------------------------------- 58
home-office deduction ---------------------------------- 61
Hospitality Desk -- 139
hot destination --- 208
Hotel Accommodations -------------------------------- 135

REFERENCE SECTION   **395**

I

Idea Art -- 72
Incentive Groups ------------------------------------- 112, 113
incentive operator ------------------------------------- 112
Insurance -- 220
insurance -- 60
International Group Tour Association --------------------- 46
International Motor Coach Group, Inc. ---------------- 230
Internet --- 27, 194, 223
invited guest --- 242

L

laser printer --- 66
legal business --- 59
Leisure Groups --- 112
liability -- 60
licensed agent --- 221

M

Making money --- 153
Managing Group Tours ------------------------------- 230
MAP --- 136
mark-up ------------------------------------- 152, 231, 233
meal program --- 136
Military -- 39
Motorcoach tours ------------------------------------- 229

N

NACOA --- 169, 178
NASTP --- 46
National Association of Cruise Oriented Agencies -- 169
National Association of Senior Travel Planners -------- 46
net airfare -- 106
net cost -- 152
net fare -- 108
net price --- 152, 231
net profit --- 152
net quote --- 160

net rates -- 152, 231
networking -- 36

O

objectives -- 22
Operating Expenses -------------------------------- 60
Opportunities ------------------------------------- 49
Optional Tours ------------------------------------ 139
Orientation Meetings ------------------------------ 138
OSSN -- 46, 220
Outside Sales Support Network --------------------- 46

P

packaging a tour ---------------------------------- 91
Paper Direct -------------------------------------- 72
Paper Warehouse ----------------------------------- 72
part-time business -------------------------------- 88
partnership --------------------------------------- 59
Passport -- 225
Passports --- 224
pax --- 89
per person basis ---------------------------------- 151
PFC Products, Inc. -------------------------------- 228
Postage --- 157
Postcards --- 216
printer --------------------------------------- 70, 71
Printing -- 154
Promotional allowance ----------------------------- 218
Promotional material ------------------------------ 156
publications -------------------------------------- 47

R

real deals -- 208
Receptions -- 138

S

school -- 174
selling price ------------------------------------- 162

REFERENCE SECTION   **397**

Senior TRAVEL tips --------------------------------------47
Sightseeing --- 137
singles groups -- 151
Site Inspections ------------------------------------ 243, 245
software --70
state licensed agent ----------------------------------- 221
stationery --72
studying by computer ---------------------------------- 169

T

tax advantages --59
tax breaks ---60
Taxes -- 140
TC --- 134
Telephone & Fax -------------------------------------- 159
telephone system -------------------------------------71
the good life --- 241
"the Good Life!" -------------------------------------- 249
The Group Travel Leader --------------------------------47
theme party -- 137
Tips on Trips --48
Tour Conductor Tickets -------------------------------- 134
tour destinations ------------------------------------90
Tour Operator ------------------------------- 102, 104, 147
Tour Operators ------------------ 114, 194, 200, 201, 218
tour package ----------------------------------- 104, 141
tour protection insurance ------------------------------ 222
tour suppliers --------------------------------------- 131
Tourism Bureaus -------------------------------------- 193
tourism bureaus -------------------------------------- 188
Travel accident -------------------------------------- 222
Travel agencies -27, 30, 73, 102, 103, 104, 146, 194, 201
Travel club --------------------21, 88, 224, 227, 229, 230
Travel delay --- 222
travel document -------------------------------------- 225
Travel documents ------------------------------------- 155
Travel Guard International ----------------------------- 221
Travel insurance ---------------------------------60, 221
Travel insurance companies --------------------------- 223

travel leader organizations ---------------------------------- 75
travel professionals --- 225
travel supplier -- 99, 101
Travel Suppliers -- 111
travel suppliers -- 205
Traveling international -------------------------------------- 228
Trip cancellation --- 222
Trip interruption --- 222
triple occupancy -- 151

U

U.S. passport -- 224

V

Visas -- 224

W

Waiting list -- 210
Website --- 223
Website address --- 71
Worksheet -- 132
Worksheets --- 34, 131